# Affordable Housing, Inclusive Cities

This book has been made possible by a generous grant from the Daida Foundation in the Netherlands.

**ORO Editions**
Publishers of Architecture, Art, and Design
Gordon Goff: Publisher

www.oroeditions.com
info@oroeditions.com

Published by ORO Editions

**Book Design:** Seema Taneja
**Copy Editing:** Meera Joshi
**Managing Editor:** Jake Anderson
**Cover Photograph:** LEVS architecten
10 9 8 7 6 5 4 3 2 1 First Edition

ISBN: 978-1-941806-19-7

**Color Separations and Printing:** ORO Group Ltd.
Printed in China.

ORO Editions makes a continuous effort to minimize the overall carbon footprint of its publications. As part of this goal, ORO Editions, in association with Global ReLeaf, arranges to plant trees to replace those used in the manufacturing of the paper produced for its books. Global ReLeaf is an international campaign run by American Forests, one of the world's oldest nonprofit conservation organizations. Global ReLeaf is American Forests' education and action program that helps individuals, organizations, agencies, and corporations improve the local and global environment by planting and caring for trees.

# Affordable Housing, Inclusive Cities

EDITED BY

**VINAYAK BHARNE & SHYAM KHANDEKAR**

"This volume offers a deeply informative range of insights and experiences on housing and urbanism. It will assist policy makers across the rapidly urbanising globe to discover unique pathways to that 'equitable middle' where the needs of all are balanced with the wants of a few – whereby a credible response to the United Nations Human Settlement Programme's Sustainable Development Goal 11 can be truly achieved by 2030."
**Jagan Shah,** Director, National Institute of Urban Affairs, India

"By looking at affordable housing in a broader context, this volume shows us inspiring new perspectives on how we can build a more inclusive society. The cases from all over the world illustrate that the targeted use of design capabilities can play a key role in this regard. This book is a must-read for architects, planners, and policy makers, who should use their powers of imagination to create social added value."
**Floris Alkemade,** Chief Government Architect, the Netherlands

"This comprehensive book outlines critical theoretical constructs and reveals on-the-ground realities that will effectively guide urban planners, researchers, policy makers and activists to create equitable cities. Covering wide-ranged geographies, protagonists of all colours and hues – especially from the bottom of the economic pyramid – it highlights views of authors with varied domain expertise. This study elucidates some of the most successful global experiments of creating inclusive cities and how those could be tweaked to local realities in different economies and political environments.

As a practitioner working with residents of informal settlements where lack of housing and basic service delivery remain formidable hurdles to accessing opportunities for betterment of life, this multi-layered book has helped generate significant strategic thinking."
**Anita Patil-Deshmukh,** Executive Director, PUKAR, India

"This volume is a comprehensive collection of essays revolving around two of the most important challenges in the contemporary city: housing affordability and socio-political inclusiveness. The editors and authors of this extraordinary assemblage do not stop their scholarly work just there; the text and its beautiful illustrations provide the clarity of content that a present-day reader requires for a preliminary understanding of housing design principles, informal and formal cities, mobility and infrastructure, socio-economic and gender segregation, public participation, community-led development, new technologies, climate resiliency, urban policies and the future of urban form and dwelling opportunities in a variety of geographic and political conditions around the world. This book offers ideas and propositions that cannot be left unexamined at a moment in which humanity is threatened by issues of over-population, resource scarcity, socio-economic differences, climate change and unbridled political struggles. This is a must-read for active participants willing to engage in an impartial and unprejudiced project toward the difficult construction of the contemporary city."
**Jaime Correa,** Associate Professor in Urban Design Practice, School of Architecture, University of Miami, USA

"Working-class housing comprises a sizeable slice of human settlements everywhere yet attracts relatively little attention from spatial design and public policy perspectives. No wonder many urban populations are forced to seek the security of shelter in slums and degraded forms of housing worldwide. Exploring the promising potential of well-designed, affordable housing to create inclusive cities – otherwise marked by a wide range of social inequalities, environmental externalities and physical hardships – this volume illustrates cutting-edge progressive efforts aimed at understanding what works and why. A must-read for everyone interested in the issues of universal housing on this rapidly-urbanising planet."
**Sanjeev Vidyarthi,** Director City Design Program and Senior Fellow, Great Cities Institute, University of Illinois, Chicago, USA

# Contents

## Inclusive Cities
### Issues, Aspirations, Possibilities

## Affordable Housing
### Global Perspectives, Local Realities

## Extreme Affordability
### Uplifting the Base of the Economic Pyramid

# Preface

This book is a milestone in the growth of My Liveable City (MLC), the India and Netherlands-based knowledge-platform created 'to Inform, Inspire and Educate in the Art and Science of making Cities Liveable for All'. With the publishing of its quarterly journal's inaugural issue, in 2014, My Liveable City was founded by Shyam Khandekar (based in the Netherlands) and Shashikala Venkatraman (based in India), with Vinayak Bharne (based in the United States of America) joining the MLC leadership in 2017.

Over the five years, My Liveable City, through its international reach and global partnerships, has established itself as an increasingly respected and influential knowledge-platform. We have expanded far beyond our quarterly into hosting conferences, organising knowledge-tours, conceiving training and educational programmes in collaboration with reputed institutes and undertaking consultancies in various aspects of urbanism. Simultaneously, we have produced 20 quarterly issues on various themes such as 'Cities for All', 'Housing for All', 'Urban Informality', 'Water', 'Mobility', 'Use & Reuse' and 'Infrastructure'. In all these endeavours, urban liveability, equitability and social justice have remained our most significant themes and central concerns.

It is therefore befitting that this first book initiated by My Liveable City is on the topic of affordable housing and inclusive cities. We are convinced that the multifaceted dimensions of this broader topic contain the basic tenets that will transform existing cities, as well as generate new ones, towards a more just and equitable future. We have therefore compiled selected essays on this topic originally written for the MLC quarterly, and created this volume along with some updates and new contributions.

Our foremost thanks go to the authors of this volume, many of whom contributed articles to our quarterly right from its early years. Many of them are leading figures in the multidisciplinary world of city making and this book is a tribute to their wisdom, knowledge and efforts.

Special thanks is due to the dedicated staff and core team of My Liveable City in Mumbai that has been part and parcel of its growth and success: Meera Joshi and Sailesh Ghelani meticulously edited this volume. Seema Taneja graphically designed it from cover to cover. And Mitali Choudhary coordinated its marketing efforts.

We thank Gordon Goff of ORO Editions, San Francisco, who took on the initiative to produce this book and his dedicated and talented staff, Jake Anderson and Kirby Anderson, for shepherding the entire production process.

We also thank Claudio Acioly (Head of Capacity Building of the United Nations Human Settlements Programme, also known as UN Habitat) for writing the foreword.

We dedicate this volume to the large group of professionals from around the world – Australia to Brazil, India to Canada, the Netherlands to Colombia, Russia to the USA – who have over the years supported and nurtured My Liveable City's mission through their intellectual rigour, knowledge base, energy and application. They are our global MLC family!

**Vinayak Bharne & Shyam Khandekar**
*January, 2019*

# Foreword

**Claudio Acioly**
Head of Capacity Building, United Nations Human Settlements Programme (UN-Habitat)

This insightful volume covering experiences across cities, regions, nations and continents unveils the strong correlation between inclusive cities and the accessibility to affordable housing. It shows us how this correlation results in the spatial inclusion of those at the bottom of the social economic ladder. It highlights examples and approaches that advocate social and spatial inclusion by means of making housing affordable for all.

The notion of inclusiveness in urban development is often correlated with the level of citizen participation and engagement in the decision-making process and governance of their cities. This means involvement on matters that directly affect the quality of life and the realisation of their fundamental rights in the city where they live and work. The achievement of inclusive cities is inexorably associated with the availability and accessibility of affordable housing options – a home that is safe, equipped with basic infrastructure and services – and access to employment opportunities. This brings to the forefront the locational attribute of housing and the access to serviced land as fundamental conditions for the realisation of inclusive cities.

The argument that the sustainable future of cities will depend on the availability and affordability of housing is reinforced by the fact that housing and residential use can consume more than 70% of the land cover in cities.[1] This is further reinforced by the fact that the housing sector has interfaces with practically every single aspect of the economy of a country. Consequently, any investment in housing will generate immediate economic impacts and influence the form and structure of cities.

Affordability represents one of the seven attributes of housing adequacy[2] under the Right to Adequate Housing as defined by international instruments and human rights legislation adopted by the United Nations. This means that every citizen is entitled to the right to live in peace and dignity and have access to adequate privacy, space, security of tenure, materials such as lighting and heating, infrastructure and location with regard to work and basic facilities and other elements – all at reasonable and affordable prices.

States and governments have committed themselves to promote the full and progressive realisation of the Right to Adequate Housing when adopting the Habitat Agenda (1996)[3] and New Urban Agenda (2016).[4] Yet, the urbanisation patterns that prevail in many parts of the developing world are characterised by social and spatial segregation and the exclusion of billions of people from accessing adequate and affordable housing. To achieve inclusive and human rights-based urbanisation through the implementation of affordable housing policies, governments ought to establish an enabling environment comprised of policy, institutional, financial and regulatory frameworks that enable individuals and households to access adequate housing and, at the same time, achieve their spatial inclusion.

In practice, this means the adoption of policies that boost the supply of serviced land at scale, programmes that improve accessibility to affordable housing finance, credit and targeted subsidies (which increase the ability of the different social groups to pay for housing while widening their freedom of choice) that will generate housing that are well-located and affordable; also policies and regulations that discourage urban sprawl and encourage land development within the urban core.[5] This is just to name a few policies that reinforce social and spatial inclusion and help to reverse the global trend of unsustainable, low density, fragmented and exclusionary urbanisation.[6] The book provides a wealth of examples of such policies and is a must-read for policy makers and practitioners working in the field of housing and sustainable urbanisation.

In reality, however, as the cases in this volume reveal, the lack of affordable housing options[7] in cities in the developing world is one of the underlying causes of informal urbanisation, which is characterised by the multiplication and persistence of slums and unplanned settlements. Data from UN-Habitat's Global Urban Observatory suggests that although the percentage of urban population living in slums is decreasing, in absolute numbers it is increasing and this trend is likely to continue for the years to come if no concerted and comprehensive actions are taken by national and local governments and the international community. In other words, the achievement of the Sustainable Development Goal 11 of the Global Agenda 2030 that aims at 'making cities and human settlements inclusive, safe, resilient and sustainable' by 2030, leaving no one and no place behind, is conditional to the realisation of the right to adequate housing and the provision of affordable housing options at scale and diversity.

This issue is especially exacerbated in Sub-Saharan Africa and parts of Asia where urbanisation has become synonymous with slum formation.[8] Worse, it remains a challenge globally and affects the sustainability and social cohesion of cities. The Global Sample of 200 Cities[9] provides compelling evidence of the global housing affordability crisis, which is further confirmed by several other studies.[10] The Global Sample demonstrates that access to housing via home ownership or rental housing remains largely unaffordable in all studied cities of the world.

The scarcity of affordable housing compels nearly one billion people to a poverty trap – a mechanism which forces people to remain poor, socially and spatially segregated and living in appalling conditions located in slums[11] in cities that perpetuate the geography of the divided city. The high numbers of slum dwellers and people living in inadequate housing in various parts of the world reveal the failure of governments in facilitating the supply of adequate and affordable housing options at scale and diversity in size, location, type, standards and prices.

By default, this means creating the conditions for cities to become 'Human Rights-Based Cities' (HRBC). It means rejecting 'cities of segregation' where everyone has obligations, but only some have their basic rights realised, while others are constrained to live in inhuman conditions. It means creating opportunity for the development of 'cities of rights' where obligations are met for all citizens.

This book is certainly a most worthy contribution towards this goal.

*Claudio Acioly is the Head of Capacity Building of the United Nations Human Settlements Programme (UN-Habitat.) He leads global initiatives linking capacity building, institutional development and policy change. An architect, urban planner and development practitioner with more than 35 years of experience, Acioly has worked in more than 30 countries. From 2008–2012, he was the Chief Housing Policy coordinator of UN-Habitat during which he led the housing policy work in Cuba, Ghana, Malawi, El-Salvador, Uganda, Vietnam, Nepal and Ecuador including housing policy implementation and slum upgrading. He is the principal author of UN-Habitat's* Housing Profile Methodology *and the* Street-led Citywide Slum Upgrading Strategy *amongst many other publications.*

# Introduction

Vinayak Bharne & Shyam Khandekar

Making cities affordable and inclusive is one of the most pressing challenges of our times. Across the world, cities have become socially segregated geographies, with the urban poor living in isolated, unhealthy environments. On the one hand, economic prosperity coupled with the inadequate distribution of infrastructure and amenities has generated massive demographic polarisation. On the other, the physical design of cities has denied fundamental aspects such as public space and transit for one and all. The challenge of making cities more affordable and inclusive has as much to do with governance and policy, as urban planning and architecture. More than an economic dilemma, it is a moral necessity.

The term 'inclusive cities' refers to a model of urban development that guarantees equal rights and participation among its citizens, including the most marginalised, and aims to end extreme poverty while promoting shared prosperity. Inclusiveness also has important spatial dimensions such as provisions for shelter and public space, and access to water and sanitation for all. But despite serious and significant commitment, building inclusive cities remains a challenge: Today, one in three urban residents in the developing world still lives in slums with inadequate services. By 2050, around 70% of the world's population will live in urban areas and most urban growth is expected to take place in the Asian and African regions that contain some of the poorest nations (World Bank, 2019). By 2025, an estimated 1.6 billion people could struggle to secure decent housing across the world (McKinsey Global Institute, 2019).

Affordable Housing has therefore become a fundamental prerequisite for making inclusive cities. It is in fact an ongoing global crisis, considering the 330 million urban households around the world who currently lack adequate shelter (World Resources Institute, 2017). Affordable housing is another term for public housing, and this rhetorical shift from 'public' to 'affordable' is today emblematic of a shift in its cultural meaning: Public housing, which was once largely if not solely within the government's domain, has today come under the purview of numerous other agencies and actors that are catering to the needs of the less-privileged in the wake of municipal and institutional underperformance. Lessons from failed experiments in our recent past have taught us that affordable housing is not just about sheltering people. It is as much about locating housing appropriately in relation to the rest of the city; in relation to land use and adequate public space, transportation and the availability of jobs and security for all.

While such aspirations and realisations may seem indisputable, the fact is that cities across the world are different from one another, less so due to their formal and spatial characteristics and more for their administrative and cultural patterns. In nations facing economic and political turmoil, affordability and inclusiveness take on meanings different from more stable societies. In geographies with land scarcity, affordable city making presents great physical challenges. Urban growth and decline, residual colonialism, population explosion, governance structures, as well as the rise and fall of industrialisation differ globally. Consequently, the actual processes and products that bring about bigger and deeper change are themselves significantly different in cities across the developed versus less-developed world. While the concern for socially and economically equitable cities falls within our global sphere of concern, its on-the-ground realities across nations and continents that are diverse and complex.

This volume contributes to this conversation. It sheds light on the exclusionary nature of contemporary planning and city making and offers ideas on how we might shift such trends towards more inclusionary paradigms. How are efforts at making cities more inclusive and equitable playing out across nations and societies across the world? How are the circumstantial differences of various places generating different strategies towards the same larger goal? How is affordable housing bridging economic gaps in affluent versus less prosperous nations? How are less developed societies grappling with the colossal challenge of uplifting the base of the economic pyramid and what might more affluent societies learn from this? The multifaceted, comparative narrative of this volume is a call for expanding the narrow focus on urban equitability towards a more integral outlook on the myriad ways through which affordable housing and inclusive cites are being generated across the world. Clearly, there are lessons to be learnt.

## CONTENT
The 36 chapters that follow were chosen from a larger list of articles. During the selection process, we recognised a number of distinct themes that wove through them. We did not think it appropriate to structure the book on these themes. But we felt it was important to mention them here, as intellectual lenses and tools for a reader to reflect upon the content:

**1. Geography** – While this volume does not make claims of geopolitical comprehensiveness, the 36 chapters that follow encompass places and projects that span Asia, Africa, Australia, Europe and North, Central and South America. One of the intents of this collection is to offer readers a sweeping overview of the overlaps and differences of urban affordability and inclusiveness across continents and nations.

**2. Recipients** – The demographics that serve to benefit from the positive efforts of this larger discourse are diverse and complex in nature. Some chapters focus on the elderly demographic; others discuss the opposite end of the age spectrum through initiatives related to children in cities. Some articles draw our attention to marginalised groups such as slum dwellers, *favela* residents and nomadic migrants. Others focus on gender-related issues and women empowerment. The book's combined narrative reveals the multiple protagonists of this broader discussion and assesses their specific needs and aspirations.

**3. Process** – The articles that follow demonstrate the multiplicity of processes and approaches – formal and informal, top-down and bottom-up. Discussions range from the planning approaches of the Dutch Social Housing Corporation that today with its 2.4 million homes owns nearly a third of the national housing stock; and the success of the Singapore Government in providing quality affordable housing to about 80% of its population through its Housing Development Board (HDB); to the Estonoesunsolar project in Spain, wherein 60 citizen associations and neighbourhood groups have helped transform empty urban lots into gardens and gathering spaces for the young and the old.

**4. Policy** – We recognise that one of the most consequential means of making cities affordable and inclusive, particularly in more legally robust nations, is through intelligent policy and administrative initiatives. This volume includes interviews with experienced and influential policy-makers and civic leaders such as Jaime Lerner (three-time mayor of Curitiba, Brazil), Somsook Boonyabancha (Chairperson, Asian Coalition of Housing Rights).

**5. Design** – In turn, we recognise that urban transformation has deep relationships with design at all scales. There are essays on large-scale implemented master plans such as Dodoma, the capital of Tanzania. There are articles on designing apartments for 'micro-living' in New York and learning from the 'chawl' typologies of Mumbai. There are commentaries by noted architects and artists such as Alejandro Aravena (recipient of the 2016 Pritzker Architecture Prize), MVRDV and Haas&Haan.

**6. Technology** – The interface of technology with affordability, architecture and urbanism is also part of this collection. Some articles focus on cutting-edge technology, such as the prefabricated Styrofoam (Expanded Polystyrene or EPS) modular shelters for migrant groups in the Netherlands. Others elaborate on low-tech solutions such as the revival of traditional tribal methods of mud-brick construction to build new public buildings in Mali, Africa.

**7. Economic Extremes** – A significant portion of this volume is devoted to discussions on what affordability and inclusiveness mean at the base of the economic pyramid. How have cities like Medellin and Bogota attempted to mediate their economic polarisations through effective public transit solutions? What might we learn from iconic cases like the high-rise slum of Torre David in Caracas? How are local non-government groups such as 'Women for the World' bringing consequential changes to the lives of the under-privileged in the developing world?

**8. Unforeseen Consequences** – There are narratives that offer lessons from the shortcomings of experiments and projects from our recent past. For example, why have the modern social housing projects of the '70s, designed in the name of efficiency, failed to produce community and public life in European cities? How is the differential between rising real estate value and affordable housing demand changing the nature of Chandigarh, one of India's modern built-from-scratch cities?

**9. Positions** – We have included analytical narratives, positions, arguments and even principles that might serve to provide a basis for evaluating housing policies and approaches. Why is low-rise high density housing a more affordable proposition than its high-rise counterpart? How might creating and improving streets and public spaces in existing slum settlements catalyse significant improvements in livelihoods, living conditions and social interactions?

**10. Utopias** – Finally, we have chosen to include compelling visionary ideas towards urban inclusiveness: How might new by-laws lead to an engineering of the 'Perfectly Pedestrian City' that reduces pollution and offers greater access to public space for all? How might affordable habitats be designed as 'self-sufficient floating neighbourhoods' in the wake of climate change and sea-level rise?

## STRUCTURE

We have organised this volume into three sections. Each section contains an editors' introduction followed by 12 chapters. The section-specific chapters were selected to offer geographic range and sequenced per a broad, though not necessarily rigid logic: Each section opens with a conversation with a prominent figure related to the section theme, then moves on to theoretical and scholarly commentaries, followed by case studies of projects and ends with visionary ideas.

I. 'Inclusive Cities: Issues, Aspirations, Possibilities' elaborates on the interface of social justice and city making in different cultures and regions. It offers comparative discussions on urban equitability through observations in affluent nations such as Australia, Austria, Japan, Singapore, the Netherlands and the United States, as well as relatively less-developed ones such as Brazil, Colombia, India, Kenya, Tanzania and Thailand. The narrative of this section, we hope, will help a reader overview the overlaps and contrasts between issues and concerns that underlie the meaning of 'inclusive cities' in various regions of the world, thereby providing a backdrop for the next two sections.

II. 'Affordable Housing: Global Perspectives, Local Realities' offers a focused discussion on one of the most significant aspects of urban equity today – the availability of adequate shelter. While the chapters in this section span a range of regions, a majority of the articles focus on successful policies, strategies and projects on affordable housing in more developed nations such as France, the United Kingdom, the United States and the Netherlands. This section is, therefore, particularly significant for its perspectives on how more advanced societies have dealt with the affordability challenge in the earlier phases of their development and what other regions may learn from them.

III. 'Extreme Affordability: Uplifting the Base of the Economic Pyramid' discusses a dimension of affordability dominating less developed societies – that today form a majority of the urban world. This aspect of affordability is often underestimated and inadvertently enmeshed in broader discussions on the subject. We believe that the challenges of extreme urban poverty cannot be compared with those in more affluent regions; they deserve their own space. In this section, we focus exclusively on the base of the economic pyramid through studies from Bangladesh, Brazil, Chile, India, Mali, Myanmar and Venezuela, shedding light on how these societies are addressing some of the most difficult socio-economic issues of our time.

The authors of this volume are both from academia and practice – politicians, administrators, policy-makers, civic leaders, activists, planners, architects, historians, conservationists – and from across the world. It is the nature and quality of these thinkers – who wrestle with complicated issues within their own cultural circumstances – that enables this volume to capture the complexity of this broader subject. As the editors of this volume, our own background (as professional architects and urbanists engaged in global practice) has enabled us to embrace the global diversity and regional specificity of what it means to make cities equitable.

That said, we must acknowledge that while the essays in this volume offer compelling advocacy for new forms of affordable housing and inclusive cities, it is not the ambition of this volume to deliver a definitive synthesis on this subject. We therefore encourage readers to understand the narratives in this collection as inspiring and provocative starting points for greater concern, further study, deeper discourse and, most importantly, consequential and transformative action towards generating a more just and equitable urban future.

# Inclusive Cities
## Issues, Aspirations, Possibilities

# Inclusive Cities

## Issues, Aspirations, Possibilities

Vinayak Bharne & Shyam Khandekar

How are cities working to empower and promote the inclusion of all, irrespective of age, gender, ethnicity, disability, religion and economic status? How are the social, political, economic and cultural specifics of various geographies generating different approaches towards the same larger goals – of reducing income inequalities, eliminating discriminatory practices, promoting appropriate policies and action, and ensuring equal opportunity and participation? This section explores the interface of social justice and city making through comparative discussions on urban equitability. In this section, we feature opinions, commentaries and case studies from affluent nations such as Australia, Austria, Japan, Singapore, the Netherlands and the United States, as well as relatively less-developed ones such as Brazil, Colombia, India, Kenya, Sri Lanka, Tanzania, Thailand and Turkey. The intent of this section is to overview the diverse breadth of issues, aspirations and possibilities that surround the idea of 'inclusive cities' in various regions of the world.

We open this section with insights by two individuals who have a proven track-record of transformative efforts related to urban equitability. Chapter 1: Building a Shared Dream is a conversation with noted urban planner Jaime Lerner, three-time mayor of Curtiba, Brazil, and the mastermind behind the city's world-famous Bus Rapid Transit system. He talks about how the roots of major urban transformation lie in small efforts that are easy to implement and that can grow in time to serve "as embryos of a more complex structure." In Chapter 2: Building for Urban Regeneration, Giancarlo Mazzanti, the architect behind the famous España Library in Medellin, Colombia, elaborates on how a community's association with a striking new building has helped regenerate an isolated district, reduce violence, improve the economy, provide social space and heighten civic pride.

The next three chapters offer narratives on harsh aspects of urban inequity, highlighting the urgency to recognise their implications and act on them. Chapter 3: Social Equity in Indian Cities - Implications for Policy and Practice uses the context of slums and affordable housing provisions to examine how social equity might be more effectively integrated in urban plans and how rising levels of extreme inequity might be contained in one of the most populous nations in the world. Chapter 4: The Basava Project: Making Space for Migrant Communities in India focuses on the bull-centric Kole Basava people. It observes how the unavailability of open spaces, drinking water and toilets keeps this nomadic demographic marginalised within cities and forces them to constantly relocate with their animals through painstaking processes. Chapter 5: Gendered Production of Spaces in Sri Lanka shows how women are subject to various forms of harassment in public spaces; how some spaces are safer for women than the others; how the time of the day affects women's use of public space; and how women are desperately coping within such circumstances. It argues for efforts to generate gender-neutral public space that can be safe for all.

The four chapters that follow elaborate on various implemented strategies and projects – as precedents for urban inclusiveness. Chapter 6: Bridging Two Extremes: Notes from Latin America showcases how innovative efforts such as Medellin's gondola lift and public-escalator infrastructure and Bogota's Ciclovia programme and TransMilenio public bus system have helped mediate social and economic polarisations. Chapter 7: Children's Right to Play in Inclusive Cities focuses on the needs of children living in crisis situations in India, Japan, Thailand and Turkey. It assesses the successes and shortcomings of various interventions by local organisations to cater to the needs of girls and boys of different ages. It argues for moving beyond the identification of risk factors in children's lives, towards protective factors that are essential for their positive growth. Chapter 8: Designing for the Young and the Old discusses how facilities in Australian cities can enable the young to socialise with all age groups and learn about the risks and opportunities of urban life, initially with parent supervision and later as independent young citizens. Chapter 9: Designing Public Spaces for All examines how community-led initiatives in Greece, Spain and the Netherlands have transformed underused urban lots into multi-purpose parks and gathering places for all ages.

Next, we have two articles on the African continent. Chapter 10: Inclusive Transport and Spatial Justice in Nairobi discusses the specifics of why prioritising mass transit and non-motorised transport over private vehicles doesn't only benefit the poor, but also meets the demands of all in Kenya's capital city. Chapter 11: Dodoma: The Burden of Planning in Tanzania is a study of the nation's planned capital city. It discusses how the gap between formal and informal planning leads to the failure of ambitious plans in African regions. It argues for a more open, inclusive approach that integrates local planners, entrepreneurs and residents, while enabling informal land management systems to participate.

Finally, Chapter 12: Engineering the Perfectly Pedestrian City bookends this section with a utopian, yet analytical vision, in which new building development by-laws, intelligent street design and walk-augmenting technology can generate a pedestrian-oriented city that offers equitable access to public spaces and amenities, reduces pollution and augments urban health and civic engagement.

Taken together, the 12 chapters in this section weave a complex narrative on the multifarious entities, phenomena, processes, approaches and strategies that frame the larger discourse on inclusive cities today. They offer, on the one hand, a vivid reminder of the gravity of the issues, as well as the plight of the entities that need our urgent attention. They provide, on the other, empirical evidence that cities across the world are indeed attempting to reorient their policies and processes to ensure that no part of society is left behind.

# Building a Shared Dream

Architect and urban planner **Jaime Lerner** shares with **Paola Huijding** his views on transforming cities as a collective endeavour

**You have been the mayor of Curitiba three times and governor of the state of Paraná twice. How important is it for politicians to understand urban design strategies and for urban planners to understand political systems?**

One of the most important issues regarding cities today is to make things happen. There is an overall paralysis that comes from constraints from many sides – bureaucracy being the main cause – but also from a fear of proposing something. To innovate is to start. We must have a certain commitment to simplicity and even to a degree of imperfection. I once read a phrase that touched me deeply, which was roughly something like this: "I'd rather have graceful imperfection than graceless perfection." Planning is a process that can always be corrected if we pay attention to feedback from the people. We should imagine the ideal, but do what is possible today. The roots of a major transformation lie in a small transformation. Start creating from simple

elements that are easy to implement and in future these will serve as embryos of a more complex structure. The system that became known as BRT (Bus Rapid Transit) and is nowadays present in over 200 cities worldwide started in Curitiba with one dedicated lane transporting 20,000 people. It evolved to an integrated transit network carrying over two million passengers per day. The contemporary world demands increasingly fast solutions and it is the local level that can provide the quickest responses.

I emphasise these points because this is where designers/planners and politicians need to find common ground. The lack of resources cannot be an excuse not to act. Some cities have seriously compromised themselves, even when resources were plentiful, with costly and equivocated interventions; elevated roads and rivers encased in concrete are good examples of that. If you want creativity, cut a zero off from your budget. If you want sustainability, cut off two! However, it is necessary to have a guiding strategic view, a future scenario. Plan for the people (and with the people), not for centralising bureaucratic structures.

Urban planning is not a product; it is a process, with a long-term timeframe. It takes time and it needs to. Politicians must understand that and have this perspective of future objectives as the guide for present action, that is to say, to bind the present with a future idea. Planners, on the other hand, need to understand that the present belongs to us and it is our responsibility to open paths,

understand the needs of political timing and the fact that if politicians disregard the daily demands of the citizens, they will lose the essential support of their constituents and will not accomplish much. Balance has to be reached between the quotidian needs of the population and the prospects of their city.

A fertile convergence ground is possible through the concept of 'Urban Acupuncture'. These quick, precise, focused interventions help generate new energy and synergy for the entire city. These acupunctures can give visibility to the long-term objectives of the planning process and provide the politicians the necessary short-term demonstration effect.

I was fortunate to be able to understand that cities are for people and must be designed to their scale and I was able to share this vision with an amazing group of like-minded professionals. Together, we were able, with the involvement and support of the population, to translate this into a shared dream for the city and make it a reality. Leadership is important, but transforming a city is a collective endeavour.

**You helped to create the IPPUC – Institute of Urban Planning and Research of Curitiba. How important is it for cities to collaborate with knowledge and research institutes in order to explore better solutions to our cities? Do you think that if today's technical knowledge (like Smart Cities), had been available earlier, the**

## If you want creativity, cut a zero off from your budget. If you want sustainability, cut off two!

**solutions you implemented 20–30 years ago would have been different?**

I believe that research and practice are the two sides of a valuable coin and should go hand in hand as much as possible. That does not mean that the production of knowledge must always have a 'utilitarian' goal, but that a wedge, a wall of incommunicability, cannot separate the world of academia, of research and the world of professional practice. Institutions are as good as the people who are a part of them. IPPUC played a key role in the development of Curitiba, helping to safeguard, from a technical standpoint, the long-term guidelines of its structure of growth. In addition, it has worked as a 'project bank', which is very important to help capitalise investments for the city in tandem with the established priorities. These are some

of the roles it has played throughout its history. Universities are, naturally, institutions dedicated to the generation and diffusion of knowledge and they have in their hands the amazing enthusiasm and idealism of youth, which is to be nourished and allowed to flourish. In teaching, I always believed in the role of architects as 'professionals of proposals' and tried to encourage that as much as possible. Fortunate is the institution, the city, the country that manages to build bridges between the realms of academia/research and the realm of the practitioners.

For me, the true 'smart city' is the one that intelligently uses its planning to integrate life, work and mobility into a sound structure of growth; that conciliates its design with nature and promotes the mixture of urban functions, of income levels,

**Tube stations of the BRT**

of ethnicities, of age groups, to strengthen its identity and foster coexistence and solidarity. It is in the conception of cities that the largest and most significant contribution to a more sustainable society can be made. Technology is an important tool, but it will not solve urban problems on its own. In that sense, I believe the examples of Curitiba hold great validity to this day.

Let me give you an example. When we were developing the 'tube stations' that are part of the BRT system (the elevated platform for the passengers boarding and alighting), there was a safety concern, as the doors of the bus needed to be perfectly aligned with the doors of the station before opening. Several technological solutions were presented, but their cost was prohibitive for us. We decided to conduct a test with one of the most experienced bus drivers we had and ask for his feedback on the experiment. The solution he pointed out was of incredible simplicity. If there was to be a mark on the side of the bus, and a mark on the side on the station, when the two of them were perfectly aligned, that meant that the bus was in the correct position and the doors could open. Problem solved at a minimal cost and a lot of ingenuity. I say that because I have been seeing so much effort invested in, let's say, driverless cars. Driverless cars will not do much to solve problems of urban mobility, because the focus is still on private, individual transportation: driverless or not, they will continue to clog our roads and demand precious space within the city. Solutions for mobility are, structurally, on a more compact urban design, on the proximity of work and home, on the priority of public transportation and the pedestrian scale. 'Smart' technologies are only as smart as the use we make of them.

**Your work as a politician and an urban planner has had a strong focus on creating equity and prosperity. The Brazilian law 'The City Statute', which has been created by means of a participatory system, safeguards the right to the city and citizen participation. How do you experience the usability of this law for urban development and in particular regarding the assignment you've been given by the current Mayor of São Paulo to develop ideas for its downtown area?**

Every city must build a shared dream, a vision for the future, which is to be created collectively, so it can have the essential support of the population. Once this desired scenario is set, it is necessary to set up the means for its implementation, which I call

'co-responsibility equations'. The name says it all: it's about how the government, the private sector, civil society and all actors involved will share the responsibilities of making these dreams come true.

Some examples from Curitiba can illustrate this point. In the early 1970s, the city had a meagre 0.5 sq. m. of green area per inhabitant and a single public park. To change that, many strategies were implemented in the following years. To increase the presence of trees along the sidewalks, the city created a campaign in which it provided the planting of baby trees and the residents were invited to water them daily, ensuring their survival. These trees grew to form a most beautiful canopy along many of Curitiba's roads. Many remnants of important green areas were located in private properties throughout the city. We envisaged a legal mechanism and fiscal incentives for the owners of these areas to preserve them, transferring the building coefficient to more apt parts of the city (a mechanism that was later absorbed in the City Statute), creating private urban reserves open for visitation or incorporating them in larger public parks. Environmentally degraded areas, such as exhausted quarries, were rehabilitated to become healing 'urban acupunctures' for the city, such as the Parque das Pedreiras, with an incredible open-air concert venue that has hosted the likes of Paul McCartney and the Three Tenors and the Opera de Arame Theatre, which is part of Curitiba's cultural scene. Because of co-responsibility equations like these, though the population has more than tripled since the 1970s, the ratio of green areas per inhabitant is now more than 50 sq. m.

The City Statute is a useful instrument to provoke the necessary discussion of a strategic vision for the city involving the whole of society and it has many helpful mechanisms to help implement the constructed scenario and even-out some imbalances. However, as with any legislation, the support for its implementation will be under the watchful eye of society and the institutions, governmental or not, that have been created. São Paulo is an incredible, vibrant metropolis and it has made a serious effort in the past years to face the towering challenges of mushrooming urban growth in a very unequal socio-economic context. It mirrors the effort of contemporary Brazil to engage competitively in the global economy and at the same time face its historical injustices. It is huge work and I'm very enthusiastic about the partnership with the Municipality in developing ideas for its downtown area; hopefully it will bear fruit for the city!

**In your understanding, cities are not a problem but a solution, which is an**

The true 'smart city' is the one that intelligently uses its planning to integrate life, work and mobility into a sound structure of growth

**integrated structure of life, work and mobility. Climate change is challenging our cities and its inhabitants are facing the consequences. Do you think that the solutions for climate change could improve the quality of people's life and could it draw scenarios for cities for all?**

Cities are home to more than half of the world's population and urbanisation is still rising; they are engines of economic growth, are responsible for about 70% of global greenhouse gas emissions and have the level of government closest to the people. Therefore, it makes sense that it is in cities that the most significant contributions towards fighting climate change and improving the quality of people's lives can be made.

I like to use the metaphor of the turtle to illustrate how cities must be an integrated structure of life, work and mobility. The turtle carries her life with her wherever she goes: she lives, works and moves 'together'. Also, her shell resembles an urban tessiture. If we break her shell into pieces, living here, working there, leisure elsewhere, the turtle will die. And this is what has happened to many of our cities and it

is a recipe for fragmentation and waste: waste of time, waste of energy, waste of creativity, waste of life. Waste is one of the largest contributors to our unsustainability as a civilisation.

A few years ago, I made a short film, called *A Convenient Start*, in the wake of Al Gore's documentary (*An Inconvenient Truth*), aiming at translating key concepts of sustainability for children. The main idea was to combat the sense of hopelessness and focus on what we know about the problem, instead of on what we do not know. And to illustrate how each one can help by reducing the use of the automobile, separating the garbage, living closer to work or bringing the work closer to home and giving multiple functions during the 24 hours of the day to urban equipment. I argue that sustainability is an equation between what is saved and what is wasted. The less the waste, the higher the sustainability will be. And a lot can be done in this regard.

It has been a common approach to deal with growing cities to meet the evolution of 'demand' with increases in scale. So it is in the account of 'excess' people and lack of resources that urban problems have been debited. It is a quantitative

*FACING PAGE*
*Top:* **Botanical Garden**
*Bottom Left & Right:* **Free University of Environment (Universidade Livre do Meio Ambiente)**

**Opera de Arame theatre, Parque das Pedreiras**

## Curitiba

*Curitiba is the capital of the state of Paraná, the largest city in Southern Brazil with more than 1.8 million inhabitants in the city itself and about 3.2 million in the metropolitan area.*

*Curitiba was born in 1693 from the combination of natives and Portuguese immigrants. In the second half of the 19th century, waves of European immigrants arrived in Curitiba, mainly Germans, Italians, Poles and Ukrainians. Due to fast economic and urban growth, Curitiba was listed in the 1970s as a city of slums, which also had the worst traffic jam issues among all cities in Brazil. It also had other environmental issues like floods and overpopulation. Jaime Lerner changed the city's planning fundamentally. The city is now one of the most beautiful and well organised in Brazil. In 1996, Curitiba was named as one of the most innovative cities in the world. In 2010 it was bestowed with the Global Sustainable City Award.*

## City Statute

*The City Statute, approved in 2001, has unique qualities that are not confined to the high quality of its legal and technical drafting. It is widely regarded as a crowning social achievement, which took shape gradually in Brazil over a number of decades. The Statute seeks to bring together, in a single text, a series of key themes related to democratic government, urban justice and environmental equilibrium in cities.*

*Bringing previously existing piecemeal laws together under the aegis of the City Statute, with the addition of new instruments and concepts, it helps to facilitate a better understanding of the urban question. Most importantly, the Statute has led to the introduction of a genuinely national approach to dealing with the problems of cities.*

problem. According to this simplistic reasoning, in case of urban congestion, for instance, if there was more money, we could appropriate more areas to build bigger overpasses to address the increasing 'needs' of automobiles. If there were resources we would win the race in relation to demand and everything would be solved.

This misconception has to be fought with the understanding that 'cities are human constructs for humans'. A more humane city is the one that focuses on enabling for its inhabitants a decent offer of housing options, an efficient public transportation system, public spaces and community facilities, ample possibilities of employment, self-development and expression.

Finally, I'd like to close these arguments with a factor that is often overlooked when discussing quality of life in cities, which is 'duo identity-coexistence'. Identity is a major element for quality of life; it represents the synthesis of the relationship between the individual and his/ her urban habitat. Identity, self-esteem, a feeling of belonging are intrinsically connected to the points of reference people have in their own city, be it built heritage, natural landmarks or cultural manifestations. These references have to be treasured and illuminated. However, identity cannot exclude diversity, respect for others, the need for tolerance and coexistence.

Cities are the refuge of solidarity. They can be the safeguards of the inhumane consequences of the globalisation process. On the other hand, the fiercest wars are happening in cities, in their marginalised peripheries, in the clash between wealthy neighbhourhoods and deprived ghettos. Heavy environmental burdens are being generated there due to our lack of empathy for present and future generations. And this is exactly why it is in our cities where we can make the most progress towards a more peaceful and balanced planet. We must fight for cities for all, or it may very well be all for nothing. •

# Building for Urban Regeneration

**Laura Amaya** interviews **Giancarlo Mazzanti**, the architect behind the España Library

During the 1980s and early 1990s, Medellín (Colombia) was controlled, de facto, by drug lord Pablo Escobar, head of the Medellín Cartel. By far one of the most dangerous cities in the world, it had an annual homicide rate almost 300 times higher than that of Mumbai (India). A highly fragmented physical and social landscape made residents feel unsafe throughout the city, from slums to up-market districts.

In 2003, 10 years after Escobar's death, Sergio Fajardo was elected mayor. His political agenda had architecture at its core; along with Alejandro Echeverri, mastermind of the physical transformation, he wanted to use design as a vehicle for inclusion and integration. Innovative transportation systems like the Metro Cable and Public Escalators came hand in hand with social initiatives such as public libraries and cultural centres. Gradually the face of the city changed; it reinvented itself to become one of the leading examples of social transformation.

Medellín sought to promote affordability through community empowerment, systematically placing the best architecture in the poorest areas. The España Library, located in Santo Domingo Savio on the Northeast Commune, was one of

the most iconic buildings resulting from that era. Giancarlo Mazzanti, the award-winning architect behind its design, sees it as a symbol of change and explains his views here.

**After a decade of horror, Medellín tried to reinvent itself as an inclusive city. How did you conceptualise the España Library as a building for all?**

The idea for the Library stems from two things: conceptualising Medellín as a landscape and as mountain geography. We were interested in understanding that the building belonged to that idea as opposed to being an object placed on a landscape. The second thing we wanted was a building that would be visible from a distance, one that could be recognised by the people of a historically stigmatised area. We wanted to make it visible and, therefore, it somehow became an element of symbolic reference.

**What is the relevance of the building as a symbol for the city?**

There is something that I think is extremely important. As an architect you do not build a symbol. Rather, a community creates the symbol

> Buildings are constructed but they become iconic references only when the community takes ownership of them

*Clockwise from Left:*
**España Library building as landscape, the interior and an aerial view**

PHOTOS: SERGIO GOMEZ / CARLOS TOBÓN COURTESY EL EQUIPO DE MAZZANTI

when it appropriates the building and transforms it into an element of belonging. Thinking that you can design 'iconic or symbolic buildings' seems naive. Buildings are constructed, yes, but they become iconic references only when the community takes ownership of them.

The España Library makes Fajardo's policy agenda clearly visible and I think that makes the building relevant as well. It becomes significant because it is striking in its geometry, because it promotes a sense of belonging in a community that feels it was given something no other community has. It is relevant because it triggers economic transformation in the neighbourhood, and that highlights a political project that goes far beyond making three buildings. The other thing that is essential is that the Library does not operate alone; it works to intensify urban connections, relationships, public spaces, infrastructure and community and social work with local residents.

### The value of the España Library transcends its design. How do you see the building as an urban destination and what is its placemaking value?

There is a deliberate contradiction between the building and the context. This juxtaposition 'signals out' the Library, making people feel a sense of pride. I think that by becoming an iconic building, the España Library has regenerated the neighbourhood's local economy. Physical transformation has promoted government intervention in terms of public space. The adjacent edges start to increase in value and housing improves, ultimately reinvigorating the local economy. There are several simultaneous processes taking place. There is physical and financial transformation, but the most important aspect is how people perceive themselves. People used to be ashamed of living in the Northeast Commune, but today they take pride in saying that they live where the España Library is.

That change has produced other very nice things. Foundations and NGOs have emerged, such as the one called Barro de Medellín, which promotes musical education for local inhabitants. Barro de Medellín is inspired by a teenage novel that revolves around two children in a poor neighbourhood who steal bricks from a library (the España Library) under construction. As they visit the library they begin to learn how to read and feel terribly ashamed about damaging the building. It is a storey for teenagers, but that produces other things. The Library transcends its original function and generates other types of situations that are now

not only physical; it becomes highly visible, both physically and as an idea of social transformation.

### How do you see the building as a catalyst for urban integration?

The Library becomes a benchmark, a reference point that attracts both tourists and locals. In a district that is very isolated (it was synonymous with violence), when a building generates other things, it reverts and connects the entire city with the site. It also produces something aided by the surrounding support programmes. Violence disappears around the immediate area because there is more tourism, more security, because the economy improves and there is more visibility, more public spaces. A sort of 'safe zone' emerges, something that is repeated in other projects we have designed, such as the Forest of Hope in Cazucá (Bogotá). When the community appropriates the building, violence tends to decrease in the immediate urban edge. The place becomes one where people can go out at night, have social gatherings and enjoy the city.

### How has the building contributed to the regeneration of the area?

After designing this Library I understood and learned many things. In the Library there was no prior process with the community; it was a competition and in that case you work on a set of guidelines. After that project, we have strived to understand how behaviours that shape collective living can allow you to think about architecture in different ways. One example is the project we are doing for Argos, in Cartagena, where we have placed the greatest value in spaces for dance and party, the basis of social life in those communities. Other activities begin to stem from these events; activities that have to do with education, with entrepreneurship. I call these elements 'social attractors', which, poorly stated, are like the anchor store at a mall. You go to the mall to buy one thing, but you find another set of activities that begin to activate different reactions. You can innovate when you begin to understand the conditions of each community.

Ultimately, architecture must be striking; it must be capable of defining the character of an area. In a very poor neighbourhood, where everything is made precariously, you cannot do something precarious. You have to do something that really goes a step further, something where people feel that they are receiving something valuable. It is not 'another school'; it is the school that nobody else has. You generate pride in the people when you give the poorest neighbourhoods the best buildings. ●

**Architecture must be striking; it must be capable of defining the character of an area**

# Social Equity in Indian Cities: Implications for Policy and Practice

**Shruti Hemani** argues a case for real social equity in cities

**Disparity in urban living environment. Urban periphery, Jaipur**

PHOTO: AUTHOR

Cities are places of exchange where different worlds, both natural and human-made, meet, merge or even collide. Although intrinsic to cities, such exchanges often present urban designers, policy and decision makers with challenges. One such test today is social inequity particularly when it is concentrated spatially.

Social inequity is symbolised by the stark disparity in the quality of the living environment. Within cities, it manifests itself as a patchwork of 'contrasting urban forms': on one end of the scale are the exclusive-luxury neighbourhoods while on the other impoverished-informal neighbourhoods. Such an urban 'contrast' is not just a physical expression of income inequalities, but a representation of more innate social conditions such as patterns of segregation and exclusion, distribution of power and public-participation and, more importantly, the access to and availability of choices and opportunities to gain full benefits of city life. Urban inequities that limit certain segments of society from fulfilling their basic needs and development potentials, create fractures within the society, leading to social unrest. This in turn threatens the national security and hinders economic growth. Increasing insecurity and fear among the citizens further shape the sprawling city

through the growth of defensive (i.e., high security, gated luxury) neighbourhoods leading to, what the authors van Ham and Clark call a 'spiral of decline', which is a combination of both, physical and social problems that reinforce each other. Described as political and policy concern, inequity can also be seen as an important structurally threatening cost to governments including social security, health, education, law and order and housing and environment disbursements.

Urban inequities, therefore, not only pose a danger to a nation's social stability and sustained economic growth but also make growth itself destabilising. Equity in the built environment, today and perhaps even more importantly in the years to come, remains an important facet of 'just and sustainable' development especially for rapidly urbanising nations like India whose massive population rise and high migration rates cause concerns about effective and equitable urban service delivery to meet citizens' basic needs.

Equity has received general recognition and has been a recurring theme in the government's policies and urban reforms right from the 7th Five Year Plan. Yet, the topic – how it can be tackled within the realm of built environment – has been less adequately addressed. This article attempts to

**The concept of equity, strongly associated with the notion of social justice, implies that the basic needs of all the people, to both survive and fulfil their development potentials, should be fulfilled**

explore the concept of social equity, its constructs and implications within the built environment. It uses the context of an informal neighbourhood (slum) and affordable housing provisions in India as a laboratory to ask questions like: How can social equity be more effectively integrated in urban development plans, in particular affordable housing? What are the opportunities for action? To this, our understanding is finally translated into a social equity framework focusing on right to space, infrastructure, access and decisions in the built environment. Once we have the answers, we will understand the social equity framework.

## What is social equity and what are its constructs?

The concept of equity, strongly associated with the notion of social justice, implies that the basic needs of all the people, to both survive and fulfil their development potentials, should be fulfilled and that economic, environmental and social benefits, damages and costs including participation

in governance need not be spread unevenly but be shared with fairness and justice across communities and neighbourhoods within a city. Within the urban built environment it suggests a requisite for minimum (preferably an optimum) level or benchmarks for satisfying basic urban needs (spatial, social, economic, environmental and political dimensions) so that everyone can enjoy all the benefits the city has to offer.

Social equity in discourses on sustainable growth and pro-poor policies has received immense recognition. Several authors have identified it as an integral component of the social dimension of sustainability and individuals and organisations have made various attempts to operationalise the concept in practice. Yet the meaning and construct of social equity in the built environment remains vague due to several reasons: **1.** The concept lacks an agreed definition; **2.** It is interpreted variously from different disciplinary backgrounds; **3.** Its measurement is difficult; and **4.** It is context dependent.

Monotonous, minimum standard imposed typology - Slum Redevelopment Scheme, Guwahati, Assam

Diverse and incremental, evolved typology - Informal Settlements, Guwahati, Assam

Although inequitable outcomes and exclusionary processes operate along and interact across several dimensions (economic, political, social, cultural and physical) and work at different levels, equity within the built environment can be seen to have three major constructs:

### 1. Availability: Provision for space and infrastructure for all

This refers to: a) equity in space, both built (housing) and open (outdoor spaces), and b) equity in infrastructure, intra-neighbourhood basic services (non-negotiable must-haves like cooking gas and electricity, drinking water and sanitation, waste management) and facilities for meeting everyday sustenance and enhancement like medical, banking, educational and open recreational facilities as well as 'daily domestic dos' such as food and groceries, fresh vegetables and fruit '*haats/mandis*' (multiple stalls), laundry and newspaper/tea stalls as well as inter-neighbourhood amenities for fulfilling regular obligations as well as leisure, shopping and restaurants, clubs and sports centres, community centres and places of worship/faith, cultural centres as well as libraries.

### 2. Accessibility: Access to space and infrastructure for all

This refers to equity in access, both physical and non-physical, actual or perceived. The ease with which the available space and infrastructure, i.e., services, facilities and amenities may be reached. (Although essential, the non-physical and perceived access is not considered here.)

### 3. Affectability: Listen to the voices of all

This refers to equity in decision-making through community empowerment and involvement in development and planning processes so as to make both approaches – top-down and bottom-up – effective in design and functioning of built environments.

Further to the above three, security (tenure), affordability and habitability can also be seen as other associated constructs.

> **There is clearly a pressing need to develop a stronger link between the conceptual/ theoretical constructs for social equity and its implications in urban design**

SOURCE: AUTHOR

STAGE **3**:

**MATURITY**
Consolidation and
Saturation

STAGE **2**:

**ADOLESCENCE**
Appropriation of
territories and
transformations

STAGE **1**:

**INFANCY**
Occupation (land
for habitation
and livelihood
opportunities)

**Stages of Development: Informal Settlements at Pravin Nagar - Gupta Nagar, Ahmedabad, Gujarat**

## How does the built environment affect social equity and what are the challenges India faces?

Design of urban built environments and policy decisions have far-reaching social equity impacts as it can either enable or restrict certain segments of the society from access to resources and opportunities offered by the city. This can influence individual, community and the country's well-being. Dempsey and her colleagues from the UK have emphasised that equity and inclusion are also critical on the local or neighbourhood scale where they relate to everyday experiences of the built environment and play a more important role especially for, but not limited to, ethnic minorities, low income residents, persons with special needs and the elderly.

Further, my research at IIT Guwahati (2012–2016) on the influence of the built environment (defined by five urban form components: density, land-use, open spatial-network, urban-blocks and built-components) on six aspects of social sustainability, clearly proves that built environment influences the level of social equity amongst its residents. 'Availability' and 'accessibility' to basic services and facilities as measures of social equity strongly influence residents' attachment to a place, which further affects their length of stay in a particular locality or neighbourhood. Length of stay, in turn, has the potential to influence all the other aspects of social sustainability such as

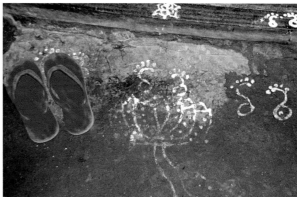

**Strong relationships between spatial organisations and the socio-cultural values of those who build and inhabit them: Informal settlements at (above) Guwahati, Assam and (below) Jaipur, Rajasthan**

PHOTO: AUTHOR. ( BOTTOM LEFT) RATIKA CHANDAWAT

residents' level of social interaction and networks, trust and reciprocity, social participation and the feeling of safety and satisfaction in an area. Locational advantage of people's place of residence is also perceived important, which includes not only convenient access to local facilities but also availability of choices and access to city-level attractions.

These theoretical investigations brought us in close proximity to the understanding of the concept of social equity, its meaning, construct and the influence of the built environment. However, our understanding concerning the social equity outputs, 'What does an equitable neighbourhood look like?' or 'How do we ensure equitable neighbourhood change?' is found to be non-existent. As a result of this, the concept currently suffers in India's development policy and practice, where it either becomes a meaningless label generally added-on to promote the message of other disciplines (such as environmental concerns) or, in some cases, ousted altogether largely on the basis of its intangible and context-dependent nature that causes difficulty in clearly defining and more so, quantifying it. While this indispensable concept is used intuitively in urban development agendas, its implications in the urban built environment, particularly design for urban poor, continues to be fuzzy. Social equity goals are usually not translated into clearly specified objectives and appropriate measures for assessing their achievement in a meaningful, disaggregated manner. Hence, social equity issues are likely to

get further reinforced or recreated elsewhere. Housing for the urban poor, therefore, continues to remain the obvious physical manifestation of economic inequity in the form of strikingly distinct neighbourhoods despite several policies and initiatives to reduce the poverty and social inequity in health, education and housing.

To add to this gap, providing a decent living environment for the urban poor remains a complex undertaking of multifaceted nature, where informal neighbourhood redevelopment has historically meant imposition of new typology of developments (high rise, minimum-size, minimum-standard apartment blocks), that rarely takes into account the economic potential and socio-cultural values of its resident community. The situation is further complicated by lack of finance, issues with respect to access to land and security of tenure, as well as pressures of scaling up to meet the heavy infrastructure and housing demands. Together, these deficiencies allow for only limited success in efficient and equitable built-environment for the urban poor and induce a vicious cycle of poverty as well as slum formation.

As India prepares for the influx of another 350 million people by developing a number of new greenfield cities whilst improving the condition of its existing urban population, there is clearly a pressing need to develop a stronger link between the conceptual/theoretical constructs for social equity and its implications in urban design, policies and practices, particularly in relation to informal neighbourhoods or slums.

> **Urban contrast that limits certain segments of society from gaining the full benefits of city life, therefore, poses a danger to a nation's social stability and sustained economic growth**

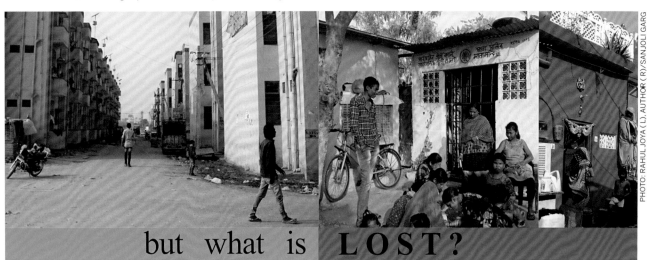

but what is LOST?

PHOTO: RAHUL JOYA (L). AUTHOR (R)/SANJOLI GARG

Modular and minimum-standard housing provided for the urban poor tend to miss the unique spatial configurations that embody rich patterns of community, family ties, concepts of territoriality, socio-cultural continuum as well as progressive change satisfying the needs for the growing family sizes and privacy of the communities they house. Although it may seem hard to argue against a policy that brings huge improvements in housing standards and sanitation, design and planning for Housing for All must weigh the improvements in housing and sanitation against the loss of all these socio-spatial factors

**Framework for Social Equity Diagram**

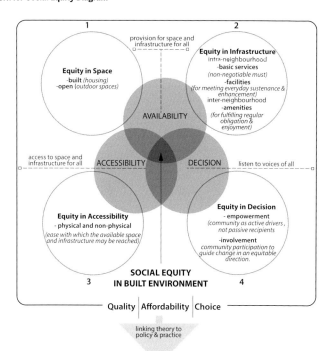

1

provision for space and
infrastructure for all

2

**Equity in Space**
-built *(housing)*
-open *(outdoor spaces)*

**Equity in Infrastructure**
intra-neighbourhood
-basic services
*(non-negotiable must)*
-facilities
*(for meeting everyday sustenance &
enhancement)*
inter-neighbourhood
-amenities
*(for fulfilling regular
obligation &
enjoyment)*

AVAILABILITY

access to space and
infrastructure for all

ACCESSIBILITY    DECISION

listen to voices of all

**Equity in Accessibility**
- physical and non-physical
*(ease with which the available space
and infrastructure may be reached)*

**Equity in Decision**
- empowerment
*(community as active drivers,
not passive recipients*
-involvement
*community participation to
guide change in an equitable
direction.*

**SOCIAL EQUITY
IN BUILT ENVIRONMENT**

3    4

Quality | Affordability | Choice

linking theory to
policy & practice

RIGHTS BASED
POLICIES

URBAN DESIGN
TOOL-KIT

5 Steps towards effective rights
based planning

Design for Social Equity (DSE) in Built
Environment . 20 Rules and Justifications

**Right to Space**
*Built- housing:* adequate housing integrated within the city for all.
*Open- outdoor:* network of purposeful & managed private/public space for all

**Right to Infrastructure**
*basic services:* basic services as non- negotiable must for all.
*intra neighbourhood facilities:* intra neighbourhood facilities readily available
for everyday sustenance and enhancement for all.
*inter neighbourhood amenities:* inter neighbourhood amenities that are easily
accessible for regular requirement and enjoyment for all.

**Right to Access**
*physical:* access to basic services, intra neighbourhood facilities and inter
neighbourhood amenities for all
*non-physical:* access to information and services on urban advantage for all

**Right to Decision**
*empowerment:* building community capacity, skills, resources and collective
ownership for mobilisation and empowerment of all
*engagement:* community governance, inclusive planning, just initiatives that
caters to the needs of all:

**5 Steps towards effective rights based planning**
1. not city planning but intense community planning.
2. not just hardware (housing as product) but focus on software (housing as
process) strategies.
3. not just minimum size, minimum standard housing but building strong
communities that last.
4. not just provision but integration into the city and society at large.
5. not just beneficiaries but community as active agents of their own change.

## How can we link the social equity concept to policy and practice and what is the way forward?

Planning and designing for social equity requires imagination. It requires a sound assessment of the ground issues allowing 'just and sustainable' growth of a city within the bound constraints of its demographic, physical, socio-economic, jurisdictional and financial aspects. An exploratory article like this calls upon further research based on a comprehensive social equity index or benchmark, which can effectively guide India's future growth and design of new cities particularly the 'smart' ones. Such evidence-based policy and design guidance can help designers, planners and decision makers in their efforts towards reducing the divide between smart growth and social justice. Emphasis on equitable processes and outcomes can foster real change that benefits local communities over time.

A framework for social equity, with two key components – planning policies and a design tool-kit – can be seen as the first attempt to initiate thinking and discourses on linking the indispensable but hard-to-materialise concept of social equity to urban design policies and practices. Responsive to the present socio-spatial context, such a framework may evolve or change in tandem with transformations in the society and its relevance may vary with time and context thus requiring regular evaluation of its implementation. A 'Social Equity Design Tool-Kit' is beyond the scope of this article.

However, five steps towards effective rights-based planning can certainly be discussed here (*see the Framework for Social Equity Diagram alongside*).

The present contrasting urban forms and socio-spatial shifts threaten the country's commitment towards inclusive, sustainable urban development by 2030 and its efforts towards becoming a smart, global player. Amidst the rapid expansion of India's urban areas alongside intense growth of informal neighbourhoods (slums), a framework for social equity in built environment that not only informs the urban practices through micro-level interventions but also becomes integral to development policies can be seen as essential to make the country's urban growth and transition more just and sustainable.

This article advocates urgent and sincere efforts to first contain and then reduce the rising levels of extreme social inequity in the built environment, to make the dream of *'acchhe din'* (good days) for the 300 million Indians – nearly a quarter of this population lives in informal neighbourhoods in extreme poverty and vulnerability – a reality. •

## THE BASAVA PROJECT

# Making Space for Migrant Communities in India

**Rajeev Malagi** explores the changing idea of 'being nomadic' in the context of Indian cities

*"I want to quit this Basava's duty, because this is considered as begging. People are happy with so many other jobs, I just want to quit this work."*
- Basavaraj, Kole Basava performer

Cities are considered large and permanent human settlements functioning as centres of growth and economy. But one needs to understand that these places are a culmination of cultures and varied lifestyles. While most of the migrant population seeks permanence in life, there are a few communities that consider migration an integral part of their profession. One of them is the Kole Basava community, a bull-centric folklore community spread across south and west India.

The Kole Basava community demonstrates an interesting human-cattle relationship through socio-cultural and economic interdependencies. The master, along with his decorated bull, travels from one place to another, performing on streets and collecting offerings made to the bull in the form of food and money; a symbolic representation of god. Over time, these communities migrated to different cities in Andhra Pradesh, Karnataka and Tamil Nadu for their livelihood. However, due to urbanisation, lack of space within the city and diluted socio-cultural belief systems, these communities have been pushed to the peripheries in search of open land close to water bodies; water being a basic need for cattle. They are currently living on temporary lands for free or for minimal cost and lack basic facilities and hygiene conditions.

This article narrates the story of the Kole Basava community in the context of Bengaluru, India. It provides a glimpse into their current profession, living conditions and the challenges they face. The interviews of the performer and the cultural expert address the aspirations and needs of the community. The intent of the article, hence, is to research the socio-cultural, economic and

> There are several nomadic communities in India for whom migration is an inherent part of their profession

**Kole Basava with its master**

**The master all set to go out with his decorated Basava**

spatial existence of nomadic communities in the context of cities taking the Kole Basava community as a case study.

The article is a derivative of my self-initiated research and documentation for my ongoing documentary film. It was carried out through interactions with the community and cultural experts. This also gave me an opportunity to experience the life of the community.

The concept of migration has existed since pre-historic times and continues till date in different forms and for different reasons. Today, the trend towards urbanisation continues. As of 2014, as per analysis done by the University of Sussex, if the urbanisation trend continues, it is believed that 54% of the world's population will soon live in cities and it's expected to reach 66% by 2050. Migration forms a significant, and often controversial, part of this urban population growth.

India is a country with a dominant rural population, where 72.2% of the population lives in some 638,000 villages and the remaining 27.8% in about 5,480 towns and urban agglomerations (2001 Census of India). In the post-Independence and industrialisation era, people continue to migrate from villages to urban centres for better economy and living conditions leading to a cultural shift.

Amidst the gamut of a changing world, there are several nomadic communities in India, for whom migration is an inherent part of their profession. These communities comprise professions like fortune-tellers, conjurers, ayurvedic healers, jugglers, acrobats, story tellers, snake charmers, animal doctors, tattoo artists, grindstone makers and basket makers. Anthropologists have identified about 500 nomadic groups in India, numbering perhaps 80 million people: around 7% of the country's billion-plus population. *(Reference: Nomads in India: proceedings of the National Seminar/Edited by P.K. Misra, K.C. Malhotra.)*

The Kole Basava community demonstrates a human-animal relationship where the bull represents a cultural and economic anchor.

## The performance and the community

The cow/bull as an animal has major significance in India. From being worshiped as a divine form of god to giving them significant rights to stroll around on the urban roads, they have become an important part of the Indian belief system. The relationship of the bull with humans exists in various forms, particularly in the Indian context. From being a source of dairy products to being a political symbol for banners, it continues to be a source of income and a socio-cultural icon for the country. One among its many avatars is the Kole Basava community.

The tradition of Kole Basava is a folk-art form in which the bulls and their masters are trained to perform various acts to entertain people. The bulls are referred to as Basava, representing the male form of god and the cows are referred to as Parvathi or Sita representing the female form. These bulls are decorated with traditional and colourful elements like *saris* (five-yard cloth), beads, bells and ribbons, handcrafted by the community. The duo walk from door to door where the master plays the *shehnai* (a wooden wind instrument) while the bull performs different movements in exchange for the offerings made by the disciples of rice, fruits, money and even clothes during festivals.

The Kole Basava community was once considered an integral part of the village, as reflected in their spatial existence in the last two decades. But the need for better economic conditions and aspirations for better living standards have led to the migration of these communities to cities. Today, these communities are often nestled on the periphery of the city. The masters along with their bulls leave before dawn and travel to the inner parts of the city covering up to 8–10 km and return by noon, which completes their day's cycle. The rest of the day is spent in recreation or preparing for the next day.

Basanna, the master, says, "Our community was considered equivalent to a higher caste community and we were respected by all. We could reside in the centre of the city near the temples and were called to perform in the temple premises."

But over time, due to migration, the nature of their profession has adapted to the context of cities. Mr. Basavaraj, a cultural expert from Bengaluru mentions that the Kole Basava

## Due to migration, the nature of their profession has adapted to the context of cities

**The Kole Basava community nestled on the outskirts of the city on vacant, private land on a temporary basis, for nominal rents**

*Top Left:* **Poor water and sanitary conditions**
*Top Right:* **Temporary shelter built by the community**
*Left:* **A master training a young bull to perform the stunt**

community follows a process of partial migration where they perform in cities for a majority of the year and return to their villages during off-peak seasons. They currently face a social, cultural, economic and spatial setback, struggling to sustain their profession and their life.

## Lack of spatial living conditions

Earlier, the performer along with the bull and the family walked from one village to the other residing within the open areas, temples, under trees in the villages where there was availability of necessities like shade, water and fodder. Over time, these communities migrated to the cities for better economy and settled in open *maidans* around the city. But the densification of the core, lack of availability of open grounds and increase in the geographical spread of the city, pushed these communities towards the periphery and continues to do so. They often locate themselves where there is availability of vegetation and water and hence ponds, tanks or lakes often become their primary consideration. Today in Bengaluru, these communities have settled on unclaimed open areas or vacant properties given for free on a temporary basis or rented out by real estate owners for a nominal price.

Basanna says, "It is hard to stay within the city as we do not find open spaces and other facilities like drinking water, toilets etc.
The cattle also need open space with tree shade and fodder. We have bought a low-cost motorbike for each family, just to fetch fodder and we take turns to do that."

Due to the temporary nature of their stay and absence of ownership of legal land and permanent shelter, people of the community are living in unhygienic conditions. The houses are built from materials gathered from surrounding construction

sites or nearby areas like waste wood, tarpaulin sheets, concrete bricks and plastic pipes. Sanitary conditions are very poor with each house having only a bathing facility and no toilets. At times, the chosen lands are unsuitable for bulls due to absence of tree shade and fodder. The sheds built for the bulls are not stable to sustain rough weather conditions.

But what goes beyond all these challenges is that when the owner of the land wants to build or sell his property, these communities must relocate themselves on fresh land repeating the entire painstaking processes. What was 'nomadic'

*Top:* **The community settled amidst the urban fabric, with minimal security or infrastructure**
*Middle:* **A member of the community on his way to the city for tool sharpening work**
*Bottom:* **Kids of the community at play**

as a profession has now changed to a need- and situation-based migration.

## The cultural shift

The bull is usually considered as holy in the cultural context of India. The Kole Basava tradition is one such profession that utilises the bull, with its socio-cultural significance in society, through folk performances. The idea of outdoor performances like theatre and street performances was a lot more prominent in the past when there was an absence of technology and minimal choices for entertainment. The Kole Basava performance was one such act, which combined cultural and folk entertainment. Mr. Basavaraj says, "The performances are unique and sometimes astonishing. A fully-grown bull weighing hundreds of kilos stands on all its four limbs on the chest of its master, who lies on the ground. It takes both physical strength and will power to perform something like this."

But people's changing lifestyles and modes of entertainment to formalised spaces and devices have greatly impacted these performances and the culture of the Kole Basava. With very few appreciating this tradition and offering money and food to the bull daily, the masters now perform only during Hindu festivals. Basanna explains, "Earlier, our forefathers used to go to a public square near a temple to play drums and

**Anthropologists have identified about 500 nomadic groups in India, numbering perhaps 80 million people**

perform. The whole town used to eagerly watch them perform. But the arrival of TV and films has changed everything. People enjoy fighting and entertainment now and not our performances."

This folklore tradition may well end up being a mere documented entity in cultural museums and may not be enjoyed by future generations.

### Security, a concern

The other aspect to be focused on is the lack of security the community faces. The Kole Basava performers moved as single families with their bulls and camped near the village. The belief of Basava bringing fortune to individual families induced the entire village to allow the Kole Basava community to build their trust with the locals and hence become an integral part of the village ecosystem. But the idea of communal living in today's metropolitan cities has changed. Everyone is more interested in just 'surviving' rather than 'integrated living'.

The variation in the degree of acceptance of these traditional belief systems is evident between the older and newer areas of the city as well. There have been instances where these communities have been asked to vacate their homes due to fear of theft or crime.

The loss of value of this culture has created a huge impact on the economic growth of the community. With the rise in global culture and cities becoming metropolitan, the Basava performance is now being considered a nuisance by the residents. This, along with their struggle to find a place within the global community (socio-culturally, economically and physically), has directly impacted their daily earnings. People of the community are opting for alternative work like knife sharpening, labour work and other minor jobs, for their survival. They now believe that the new generation should not continue their age-old profession and would rather educate the kids for better jobs yielding substantial income.

The master returning to his community

If this continues, it will lead to the death of this culture.

### So, what's next?

The Kole Basava community were once nomadic by profession, but are now attempting to settle down due to lack of livelihood and security. The challenge is in integrating these nomadic communities as a part of the city's ecosystem and bringing a sense of permanence to their lives. City folk may view these communities as novelties, but the communities, on the other hand, want to upgrade their skills and profession to lead lives like the rest of the world. So, the question is, how do we strike the right balance between the two where the communities can retain their art and yet manage to earn enough to sustain their families? Can the idea of 'cities for all' justify the existence of these communities where we accept them as a part of the city's spatial ecosystem? Can these rich yet dying cultures be intertwined with modernity to create a contemporary twist, which can in turn strengthen their relationship with the people of the city? Can we really design cities for all? ●

# Gendered Production of Spaces in Sri Lanka

**Kaushalya Herath** walks the mean streets of Colombo

One night, my family dropped me in Pettah, Colombo, at around 8:00 pm so that I could take a bus to Moratuwa. Just after they left, as I was walking towards the pedestrian crossing to get to the bus stand, a man holding the hand of his elderly mother gave me a questioning look as if wondering 'where do these girls go alone late at night?' Another guy who noticed this incident began stalking me so, as a precaution, I took refuge by joining three guys who were about to cross the road. But they started to make fun of me. One guy said, "Ah you waited for us to cross the road with you, right?" "Do you want us to die for you?" the second guy interjected. The last guy even invited me to join them. Then they all kept repeating, "Will you come?"

These men made fun of me because they perceived me as an object to release their stress. I'd had a really long day, was exhausted and using public spaces added an extra pressure to my day because I am a woman. Fortunately, a bus came along. Most of my Sri Lankan friends with whom I shared this story insisted that I should not have walked alone in Pettah that late at night. Some other women were curious about why my family left me alone in Pettah and exclaimed, "My family would never do that."

Street harassment of women is a real problem in Pettah, although not limited to the area. Women get harassed on the streets, at bus stands, railway stations and this clearly shows that spaces in Pettah are gendered. Time of space is gendered. This is an important concern for urban planners in Sri Lanka.

It is important to understand the dynamics of Pettah in order to understand the gender in spaces. Pettah is a highly commercialised district in Colombo, the commercial capital of Sri Lanka. Colombo was the colonial capital under the Portuguese, the Dutch and the British for centuries. Colombo Port and colonial rule played a huge role in producing Pettah. Nihal Perera (1998, 2002, 2015) has discussed the colonial production of Colombo and also the indigenisation and feminisation processes of Colombo in general and Pettah in particular. Pettah is one of the most multicultural spaces in Colombo. The indigenisation and feminisation process of white male Christian Colombo (Perera, 2002) happened over many decades, but even today I observe Pettah as a masculine space.

This article reflects my own experience of gendered spaces during an ethnographic study in Pettah in 2014. I took the stretch of road between Colombo Railway Station and the Wimaladharma

> The indigenisation and feminisation process of white male Christian Colombo happened over many decades, but even today I observe Pettah as a masculine space

*Left:* **One of the Cross Streets in Pettah on a Friday morning**
*Right:* **Bogaha Handiya**

Clock Tower along Malwatta Cross Street every Friday evening and Monday morning for four months. I chose this road randomly. In addition to this walk, I went to Pettah for interviews and other regular uses from time to time. Malwatta Cross Street and other cross streets of Pettah are usually full of men. According to my basic observations, during many visits, the ratio of women to men on Malwatta Cross Street on a weekday was about 1:10. At night, this ratio drops. There are also queer people in Pettah, perhaps because it is relatively easier for different people to coexist in more multicultural places. The number of women on the Main Street and second Cross Street are higher than other streets. Women who use Pettah as a transit route add up to the number of women who are present on the main road in Pettah. As Pettah is probably the most diverse place in the entire country, women in Pettah also represent different class, caste, ethnicity, religion, age, disability and education levels. I also tried to capture this intersectionality in gender in my observations.

## Gendered Spaces in Pettah

Every time I walked along Malwatta Cross Street, I was subjected to eve teasing. Street vendors made comments such as, "Ah *nangi* (hey sister), why are you alone?" "Just give us a smile", and "You are beautiful". Very recently (January, 2018), I was walking in Pettah with a group of about 20 men and women. Even then, on a busy street, a vendor mumbled into my ear with a sexual tone, "What are you looking for?" I interviewed some women who were walking alone. These women mostly work in the municipal council cleaning service and shops, or use Pettah as a transit place, or they live on the streets. Other women who visit Pettah for shopping are, more often than not, never alone.

Anyone going from the SLTB (Sri Lanka Transport Board) bus terminal to the Main Street has to walk through the Fose Market, a sheltered market built by the government to house all the informal street vendors. Almost all the vendors and shopkeepers in this market are men. Alleyways inside the market are narrow and women have to tolerate men gazing at them and passing comments. The alleyway from the Main Street to the private bus terminal on Bastian Street is also the same.

Women from different backgrounds, using Pettah for different purposes, said that these comments with sexual undertones make them feel that women don't belong in Pettah. This idea is also supported by the common perceptions about Pettah. An undergraduate of Colombo University from a rural village mentioned that her parents advised her

**A Muslim woman in Pettah**

that Pettah is not a good place for women, especially for young women. She said, "It would be great to be able to walk around Pettah without listening to rude comments and feeling like I am naked and exposed."

## Stereotyping Gender and Spaces

In order to reveal real issues, it requires us to deconstruct and unlearn some stereotypes and perceptions attached to gender and space. Let's unwrap some of the stereotypes attached to Pettah and the women there. Outsiders who come to Pettah think that women who are alone and well-dressed are prostitutes. According to them, Pettah is not only a man's place; it is also a place of 'bad' women. This dominant idea from outsiders is very powerful in restricting women's use of Pettah. As Shilpa Phadke writes, women are not privileged to loiter in most South Asian cities. Women have to have a purpose for their trips and are expected to travel only from one sheltered space to another. The same ideology is reflected in spaces in Pettah. Once I was waiting in Pettah for a friend and suspicious looks came my way. Later I was told by some of my friends that it was because I was waiting by a place where sex workers usually hang out. It's not only the spaces that define the women, but also their presence, whether they are sex workers or not, that changes the meaning of spaces.

'Genderedness' of the spaces in Pettah has two edges: spaces are not safe and women get harassed when using public spaces; and on the other hand, the fear that spaces are not safe, discourages women from using public spaces. This worsens the issue and makes spaces more unsafe. Some women avoid coming alone to Pettah and others use Pettah only

*Top:* **Inside Fose Market**
*Bottom:* **A man staring at a woman walking through a narrow alleyway**

as a transit point simply because it is necessary to do so, but they make sure they have company. The perception that Pettah is not a safe place for women is influencing women's use of Pettah more than the actual issues that make it unsafe for women.

Once I was walking through the shops in the Fose Market and a shopkeeper passed some comments. I stopped and smiled at him. He immediately turned into a nice person and asked me what I wanted to buy. I explained that I was there for research and asked if he was willing to help. I asked him, "Why do you make fun of women who pass by?" He said, "It is just for fun, I don't think there is anything wrong in it. Sorry if my joke upset you, but most women enjoy being teased." Some other men also agreed and believed women didn't feel unsafe and abused by the unnecessary comments. On the contrary, a few women I interviewed who use Pettah regularly disagreed that they enjoy teasing. They stressed that they expected Pettah to be harassment free.

Pettah is a transportation hub in Sri Lanka: the Central Bus Terminal and the Central Railway Station of Sri Lanka are located here. There is a large number of transit population in and around Pettah. After dark, the transit population mostly consists of men. Sometimes, men stay the night in places around the bus terminal to take a bus the next morning. Prem and Manoj used to take a bus to Pettah from the Eastern province and would arrive at Pettah around 3 a.m. on some Mondays for a few years. While waiting for a bus to Moratuwa in Pettah, they had observed men waiting for buses by the roadside, male labourers and other male users of Pettah taking naps on the pedestrian paths and in front of shop spaces. Some women had approached them on many of these mornings, and they believe that these individuals were sex workers.

## Making Spaces More Inclusive for All

There are 'street women' in Pettah; these women are identified as beggars by the general public, but not all these women beg for money. Some of them have small businesses or are labourers.

A woman of Hindu origin was living near the Wimaladharma Clock Store with her son. She (Rani) said her husband left Pettah to go to South India to find a job and never returned. Rani sends her son to a school nearby. She has negotiated with the security officers of the Wimaladharma Clock Tower to be able to stay within the railings of the store where it is safer for her and her son. She does some labour work and helps clean the store front to earn a living.

Malkanthi is another woman by the clock tower, coming from a housing scheme in Maradana to

*Top:* **On a Friday morning in front of the SLTB bus terminal**
*Bottom Left:* **A woman from the Colombo Municipal Council Cleaning Service**
*Bottom Right:* **A small shelter set up by a woman near a store front**

Pettah every day to sell betel chew. A mother with her disabled son from Ambilipitiya, a town faraway from Colombo, also used to come to Pettah during the weekends. She stays at a church nearby at night and begs for money by the clock tower on Saturdays.

These women have redefined the spaces by changing their meanings, adding small spaces that are safe for them. Just the presence of women in public spaces can make spaces safer for all. When there are women with their 'eyes on the street' (Jacobs, 1962), it makes the spaces safer for other women who visit Pettah. I felt safe as I hung around near the Wimaladharma Clock Tower due to the presence of these women and on the other occasions I went to Pettah, I felt even safer because I knew these women.

Women in Pettah represent different age groups too. There was an elderly mentally challenged

woman who lived on one of the cross streets. She had created her own shelter with plastic sheets and other temporary material. One morning, I observed some shopkeepers were making fun of this woman by throwing plastic bags filled with water at her. She was yelling at these men. It seems that the shopkeepers enjoyed watching this woman yelling indecent words and throwing tantrums. It is interesting to see how women with physical and mental disabilities, women of minor ethnicities and women of different age groups are treated in Pettah. Intersectionality of gender is a very important dimension in understanding gendered spaces.

Women in Pettah also familiarise spaces by changing themselves. Some women try to adopt some characteristics that are perceived by popular culture as masculine. One of the women attached to the Municipal Council Cleaning Service said she finds it easier to survive in Pettah when she dresses "like a man". One visitor mentioned that, "even the women in Pettah are like men." According to him, women in Pettah also use dirty words, which also highlighted the idea that the language is gendered. Women use this as a strategy to fit into the masculine spaces in Pettah.

## Mainstream Planning and Gendered Production of Spaces

Mainstream planning and development projects by the government and capital investments by the private sector fail to notice the gendered spaces and the production of spaces by women. A labourer in Pettah once said, "We want no development from the government, because what they call development is a city without us." When the government formalised the informal trading and vending activities in Pettah a few years ago, several new market complexes were introduced and trading activities were relocated. Some people who had small stands by the roadside to sell some items were neither given a new shop space nor were they allowed to do business in their original location, as it became illegal with the new formalisation process. A woman who sells betel chew by the Pettah Bogaha Handiya (junction by the bo tree) said, "Only thugs with political support got shops at the new places. I was here doing business since I was born (an exaggerated expression), but they (government and planners) refused to acknowledge that." She believes that it is very rare for women to be acknowledged for their presence and activities in a place like Pettah, particularly when it comes to business and development.

## Conclusion

Spaces are gendered in Pettah and women face various issues in public spaces; some spaces are safer for women than others and the time of the day affects women's use of spaces. Most of the women shared that they don't feel like they

Floating Market Area

*Top:* **Fose Market stage 1**
*Bottom:* **A betel chew vendor by the Bogaha Handiya**

belong to Pettah. Women use Pettah only if they have a reason to do so. Even then they usually accompany another man or a woman to make it more comfortable and safe for them. In Pettah, most of the labourers, bus drivers, taxi drivers, street vendors and shopkeepers are men. Most of the people who live on the streets are also men. This discourages women from visiting Pettah alone. After dark, it is very difficult to find women on the streets.

Despite the fact that the spaces are gendered and women face different issues in Pettah, women are familiarising the spaces. This familiarising process is twofold: they transform spaces to be more inclusive and also change themselves to fit into masculine spaces by adopting some characteristics defined as masculine. Mainstream development discourse is unable to read and understand these familiarisation processes. Instead, these processes create alien and formal spaces that are not inclusive for all the genders. It requires one to pay enough attention to how gendered the spaces are and the women's process of producing spaces in order to develop more inclusive and sustainable cities. ●

# Bridging Two Extremes: Notes from Latin America

Bridging the gap between the rich and the poor isn't always about income equality. Sometimes, the way we create urban spaces can give people a sense of inclusion that is just as valuable. **Vinayak Bharne** shows us how

It would be wonderful if the right to the city were equitable for one and all. If the wealth of public places, access to jobs and privilege of easy mobility were available to everyone, irrespective of social class or income level. If our cities were not enmeshed in tensions between power structures and economic hierarchies, but displayed an altruism that sought to reward everyone in various ways. If the right to the city was not decided by who had power and who did not. But this is not the way the world works. All cities in some form or the other have economic poles; some far starker than others, and between them there's a mundane middle that sustains both. The nuances of how these poles struggle and negotiate this middle, intentionally, unintentionally or inadvertently, are what the shaping of an affordable or, in turn, unaffordable city is all about.

## Unfair City: The Widening Gap Between Two Extremes

Questions such as who should share the public offerings of the city, by what means, and on whose consent, encompass every city. They are difficult questions, as deeply philosophical as political. In the United States for example, over the past few decades, most cities have sprawled – legally – into vast automobile-dependent places where only the rich can afford to live and the poor cannot. But there is a bigger irony at work here: these affluent places are fed by highways, malls and job centres, where the less-affluent have to commute long hours for work. In other words, the poor have to pay for more gas and more taxes, which in turn funds more highways that ironically exclude them. As such, the least affordable cities in the United States are born out of a gross disconnect between housing and transportation costs compared to

**Sprawling cities actually turn out to be far less affordable than compact cities with public transit because of their high cost of driving to spread-out locations**

PHOTO: PHOTOPIPPO, WIKIMEDIA COMMONS

Cityscape of Santa Barbara, California. The average house price in Santa Barbara is over a million US dollars, making it one of the most expensive markets in the United States

typical household income. The poorest fifth of American families pour more than 40% of their income into owning and maintaining cars. And this economic gap widens further through other social fissures. In Los Angeles, for instance, the subway linking downtown to the Pacific Ocean in Santa Monica was in fact delayed for two decades because wealthy residents of Hancock Park and Beverly Hills did not want their community to be directly accessible to the poorer residents of east and south Los Angeles.

As a contentious terrain between two economic extremes, the unaffordable city has various global guises. Singapore today is not only the most expensive city in the world, where the import of chewing gum is banned and where there are fines for irritating people with a musical instrument, but it's also one whose liveability quotient is synonymous with an impeccable cleanliness and urban order. Aberdeen (Scotland) is an almost solely private sector city, boasting the highest concentration of millionaires in the United Kingdom. Paris, which now ranks as the second-most expensive city after Singapore, has rental accommodation at prices so high that modest-paid

workers have taken up illegal and substandard rooms, even as the poor and elderly are carted out to the urban edges. In Caracas, Venezuela's capital and also one of the world's priciest cities, high inflation rates and chronic food shortages are driving up the average living cost even as gasoline remains cheap. And even though Tokyo is no longer the most expensive city in the world as it was in the '80s, with the Fukushima disaster prompting a shutdown of all 50 nuclear reactors across Japan, residents are paying more than ever in household electricity bills.

Meanwhile, with nearly 50% of Asia's and Africa's populations becoming city dwellers, and more than 75% of Latin America already there, inner city poverty is now the biggest challenge of our time. With infrastructure hardly developing at the same pace as the largest and fastest-growing cities in Africa, Asia and Latin America, the demographic bulk fueling this growth has to live in temporary shelters and slums, symbolising the other extreme of the unaffordable city. Weak ownership rights to the land leave slum residents economically vulnerable and unable to build safe, sturdy houses and these habitats consequently

Singapore Boat Quay and skyline. Singapore is the world's most expensive city, according to research by the Economist Intelligence Unit (EIU), followed by Paris, Oslo, Zurich and Sydney

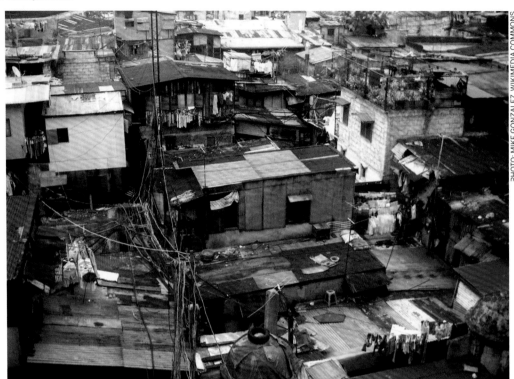

PHOTO: MIKE GONZALEZ, WIKIMEDIA COMMONS

**Shanty town, Manila, Phillippines, seen from Recto LRT Station**

become easy victims to weather, fire and crime. The lack of safe, clean water means that families often have to buy it at a high price from vendors. Inadequate sanitation and waste disposal means disease and illness means loss of livelihood, leaving families struggling to buy food.

There is also a deeper environmental consequence to all this: urban poverty endangers the lives of millions of urban residents and simultaneously damages the environment. But environmental degradation continues at an even bigger scale through middle and upper classes' over-consumption and increasing industrial production, both of which damage natural resources. And even as the poor are denied access to fundamental infrastructure, governments are financially unable or often even refuse to invest in efficient systems. The challenge of the polarised city is as much environmental as it is political, as much about sound governance as efficient management processes and as much about concerns of social justice, as experimental efforts in human psychology.

### Towards a Fair City: Transforming the Mundane Middle

How can we make the city more equitable for everyone? How can we help a polarised city feel more balanced? How and where do we begin to bridge the ends of urban inequality? There is no question that the numerous bottom-up practices and campaigns by activist and non-government organisations and their ability to grapple with extreme issues at the bottom of the economic pyramid – poverty, informal economies, social injustice etc. – cannot be underestimated. But the unaffordable city has many other broader, yet more nuanced dimensions as well: rampant sprawl, bad mobility, rising home prices, the looming water crisis, urban pollution, gridlock, toxicity and the erasure of agrarian landscapes. These issues are equally pressing, for they are destroying the long-term viability of cities for both the rich and poor and everyone in between.

For example, there is a direct relationship between walkability, transit and affordability. Sprawling cities actually turn out to be far less affordable than compact cities with public transit because of their high cost of driving in spread-out locations. New York City and San Francisco have relatively high housing costs, but they also rank among the lowest-cost cities for transportation, because of their relative urban density that facilitates walking and their extensive and heavily-used mass transit networks. In cities with the dire need for bridging polarised extremes, the answer

**In the shaping of the affordable city, feeling equal matters as much, or perhaps even more, than actually becoming equal**

SOURCE: MORIO, WIKIMEDIA COMMONS

*Top:* **Bus stops in Curitiba, Brazil**
*Bottom:* **The TransMileneo bus system, Bogota, Columbia**

then might actually lie somewhere in between, that is, in transforming the mundane middle of the city and letting it nudge the two extremes together.

Curitiba stands out in this regard. By 1960, this Brazilian city's population had surged within two decades from 120,000 people to 361,000. Even as planners were contemplating widening roads for more cars, Curitiban architect Jaime Lerner took office as mayor in 1971. He introduced dedicated bus lanes along the city's main arteries, with stations placed on medians along the routes. The intent was to allow buses to run at speeds comparable to light rail, while dramatically reducing the cost. Lerner made a bargain with private bus operators to partly pay for the creation of the new infrastructure, giving them the vehicles in exchange. With this trade-off in place, the first rapid-bus lanes of Curitiba ended up costing 50 times less than rail. The first line opened in 1974 and, by 1993, with new routes added, it was carrying 1.5 million passengers a day. Today,

the Rede Integrada de Transporte has 157 bi-articulated and 29 single-articulated vehicles and is used by 2.3 million passengers of all income levels and class each day, together representing 85% of Curitiba's population.

Bogota, Columbia, is another compelling case in point. Before Enrique Penalosa became its mayor in 1998, the city was getting technical and planning advice from the Japanese International Co-operation Agency (JICA), and they had prescribed a vast network of freeways to ease the city's congestion. This is what Penalosa threw away. He hiked gasoline prices and poured revenues into an ambitious agenda putting public space and public transit at the forefront. Inspired by Curitiba, The TransMilenio bus system was introduced and given the best space on the city's avenues in exclusive lanes, making cars and minibuses secondary. The sleek red look of these buses and the use of high-quality finishes in the bus stations was an additional strategy to boost the status of

SOURCE: PEDRO FELIPE, WIKIMEDIA COMMONS

public transit for one and all. The TransMilenio began to move many people of all income levels so effectively that general commuting time across the city plummeted making things efficient for everyone. Curitiba's bus rapid transit and Bogota's TransMilenio not only successfully bridged the economic extremes of their respective cities bringing benefits to all sections of society, but did it at a fraction of the cost.

Columbia has two other worthy cases in nudging the rich and poor together in cities with rigid class lines and rampant violence. One is the now famous Ciclovia programme. In 1994, when Enrique Peñalosa lost the mayoral seat to Antanas Mockus, his younger brother Guillermo was hired as the commissioner of parks, sports and recreation. He recast the Ciclovia programme that had originally in 1974 barricaded eight miles of roads every Sunday and opened them only to cyclists and pedestrians. Penalosa supersized this concept to more than 60 miles of the city's major streets. Gradually, more than a million skaters, joggers and strollers began coming out to enjoy this new 'park' that was now open to everyone. Less-privileged residents who had no backyards or cars to escape the city, in particular, now had a public space of their own. As a unique experiment in social equitability, the Ciclovia programme closed the gap between the rich and poor who gathered together happily in a common setting.

The other case is Medellin's visually striking 385-metre-long escalator installed in Comuna Trece, one of the poorest sections of the city. It opened in 2011. The escalator operates on weekdays from 6 a.m. to 10 p.m. and on weekends from 8 a.m. to 9 p.m. It is busiest in the evening when people return home from work and on weekends the area around the escalators turns into a social space. More than giving the people in Comuna Trece access to the city, the escalators have paved the way for the city and in turn its institutions to gain access to one of its remotest areas. Consequently, it has been easier for the municipality, non-profits, police and housing corporations to improve public services, bring in subsidies for housing improvements, create social programmes for children and young mothers and help the younger demographic resist the temptations of gang involvement. The escalator has not directly ameliorated the Comuna's physical conditions, or helped it produce higher incomes. And neither has it reduced the city's overall income inequality.

But for the first time, there is a new sense of pride, dignity and inclusion among the local residents. For the first time, residents of Medellin's poorest neighbourhoods have felt a real connection to the city and vice versa, giving both a greater

> **The Ciclovia programme closed the gap between the rich and poor who gathered together happily in a common setting**

PHOTO: NAT_FG. WIKIMEDIA COMMONS

Ciclovia, circa 2009, Bogota, Columbia

**Medellin also has a gondola lift system called Metrocable. It was implemented by the Medellin City Council to provide a complementary transportation service to Medellin's Metro, and designed to reach some of the least developed suburban areas of the city**

sense of belonging. As Charles Montgomery suggests in his book *Happy City*, the biggest lesson to learn from Medellin is this: In the shaping of the affordable city, feeling equal matters as much, or perhaps even more, than actually becoming equal.

## In Summary

The most significant thing in the cases discussed is that they are neither perfect nor radical. Bogota's efforts have not directly mitigated the city's inequalities and the TransMilenio is currently plagued by desperate overcrowding.

But as sincere, practical, conscious efforts towards the making of an equitable city, these experiments have actively redistributed the city's benefits to make it fairer and more accessible to the largest number of people and within their own specific means. They affirm that by spending resources towards designing cities to be more generous, we can in fact make cities stronger and more resilient. They affirm that striving to help people feel more equal is a very worthy policy goal.

The other important thing is that all these ideas and initiatives have happened without the necessity of guerilla tactics or alternative means; they have emerged as government and municipal

initiatives with an intimate understanding of the pulse of their cities and people. If then, as Michel de Certeau has noted, 'tactics' are employed by citizens to negotiate daily life in the city, and 'strategies' in turn emanate from the state and corporations in the form of government regulation, Bogota's TransMileneo and Ciclovia, or Medellin's escalator are lessons in how to blur the boundaries between the two.

From social housing to public transit, from job creation to public space, the struggle to shape the affordable city is the struggle to confront the unfairness wrought by market forces, cultural biases and social pressures and the struggle to answer the fundamental question: Who is the city for?

If, as Enrique Penalosa remarked in his inauguration mayoral speech, only a city that respects human beings can expect citizens to respect the city in return, then shaping the affordable city is a continuous, dedicated campaign towards urban fairness and the place to begin this change is not at the extremes but in between. We must recognise the transformative potential of the mundane middle of our cities and we must believe in this change and act on it. Let's get to work. ●

# Children's Right to Play in Inclusive Cities

**Sudeshna Chatterjee**, from Action for Children's Environments, argues for safe, child-friendly cities in contexts of crisis

The International Play Association (IPA) carried out research to understand the play rights and play needs of children living in situations of crisis in six countries: India, Japan, Lebanon, Nepal, Thailand and Turkey (Chatterjee, 2017 & 2018). The urban research contexts in the study represented a diversity of crisis situations, ranging from everyday crises in an illegal squatter settlement in Kolkata, India, and in Burmese and Cambodian migrant settlements in Thailand; the humanitarin crisis of the continued exclusion and discrimination against the Roma people in racially mixed neighbourhoods in Istanbul, Turkey; and the crisis precipitated by the enormous triple disaster following the Great East Japan earthquake in 2011, which ravaged the eastern coast of Japan.

## Migrant communities in Thailand
Since 1984, 80% of all migrants in Thailand are Burmese who fled their homeland. The

IPA research engaged with an urban Burmese community who lived around a fishing dock in a high-risk landscape dotted with abandoned buildings and dark swampy mangrove areas. Parents worked at night leaving children unsupervised and vulnerable. Various coping mechanisms had evolved including women taking turns to coordinate off days to watch over the children at night.

Children's play typically involved exploring the many safe as well as unsafe places in their surroundings. In contrast, a Cambodian migrant community included in this study, actively prevented children from playing outdoors. The Cambodian migrants, many of whom were illegal, lived in a busy port area where sand trading took place bringing in much heavy vehicular traffic and unchecked workers. Parents feared for their children while away at work and prohibited playing far away from home. Some of the children had no permission to leave the house at all and

> **Children's play in such limited and often aggressive ways was perhaps a way of coping with the violence embedded in their community**

Access to housing through a dark, swampy mangrove area

SOURCE: JHALAPALA

SOURCE: CHILD AND YOUTH MEDIA FOUNDATION (CYMF), THAILAND

were locked up at home while parents were away at work. They were given cell phones as a communication lifeline.

## Illegal squatter settlers in Kolkata

The site of the IPA research study in India was a squatter settlement where people lived without any security of tenure and in abject poverty in an extremely hazardous environment. The squatter huts were located on either side of a railway track and to the east of the squatters was the River Hooghly. Growing up barely three feet away from a busy rail track with inadequate signaling, children and families considered the train track a lesser hazard than the river. The river was unpredictable, particularly during a tidal bore, when a sudden backward surge from the estuary swelled up the river with strong currents. Two children died in the river during the rainy season last year.

By far the riskiest play witnessed during the course of the six-country research was seen in Kolkata where boys from the age of eight built rafts from found loose materials and navigated the Hooghly River. The process of resourcing materials for building the raft, and later using and protecting it, demonstrates the highest form of resilience in the face of tremendous structural challenges.

This was the favourite play of boys living in Nimtola Ghat, Kolkata. The raft was locally called a 'trawler' or 'shola', and they made it themselves for sailing on the river even during high tides or during the tidal bore. They held floating parties on the trawler, used it for sailing on the river and also for crossing over to the other side. Particularly during summer, boys used the trawler extensively to float in the middle of the river. In an environment that had no safe spaces for children to play, the trawler was an innovative way to claim territory in the biggest open space available to the children in their city: the Hooghly River.

## Growing up Roma with structural discrimination every day

The three Roma neighbourhoods (Sulukule, Tarlabasi and Kustepe) under this study in Istanbul were all poor, lacked open spaces for outdoor play and had unsafe public places. Parents told stories about kidnapping, burglary and street fights to scare children from venturing out too much. The only places that were considered safe spaces were the children's centres run by different organisations and university volunteers.

In one of the neighbourhoods, a lot of aggression was witnessed in the street play of young Roma boys during the fieldwork for this research. The boys fought with knives and also burned trash. They acted like the men around them: aggressive and tough. Children's play in such limited and often aggressive ways was perhaps a way of coping with the violence embedded in their community; it may also be indicative of internal distress. In either case it does suggest the need for specialised interventions to reduce the risks and vulnerabilities in children's lives while promoting the right to play in these contexts.

## Disaster destroys play opportunities in Japan

Japan is one of the most earthquake-prone countries in the world and also one of the best prepared. Immediately after the magnitude 9 earthquake and the tsunami on the coast of the Tohoku area, people were evacuated to schools and large halls and lived in overcrowded conditions for about six months while temporary housing was being constructed by the government.

After the evacuation stage, different types of temporary houses were made available but there were no play spaces. Irrespective of where children were staying – the evacuation centres, at a relative's house, or public temporary housing, or even when children returned to their original

*Right:* **The trawler being taken out for a test run along the river banks (Kolkata)**
*Left:* **Cambodian migrant children playing on a construction site**

SOURCE: HITOSHI SHIMAMURA

SOURCE: JHALAPALA

house directly from the evacuation shelter – they had no adequate space or opportunity to play. The parks and schoolyards became dominated by construction work for temporary houses and leftover spaces around them were covered with tarmac and used for parking cars. The landscape of devastation coupled with lack of permission to play, inspired aggressive play outdoors or playing video games indoors.

## Coping through play

Sneaking out to play was the most typical coping mechanism observed and reported by children across all the IPA research sites. While staying in the evacuation centre in Japan, boys and girls tried to seek out secret places such as under the bridge, a place they had no parental license to explore. They enjoyed catching fish in the river. More importantly they cherished the riverside as a place to have contact with nature. In the context of everyday crises, despite lack of permission, children played in unsafe places where adults prohibited play; children could do this very well since their parents were often not around. This was particularly true in Kolkata and Thailand. The prohibited places were the places they liked to visit the most. Those places were often places with water (for example rivers, river banks, ponds, canals, waterways or waste water pipes) and were challenging and exciting to explore so children often sought them out secretly by themselves or with friends.

## Interventions for children

Across the IPA research contexts, attempts to promote the right to play by different organisations were most notably seen in Japan, Thailand and to a lesser degree in Turkey. In

India, where much free play was witnessed but under the most hazardous conditions, securing the right to play depended very much on the individual creativity and resilience of children living in squatter settlements and some parents who sometimes facilitated play by making play objects for children.

The Japanese Adventure Playground Association supported local volunteer groups to set up temporary pop-up playgrounds. Eight adventure playgrounds were built in Ishinomaki City after the disaster. Japan, which already had a culture of mobile play through Play Cars (vividly painted cars carrying play materials to different locations for setting up temporary/pop-up play spaces), saw escalated mobilisation after the disaster through the work of various non-profit organisations and some support from the UNICEF National Committee in Japan. A two-day festival called Mini City Ishinomaki has been held every year from 2012 since the disaster. Modelled after Mini-Munich, which creates a mini city where everyday life in a big city is simulated through play, Mini City Ishinomaki reclaims the city centre that has been partly abandoned by businesses after the disaster and recreates the city's life. It also offers a networking platform for all organisations committed to rebuilding activities after the disaster.

In Thailand, the Foundation for Child Development built a playground with the help of the community by reclaiming a muddy patch between two residential buildings. When it was finished, people in the community called it 'Salor-Lukui-Sukretaw', which in the Karen language means 'This Place Is the Best'. Salor-Lukui-Sukretaw is more than a safe playground for children; it is the first leisure and creative place for migrant children and also a socialisation space for parents. The community

*Left:* **Children, community and volunteers built a playground in a temporary housing site in Ishinomaki City, Japan, one year after the disaster**
*Right:* **Children's favourite play space by the river in Kolkata**

Sneaking out to play was the most typical coping mechanism observed and reported by children

SOURCE: HITOSHI SHIMAMURA

*Right:* **Mini Ishinomaki City being set up, a recurring event since 2012 after the disaster**
*Bottom:* **A community-built playground in the heart of an urban Burmese migrant community in Thailand**

SOURCE: AUTHOR

volunteers manage to keep the place safe and clean. This is a good example of the implementation of one of the Sustainable Development Goal (SDG): ensuring healthy lives and promoting wellbeing for all at any age.

## Conclusions

For building safe, inclusive and resilient cities that will enable the children living in squatter settlemens in Kolkata, in migrant communities in Thailand, in poor racially mixed neighbourhoods in Istanbul and in the disaster ravaged landscapes in Japan, to thrive, we need to move beyond and away from identification of risk factors in children's lives to protective factors that are essential for positive outcomes for children.

There is a need for advocacy at the highest level to ensure that city planning considers children's rights in the creation of safe urban communities while paying special attention to the right to play of children in urban spaces. Play is the only spontaneous activity of children that is structured and controlled by children. It is by far the most important component of the pleasure of childhood. If our cities do not provide for play and recreation in appropriate ways, children will forever be at risk while seeking out opportunities for play even within the harshest environments.

Beyond advocacy there is a need to provide numerous interlocking spaces of different scales and character to cater to the needs of girls and boys of different ages and providing safe access to them across the city space. Adults in residential areas and schools who understand the importance and characteristics of play and recreational activities of children should support these spaces. The SDG goal 11 can most effectively be realised in each and every neighbourhood only through community-based participatory processes of planning and design to collectively and incrementally create a safe, inclusive and resilient city that works for children.

*(For more details about this research see: http://ipaworld.org/what-we-do/access-to-play-in-crisis/apc-research-project/)*

# Design for the Young and the Old

**Bruce Echberg** on how Australian cities can be made timeless

Australian cities and towns face considerable challenges in meeting the needs of the young and the elderly over the coming decades. Both groups are easily overlooked as we reshape our cities for the future. Although they have a small voice in the planning and development of cities, we will have gone a long way towards creating true 'liveability' for future generations if we take their needs seriously.

With a lot of overlap in what the young, the elderly and other disadvantaged groups need from the places in which they live, improvements for one group will often benefit all.

## Children in Australian cities

Children and young people as a group can be described as everyone from birth to 18 years of age. The proportion of children and young people in the total Australian population is decreasing, however, the number of children living with their families in Australian cities is increasing.

## International policy on children in cities

The Child Friendly Cities (CFC) initiative of UNICEF is aimed at realising the UN Convention on the Rights of the Child at the local level. This initiative describes a Child Friendly City as a local system of good governance committed to fulfilling children's rights. More specifically, a Child Friendly City is actively engaged in fulfilling the rights of every young citizen.

## The elderly in Australian cities

People aged 65 and over constitute Australia's fastest growing age group. In 2013 they represented almost 15% of Australia's population, with growth

**A central city 'nature' themed playground that aims to give urban children contact with plants and natural materials**

A typical suburban play area with equipment zones to cater to different age groups

projected to continue into the foreseeable future as living standards and the quality of public health continue to rise. It is vital, therefore, to create 'age-friendly' cities and towns.

### Common issues for the young and the elderly
The needs of both groups are easily overlooked in planning and development processes and should be given a greater voice.

### World Health Organisation recommendations on age-friendly cities
The World Health Organisation (WHO) has established a framework of eight interconnected domains that recognise older persons' needs in the urban environment. WHO's global network of age-friendly cities and communities aims to make communities a great place in which to grow old in and to share mutual learnings, knowledge and support.

The WHO approach stresses the importance of accessible transport for older people within cities, including access to public transport, parking and accessible driving conditions. Affordability and access to health care services is also crucial to keep older people independent and active in the community. Appropriate housing design in proximity to services can reinforce social participation. Another key issue is the importance of social inclusion in the social, civic and economic life of cities. Cities and communities should consider becoming part of the WHO's Global Network of Age-friendly Cities and Communities. To date, eight Australian cities have joined the network.

### Participation in the social life of the city
Young and old people need to be active participants in family and social life in cities. The young need to socialise with all age groups and learn about the risks and opportunities of urban life, initially with parent supervision and later as independent young citizens. Safe social interaction, both organised and informal, is also valuable for the elderly to enhance their quality of life especially when they have more leisure time after retirement.

**A Child Friendly City is a local system of good governance committed to fulfilling children's rights**

55

## Healthy lifestyles for the young and the old

Health care and education are important to the young and the old. The development and design of cities can do much to enhance the physical development and health of the young. The elderly also have time and the need for exercise. Both groups value independence and the ability to engage with urban life without being car dependent. Access to sporting facilities and ability to safely ride or walk to destinations or use public transport is of primary importance to the young and the old.

## Safety

Cities, therefore, need to be safe and accessible to all ages both in the day and at night. Urban living environments need to be free from pollution with public spaces providing free access to drinking water, sun, shade and places to stop, sit and socialise. Public space and city services need to be accessible to all regardless of ethnic origin, religion, income, gender or disability.

Conflict between cars, bikes and pedestrians is an ever present issue in all Australian cities and towns with a high degree of regulation through road authorities and local councils that have tended to favour the safe and efficient operation of cars, are gradually focussing more on the needs of pedestrians and cyclists who are often children or the elderly.

Design of public space needs to consider principles of CPTED: 'Crime Prevention Through

Southbank Boulevard as it was earlier

Environmental Design', a theory that has developed since the era of Jane Jacobs in the 1960s. Most states in Australia have produced CPTED guidelines to assist the planning of new urban areas and retro-fitting of established areas where people feel unsafe or crime is more prevalent.

## Nature in the city

Convenient contact with nature through access to parks, gardens and well-designed streets should be available to all citizens and especially the young and the elderly.

Urban Australian children are increasingly disconnected from nature, often being driven to and from school and increasingly growing up without the traditional Aussie backyard, not to mention more and more time spent with phones, computers and digital devices. Play areas are now

*Top:* The city of Melbourne has recently just committed to convert a section of Southbank Boulevard that was built as a wide two carriage-way, tree lined avenue in the 1970s, to accommodate 2.5 hectares of new public space for the rapidly-growing residential population. The design involves removing one carriage-way currently dedicated to traffic and parking and replacing it with a series of new open spaces. The project is budgeted to cost 35 million Australian dollars and will be funded by the City who may eventually get a return from increased rate revenue due to property value uplift. This is a great model for how open space can be effectively created without the need to purchase high value land when high-density residential development occurs in inner city areas with generous road reserves. The new park space will allow residents to stroll, hold events and children will have play spaces and an off-roads bike path. Similar projects of lesser scale that displace bitumen for new urban public space are happening elsewhere in the city of Melbourne and around the county

Walking and cycling paths are a feature of most cities and towns on the coast and inland towns may have equivalent facilities around parks or along waterways. They are well-used by young and old. Skate facilities have been developed in many towns and suburbs in Australia to provide for youth and to try to discourage use of the streets, car parks and public plazas for unsupervised skating being designed to partially compensate, but there is no substitute for spending extended, relatively unsupervised periods outside with dirt, sand, water, pets and plants whether it be at the beach or in the bush.

Studies have also shown that spending extended time in gardens and parks enhances the mental well being of the elderly. Horticultural Therapy is a recognised body of knowledge that promotes the health and psychological benefits of interaction with plants, especially for the young and the old in developed countries worldwide.

Special gardens are often developed for children and the elderly with special needs including those with dementia or lack of vision. Learning how to grow and cook food is increasingly taught in Australian primary schools and communities. Gardening is also valued by many Australian retirees for both the exercise and satisfaction of growing their own produce.

## Streets for children and the elderly

Australian cities and towns have been largely developed around the car in the post-World War II era.

Inner city areas of Australia's larger state capital cities, especially Sydney and Melbourne, have good public transport that predate the era of the car, including rail and tram, networks that are now at capacity and expanding to meet increased demand. These higher density areas are in many ways more suited to independent living for the young and the elderly because of the public transport systems, walkability of their streets and the access available to a wide range of facilities and open space without driving.

Lower density suburbs and rural towns throughout Australia developed over the past 70 years are very dependent on the use of the private car. They often have parks, schools and other community facilities, but because of the lower density, access to them is most convenient by driving, which limits the young and the old to some degree and of course requires consumption of energy. The carbon footprint of development was not considered when these suburban areas were planned.

In the future, autonomous electric cars may offer a partial solution, but continuing to accommodate growth in this fashion is unsustainable because of the high cost and the fact that sprawling suburbia takes up huge areas of land, the supply of which is limited. The future of our cities revolves around finding new ways to retrofit existing suburbs with nodes of employment and higher density mixed-use development that maximise use of existing services and infrastructure including public transport.

The next generation of ageing population: 'the baby boomers' (those born in the decade or two after the World War II), have different housing needs. They will need streets and parks where they can walk or ride bikes for exercise and, ideally, access to a wide range of facilities and social and recreational opportunities as well as daily contact with nature. The 'baby boomer' generation is relatively wealthy, healthy, active and independent and keen to live out the major part of their final few decades independently in their communities. Cities will have to be better designed to fully cater to these needs.

Better housing is important, but it is the quality of the public realm that needs the most effort; streets need to be more than a space for cars, they need to be designed for pedestrian comfort, safety and convenience. Landscaping within cities now needs to be carefully considered to maximise their cooling effect in hot weather, something that will increase in Australia over the coming decades, exacerbating the risk of death for the elderly. The effect of climate change will also lead to increasing storm events and water shortages, so urban landscapes need to be designed to capture and re-

*Left:* **Water play is being developed in cities to enable children to explore nature. This play area is in Darling Harbour, Sydney**
*Right:* **Royal Park in central Melbourne has extensive walking and cycle paths that enable people of all ages to experience nature, fresh air and the open sky**

Australian suburbs and county towns all have sports fields for children to play a wide range of team sports

use storm water at every opportunity.

Because Australian cities have all been planned with generous road reserves – with some inner city areas undergoing an unprecedented boom in high density housing development, often displacing industry and lower density retail, commercial or office uses – there is a new emerging interest in retrofitting streets by displacing bitumen for green space including cycle paths and public plazas and play areas.

## Parks and green space in cities

As cities increase in density and the effects of climate change take effect there will be a need to ensure networks of public and open spaces are retained, expanded where possible and enhanced to meet the needs of all citizens, especially the young and the old. Parks and streets will have to work harder to provide for both young and old to move freely and exercise and socialise in the public realm. New forms of open space will need to be developed to better cater to the young and the elderly.

Parks in Australia already do quite a good job providing for the young. Children's playgrounds are widely distributed through residential areas and are subject to safety regulations. Successful playgrounds provide a range of play equipment and age appropriate zones allowing for creative,

adventure and nature play. All kinds of sports are catered to from skateboarding to club sports to sophisticated indoor courts and swimming facilities.

The elderly are catered to with golf, bowls, gyms and swimming facilities as well as safe walking and cycling paths especially in parks and along rivers and coastlines, but much more can be done to extend and enhance these systems. Demographic trends in Australia suggest that catering for the residential, health and recreation needs of retirees will become increasingly important over the coming decades.

## Conclusion

Australian cities do provide many facilities and opportunities for the young and the old to participate, however urban areas are in transition in many places, as we cope with growth and we slowly begin to reduce the carbon footprint of towns and cities. We also need to adapt our cities to improve resilience in the face of climate change.

This needs to be done with a clear eye on the interests of the young and the old. Increased density need not disadvantage these sectors of the population. Better public transport and well-designed streets and public space developed using democratic consultation processes can work to the benefit of all. ●

# Designing Public Spaces for All

**Liesl Vivier, Annemiek van Koldenhoven** and **Nikos Margaritis** give us some examples of community-led developments that have helped build better neighbourhoods

The urban public spaces, as spaces where the social nature of human beings can be expressed, are concurrent to the notion of City/Polis itself. Public spaces are where social interaction, commercial activity, recreation and even political expression take place. This has been so for many centuries. It is not a coincidence then that any kind of societal change affects the design of urban public space or that public space design influences the societal structure and behaviour of people.

This relationship between design of the public realm and behaviour of people is an ongoing one. The 21st century is the most urbanised century of humanity and has also brought extreme challenges to the global urban population: natural disasters, financial stress and inequality, immigration etc. All these challenges will deeply affect the character of urban space. The question that arises here is

how social problems can be addressed by imposing changes onto the character of urban, public space and how the local population can be involved in the process. Can inhabitants initiate change in a successful way? Some examples from Europe can help us understand how easily this can be done.

## 'Estonoesunsolar', Zaragoza

The city of Zaragoza in Spain experienced 21st-century challenges: the combined forces of the fading industrial power of the city and the global financial crisis of 2008 had a strong impact on the local population. After 2008, the unemployment rate radically increased and social relations were disrupted on many levels. That was the moment when local authorities and architects decided to combine forces in order to reverse the loss of social cohesion by intervening in the urban, public and private space. An analysis of the urban tissue

> **Zeeheldentuin is a good example of how people's willpower can drive the transformation of public spaces**

SOURCE: GRAVALOS AND DI MONTE ARCHITECTS

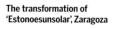

The transformation of 'Estonoesunsolar', Zaragoza

of Zaragoza showed that there were numerous vacant public and private plots, disrupting the normal functioning of the city. The design team interpreted these empty plots as areas that destroy the coherence of the city. The assumption of the designers was that a city could only function well when it has a continuous narrative for its users.

The proposed solution was the 'estonoesunsolar', meaning 'this is not an empty site', programme. Firstly, the local authorities hired a few dozen people to clean the abandoned, empty plots of the city. Later, a team of architects extended the idea and proposed to redesign the emptied plots. Together with the municipal services and the architects, more than 60 citizen associations, neighbourhood groups, community organisations and citizens were involved in a creative process, which encompassed the whole design and implementation phase of each selected spot. Through the programme, a series of new urban spaces were introduced targeting different age groups and different social groups. The empty sites were transformed into urban gardens, green spaces, playgrounds, street bowling areas for older people, an all-ages game centre and gathering spaces. The diverse uses implemented within the different spots reflected the needs of the local population: recreation and educational uses, such as dance classes, architecture workshops for children as well

as horticulture programmes for adults.

The effect of this initiative was manifold. The unemployment rate dropped while the city acquired and cleaned the vital urban spaces. By adding design qualities to the unused plots, the urban tissue became stronger and added a new range of uses, qualities and experiences to the city. Additionally, the estonoesunsolar team spoke extensively to the local people to determine existing community needs before embarking on the design process. The programme was such a success that it has now been expanded to more city areas.

### Zeeheldentuin, The Hague

While estonoesunsolar in Zaragoza is a good example of how interventions in the urban tissue of a city with a problematic structure can be extremely effective, other examples in cities with fewer social problems and a well-organised, state-oriented public realm design policy also show that city dwellers often recognise the importance of public space and try to optimise it according to their everyday needs. As is the case with Zeeheldentuin, very close to the city centre of The Hague in the Netherlands.

In the Zeeheldenkwartier, a comparatively wealthy neighbourhood of the city, the old Maria School was destroyed in 2006 by a fire leaving only ruins within a fenced plot. The efforts to convert

**Bird's-eye view of Zeeheldentuin, The Hague**

**Residents using the park 'lounge', Zeeheldentuin, The Hague**

the remains of the building plot into social housing units were not successful and so people living in the surrounding area decided to take action and claim this space in order to fulfill their needs for more public space. A group of volunteers consisting of designers, artists, botanists and citizens together with the local landscape consultants DGJ formed a Foundation, and through an open, participatory process they managed to design and find sponsors to construct a very successful mini park central in the neighbourhood.

What makes Zeeheldentuin unique is that due to the participation of many locals and the wide representation of social groups within the design team, several different uses were combined in the garden. A wilderness playground for children, a flower garden, an open play field, vegetable and collaborative gardens, a fruit orchard and a lounge, all fitted perfectly within the limited space available. The creation of the garden had a huge social impact in the neighbourhood. The board of the mini-park initiated co-operation with local daycare facilities for children and the elderly. The former school was transformed into new housing units, increasing the social occupancy of the place. In the present situation, different social groups co-exist all day long in the garden in a harmonious manner. The project has received several local awards including the European Green

**The construction of the park: Do-it-yourself day, Zeeheldentuin, The Hague**

Infrastructure Award 2015.

Zeeheldentuin is a good example of how people's willpower can drive the transformation of public spaces, but we should keep in mind that this happened in The Hague, in a country where the state has created the legislative context for such moves and with plenty of experience from past years.

### Navarinou Park, Athens

While in some countries similar state or municipal-oriented programmes are common, the question remains whether initiatives such as the Zeeheldentuin are possible in cases where the authorities do not have the financial or executional power to start and support such initiatives. A

**Navarinou Park is continually evolving as per people's needs**

perfect example is to be found in Athens, the city that was hit most severely by a combination of two types of crises, the global financial crisis and the refugee crisis.

Athens, in Greece, a city of approximately four million inhabitants, has faced several problems for decades. The rapid urbanisation of the city, which followed the establishment of the Greek state in the 1830s led to degeneration of the urban tissue. And the complicated building regulations, which came in force after World War II created an almost inhuman urban landscape. The problems in the city centre of Athens were exacerbated after the 1990s, when poor immigrants and refugees started renting cheap, empty apartments in the city centre abandoned by Greeks who had moved to the outskirts of the city. Because of this, the state and locals neglected the urban space. It was a period when the necessary and hard-to-find public space of the city centre of Athens was ignored by its owners.

The image of this part of the city is one of massive, dense, derelict concrete structures, an absence of green spaces and an abundance of empty plots and dirty fields looking like they did not belong to anybody, but in anticipation of

**Navarinou Park in Athens: visitors using the open amphitheatre of the park**

becoming a building someday.

In Exarchia, a very vibrant sub-area of the city centre of Athens, where political and artistic movements have always flourished, locals decided to create a neighbourhood park on an empty plot between multi-storey buildings that was being used as a parking lot. The plans by the city to transform the same plot into a multi-storey parking garage were blocked by the movement started by the locals.

The idea of making a new green oasis became the reason for locals, immigrants and visitors to band together and fight for their public space. Without any structure or help from the state or the municipality, even without the existence of any relevant legislation, the neighbourhood managed to organise themselves to create the ideal public space designed for their specific needs. Together, locals and foreigners, children and adults, people living there for ages and newcomers, managed to achieve the desired result.

The park itself, the design of which occurred by involving many different people with different backgrounds without any central control, is very innovative within the Greek public space design context. Even though it is not an official park with legal validation, but rather an occupied plot, it has high quality vegetation and hosts uses for people of different ethnic backgrounds, ages and social or educational levels: a playground, an open-air cinema, vegetable gardens and meeting points.

Interestingly, after the completion of the park the people involved in the creation of the park formed an assembly that meets weekly in order to manage its maintenance. The park has been beneficial in many ways: people started using the public realm again, the area became safer and locals cooperated and met one another in the newly designed park. Because of the unique social structure that created the park and the absence of any central control, Navarinou Park is continually evolving as per people's needs. Recently, a new segment of the park with organic agriculture opened. A compost production area is planned in order to reduce waste in the neighbourhood and also to provide the park with natural fertilisers. The park can be seen as a constantly changing open, urban lab, which everyone can be a part of.

## Kerckebosch, Zeist

The above examples are all relatively small interventions, where pockets of public realm were recreated to be all-inclusive. There are, however, also examples where larger urban areas have been redeveloped to be more inclusive. An example of this is Kerckebosch Housing Estate on the outskirts of Zeist, in the Netherlands.

Kerckebosch, designed in the 1950s as a social housing estate for low-income families had approximately 700 housing units surrounding a centrally located forested area. At the beginning of this century, the buildings and the public realm, which were both showing signs of wear and tear, were due for a major renovation. Neglect of the forests within the estate had resulted in dense vegetation, which was unsafe, unattractive and impenetrable. Also, the concentration of low-

> It is important that the input and the opinions of the participants bear equal weight in the design process

*Left:* **Vision drawing, Kerckebosch, Zeist**
*Right:* **Informal play area**

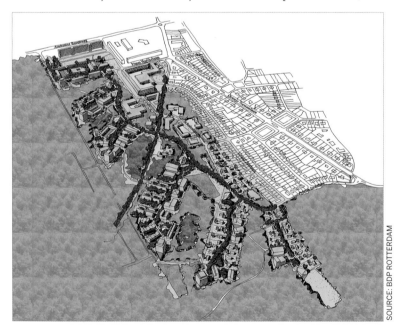

SOURCE: BDP ROTTERDAM

SOURCE: WURCK, KERCKEBOSCH, ZEIST

**Energy plaza, Kerckebosch, Zeist**

SOURCE: WURCK, KERCKEBOSCH, ZEIST

income families had resulted in a neighbourhood with a one-sided social structure and relatively high unemployment rates. In 2005 the housing corporation and the owner of the estate joined forces with the local council and took the radical decision to demolish almost all the social housing and build new housing to cater to a wider range of incomes. The Rotterdam studio of the international design consultancy firm, BDP, was commissioned to design an urban vision for the new neighbourhood. The theme 'Living in the Forest for Everyone' was coined as the design motto for the urban vision.

Through the vision, a more diverse and inclusive neighbourhood was proposed. Homes for families and single urbanites, social housing for low income families and privately-owned homes for high income families, special care homes for the elderly and a home for mentally challenged people were proposed. A new, centrally located 'Multifunctional Accommodation' housing a health centre, a music school, a small sports centre and a café where residents could meet, was proposed at the heart of the scheme. The existing cluster of schools in the neighbourhood was redesigned as a 'school campus' – accessible and open for all. In the vision, the forest weaves through the neighbourhood to maximise access to the forest. The vision proposed to limit the size and number of private gardens – the idea being that the forest, which belongs to everyone, is a large collective 'garden' for all and forms the primary space where the inhabitants, with their diverse backgrounds, will meet.

The 'interactive neighbourhood' idea was carried further by the design consultancy company Wurck, a Rotterdam-based design firm, which was responsible for the design of the public realm of Kerckebosch. Wurck made the forest more accessible by designing an intricate network of footpaths, which carefully avoid the trees and link the different built clusters together. Parts of the forest have been opened up to bring back the indigenous heather-plants and to create vistas. Felled trees are reused in the public realm as playing objects or informal seating areas. A new unfenced central playground has been designed between the schools, to be used by children from the neighbourhood after school hours. A public outdoor Calisthenics exercise park has opened next to the Multifunctional Accommodation for the use of sports-fanatics.

The new Energy Plaza, with its own WiFi-hotspot, caters to the needs of teenagers (and the young at heart). A feeling of ownership of the public space was developed among residents by actively involving them in the design process through public consultation sessions and involving them in activities such as Tree Planting Days and Neighbourhood Nature Days when forest maintenance takes place. This has contributed greatly to the success of the neighbourhood because residents take pride in 'their' forest and thus treat it with respect.

## Conclusion

Public spaces should be open, free, democratic and accessible for everyone and cater to the needs of all. These case studies show examples of inclusive public spaces that are used by people of different ages and backgrounds. A common thread in all these examples, whether they are their own initiatives or organised developments, is the direct involvement of the users in the design and execution of the spaces. In this it is important that the input and the opinions of the participants bear equal weight in the design process. One could conclude that the active involvement of the end users in the design of the public space is a prerequisite for public spaces to be enjoyed by everyone. ●

# Inclusive Transport and Spatial Justice in Nairobi

**Dorcas Nyamai** argues a case for a more just spatial system in a city that values fancy cars over people's lives

PHOTO: ©MUTUA MATHEKA/PROKRAFT AFRICA

**Nairobi City**

## Current state of urban mobility

Five in the morning! That's the average time a person living in Nairobi has to wake up to be at work by 8 a.m. Battling traffic, risking life to cross the busy highway after alighting from a bus and a hop, skip and jump over neglected and divested pedestrian footpaths, then working until 8 p.m., because the rush hour will not let you leave work at 5 p.m., unless of course you are willing to spend a good two hours in traffic to get home. Waiting to leave at 8 p.m. would mean that you get home in 20 minutes. This is the beginning of the end of a social life and a slow but sure death of a healthy life given all the exhaust fumes breathed in every day, thanks to the numerous vehicles that are now choking the once green city under the sun.

The typical everyday life of a Nairobi resident has been made difficult by the lack of efficient public transportation, endless traffic congestion, air pollution and divested pedestrian paths. People are getting angrier as they are forced to sit in traffic all day. We should have better roads, inclusive transport that also caters to non-motorised

transport and an organised and efficient public transport system. But we don't. Instead, we buy more cars and even a nine-year old can tell you what model of a car he would buy when he can afford one. No one thinks of owning a cool 'gazelle' bicycle.

In the last decade, Nairobi, Kenya's capital, has witnessed growth both skyward and outward, swallowing formerly rural and suburban areas. Nairobi's population is approximately four million at present and is projected to be 14 million in the next three decades. The challenge of a growing population has been compounded by the growing middle-class buying vehicles as soon as they can afford them, to the tune of 5,000 vehicles imported every month, that is, 60,000 vehicles every year, while the most popular public transport and non-motorised transport are squeezed out to make way for the car, which has dominated much of the available urban space, contributing to spatial injustice. It is common practise to react to traffic flows exceeding road capacity by expanding and growing the existing roads. However, this only favours more car use,

**The air pollution in Nairobi is 30 times worse than that in London**

but does not contribute to better flows in terms of persons moved within the city.

The number of vehicles in the city has increased dramatically making traffic congestion so terrible that it makes headlines, not only for the frequent long jams, but also for the health hazard it has become. Scientific researchers have revealed that the air pollution in Nairobi is 30 times worse than that in London; the prime cause being the number of motor vehicles releasing exhaust fumes into the air. Everyone in Nairobi breathes huge volumes of exhaust given the number of hours one has to stay in traffic.

Having been away from Nairobi for a number of years, returning home was a little shocking to realise that traffic starts piling up at 6 a.m. It is now commonplace to spend two hours in traffic on a journey that would otherwise take just 20 minutes. Besides the wasted human hours, which costs the nation more than half a million dollars a day in productivity, most people have too little time and energy for family and other social activities, consequently lowering the quality of life as research on happiness has revealed that lengthy commutes make people unhappy.

## Public transport situation in Nairobi

For the majority who own vehicles in Nairobi, car dependency has become an addiction and as most addictions start with use, they only become manifest when non-use has a negative influence on wellbeing. Car dependency has produced a situation where the users do not see any alternatives or at least have the perception that alternatives are lacking. The government is to blame for this due to the poor and inefficient public transportation that exists in the city. As someone who prefers using public transport in Nairobi, I find that the government's public transport policy is forcing me to get a car; at least for my convenience and to preserve my life as cycling is a risky affair.

Nairobi has a severe public transportation problem with a system that is bursting at the seams. Using public transport means having to wait, in most places in Nairobi, for as long as 15 minutes to see an empty public service vehicle or *matatu* and if you are lucky to find one, you may have to wait for an additional 15 minutes for the *matatu* to fill up before you can embark on the journey to sit in traffic. The drivers are ruthless and prices are usually hiked without notice. God-forbid that you have to get a *matatu* on a rainy day as it would mean waiting for about an hour or two and having to pay three times as much as the regular charges. In some neighbourhoods, *matatus* are barred from going into residential areas forcing those who can afford it, to buy a car, adding to the urban blight of traffic-related problems.

When I was growing up in Nairobi, the Kenya Bus Service, run by the County Council of Nairobi, used to manage the buses, which ensured efficiency, as the route was circular and on time. Nowadays, the bus system is privatised and operates in the same manner as *matatus*. The Nairobi County Government has been piloting

*Left:* **Pedestrian flows and public transport buses caught up in a traffic jam**
*Right:* **A signpost by the Kenya Urban Roads Authority barring** *matatus* **from residential areas**

a Bus Rapid Transit (BRT) system, ostensibly to help reduce traffic congestion and improve urban mobility in the city, but the buses have been sharing the same lanes with other road users, defeating the purpose of rapid transit, while they should instead have dedicated lanes, which would increase efficiency and reduce traffic snarls.

## Are there other alternatives?

The other alternative is walking to work. Research has shown that approximately 54% of the population of Nairobi walks to work. This is nearly the whole of Paris or to put it in the African context, the whole of The Gambia. The numbers may even be understated because those who combine walking with public transport are excluded from the figures. There is, however, a disregard for the lives of pedestrians and cyclists, which has led to deaths. A majority of the roads are high risk for pedestrians. An assessment by the International Roads Assessment Programme (iRAP) in Nairobi found that 95% of roads assessed have high pedestrian flows, yet only 20% have pedestrian footpaths, forget cycling lanes. It is unnecessarily dangerous and sometimes impossible to walk. Pedestrian paths have been divested and used up as parking places forcing the disabled to pull wheelchairs on the same road space as the motorists with the hope that some unruly driver will not knock them down. Records show that more than 60% of the 400-plus deaths recorded in Nairobi in 2016 involved pedestrians and the numbers continue to rise with each passing year; this despite the existence of a non-motorised transport policy.

Another private alternative to the public problem has been the two-wheel motorcycle otherwise known as *bodaboda*. Their numbers have increased in recent years providing speedy and reliable transport due to its ability to manoeuvre traffic and reach places that public transport cannot otherwise reach. The industry has grown from $4 billion in 2015 and is set to rise to $9 billion in 2021, especially due to the absence of a reliable and efficient public transport system that cannot cope with the increasing urbanisation rates and traffic congestion.

## Aspirations to modernity

The explosive growth in the automobile population needs to be checked quickly by adopting an inclusive urban transport system that would increase the use of public and non-motorised transport. It is clear that the prioritisation of private motor vehicles over other forms of transportation impacts a divide in mobility and contributes to the differentiation of the network, rather than making it more inclusive. Most urban transport planners agree that people will have to stop driving their own personal cars and use public transport or non-motorised transport if cities are to cut congestion, but this will mean that the transport system will have to be aesthetically valuable and extremely efficient.

Efficiency in transportation will be achieved by moving people around a centralised system that incorporates and coordinates data across public transport and non-motorised transport. This will require ingenuity and collaboration among all the stakeholders and significant financing, both from

**Everyday traffic congestion in Nairobi**

PHOTO: ©MUTUA MATHEKA/PROKRAFT AFRICA

## It is paramount to plan for the city based on the movement of people rather than vehicular movement

PHOTO: ©MUTUA MATHEKA/PROKRAFT AFRICA

**Nairobi City CBD**

public and private sectors. It will address long term goals for many generations to come as well as change the city's economic and social outlook but first, addressing the immediate needs of the majority, i.e., improving pedestrian paths, will require immediate implementation. Additionally, excluding affordable transportation from road designs only holds back the advancement of Nairobi's working class and the urban poor, most of who walk or cycle to work.

Vouching for non-motorised transport in Nairobi would be making a foray into a system that is dominated by private vehicles, but this might just be a breakthrough for economic and social progress in the city. The health-related problems caused by inhaled exhaust fumes would reduce and consequently so would the amount of money spent on medical bills. A success story is Lithuania, where bicycles outsold cars a little over nine times and saw the economy grow by 3.6% in 2012. Cities such as Copenhagen, Amsterdam and Rotterdam cannot stress enough about the merits of cycling for urban development. These cities have reached a common conclusion: that efficient inclusive transport is the solution to clean and green cities free from congestion.

Long-term investment in urban mobility is a critical part of increasing economic opportunity and reducing poverty. Mobility is the most salient aspect for any progressive economy. People's movement is necessitated by the need to get access to spatially disjointed activities and services that can improve one's wellbeing and livelihood. When people are cut off or divested from other places in

the city as a result of inefficient transport, spatial injustice prevails.

There is a need to establish a trajectory of structural transformation in the transport sector in Nairobi and to get in tune with everyday realities by considering more sustainable means of transport while bearing in mind that the conventional short term solutions to long term problems only serve as an impediment to growth. Safe pedestrian movement, efficient public transport and promoting non-motorised transport will contribute to spatial justice in the city as the efficiency of the entire transport system will place utmost focus on human movement and not vehicular movement. It is people who move from one place to another and not their cars.

It is paramount to plan for the city based on the movement of people rather than vehicular movement. In Nairobi, it is evident that people with cars have more capacity to influence design. The private vehicle is placed at the centre of decision-making leading to spatial injustices as public transportation and non-motorised transport gets the least share of the bargain. The city needs an agreeable urban transport system that is spatially just and under the control of the society; a system that not only benefits certain social classes but is available for all and meets the demands for all.

Mass transit and non-motorised transport should not be seen as a 'system for the poor' but rather for all to move effectively around the city. It could be that the bicycle may be the one solution to many problems and a door opener to many other opportunities, especially in the case of Nairobi. ●

# Dodoma: The Burden of Planning in Tanzania

Throughout history, African cities have always attracted large master plans. Dodoma, the capital of Tanzania, is an interesting example. Planned as an African city, inspired by Maoist ideals, designed by Canadians, built by Europeans and Asians, and soon to be re-built by South Koreans, this hidden place has been flooded by global interest. **Sophie van Ginneken** tells us how African cities can learn from experiments of the past

PHOTO: SOPHIE VAN GINNEKEN

**Central shopping street in Dodoma**

"Anyone going to Dodoma?" the pilot asks his passengers. I raise my hand, as the only one of five in total. The single engine plane is about to take off from Dar es Salaam for Dodoma. At least that's what the schedule says. Despite Dodoma being his travel destination, the pilot apparently has other plans. In reality, Dodoma is not the most obvious place to go to, neither for Tanzanians nor for tourists. "All right, we'll stop over at Dodoma then," the pilot adds. This would be the first and probably the last time that a plane hit the ground for me alone. Not quite what you would expect while visiting a capital city.

That was two years ago. This African New Town, where I spent a week doing research, is obviously not the urban heart of the nation. In fact, with its calm and dusty streets, a few cars and not a single tall building, it's more like a large village. Today, 40 years after Dodoma was declared the capital, several reports state that the capital city project is finally taking off. In December 2013, a brand new master plan, made by SAMAN Corporation (a South Korean engineering firm), was presented to the national government.

With a target population of three million people and the ambition to finally live up to its political status, Dodoma is soon to be 'remodelled' once more. It all started in 1973, the year that Dodoma was declared the new capital of Tanzania by the legendary first president Julius Nyerere (1922–1999). As in other African nations, leaders in the era following independence sought new symbols of national identity. Often, these ambitions were channelled into the building of new cities. Other examples are Tema (Ghana), Abuja (Nigeria) or, more recently, Ramciel (planned in 2011 as the new capital city of South Sudan). Located in the middle of the country, the then small and sleepy town of Dodoma was chosen as the site of the new capital city to replace the existing capital Dar es Salaam. Here, a brand new 'city of self reliance' was to rise, as an embodiment of Nyerere's ideology of African Socialism, named *Ujamaa*. Based on equality and collective rural life, *Ujamaa* (Swahili for 'family hood') referred to traditional African values and culture. The need for a new capital city was thus justified as not only a political or symbolic decision, but also an economic and social one.

One of the ideas was that a city in the countryside would mostly benefit peasants who were living in the least developed part of the country. Peasants who, according to Nyerere, were the 'true' builders of a new society as opposed to urbanites who he saw as their exploiters. In this, he chose the exact opposite policy from Kwame Nkrumah, who at the same time reformed the newly independent Ghana favouring industrialisation over agriculture. Nyerere expected the peasants, 'working together for the benefit of all', to have the potential to turn Tanzania into a 100% rural, self-reliant economy. A planned pattern of thousands of newly established villages, evenly scattered throughout the country, was the physical expression of the socialist reform agenda. Dodoma was planned as the centrepiece of this huge *Ujamaa* Villagisation programme: a model African city, without skyscrapers or super highways, a rural city produced and inhabited by peasants.

As the geographer Garth Myers puts it, *Ujamaa* was "one of the most significant 'alternative visions' of urbanism and human settlement that has emerged from post-colonial Africa". With the idea of an autarkic city, reconciling agriculture and urbanism into a self-reliant rural economy, Nyerere took a unique standpoint. At the same

time the idea of 'collectivisation' of the country's agricultural system was heavily inspired by Chinese Maoist reform plans. Given the socialist aims of the new city and Nyerere's heavy reliance on local traditions and rural habits, it is fairly ironic that a Canadian office was asked to design the master plan. Landscape architect Macklin Hancock (1925-2010) from Toronto, principal consultant of Project Planning Associates Ltd, designed the new capital for which he, in turn, borrowed the American suburban planning model.

The outcome of the rather strange partnership between the Tanzanian government and the Canadian consultants was a very western, typical New Town plan, while simultaneously conveying Nyerere's message of a rural self-reliant city. In reality, the plan had nothing to do with Ujamaa or even 'just' socialism. In fact, the scheme holds striking parallels with Don Mills, a 1950s suburb

*Top:* **Dodoma is a regional distribution centre for agricultural products – central market place in the middle of town**
*Bottom:* **Bar and a typical 'duka' (small shop) in the Canadian neighbourhood 'Area C'**

PHOTOS: SOPHIE VAN GINNEKEN

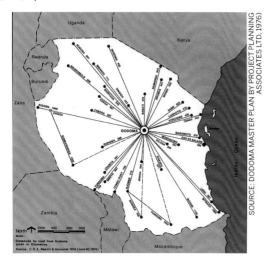

SOURCE: DODOMA MASTER PLAN BY PROJECT PLANNING ASSOCIATES LTD. 1976

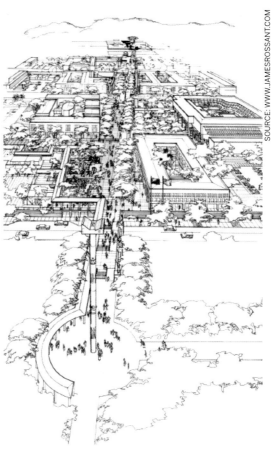

SOURCE: WWW.JAMESROSSANT.COM

*Left:* **Dodoma in the geographical middle of the country**
*Right:* **Design for the National Capital Centre by the American architect James Rossant (unbuilt)**

of Toronto, also built by Hancock. This famous Canadian experiment, a physical example of Clarence Perry's neighbourhood unit, shows typical New Town characteristics such as the hierarchical setup into neighbourhood units, the separation of vehicular roads from pedestrian paths and spaciously designed cul-de-sacs.

Though largely unrealised in its architectural ambitions, the 1976 Canadian master plan has always been the leading scheme for Dodoma – up until now. Western ideas have been copied to help the city 'move forward' in the march of civilisation, such as a free bus lane, large open spaces for leisure activities and European style houses with private gardens and patios. The finely detailed road network was remarkable in this context, where only few people had access to a car. The plan was to set an example for the future in which everyone had a proper home and a car, commuted daily to the central business district for work, and at the end of the day enjoyed family life in the garden or played football in one of the numerous parks. Not quite a rural 'Ujamaa' city, but rather a classic North American suburb.

The huge wave of optimism following the planning of Dodoma and generally accompanying the planning of New Towns anywhere, attracted Canadians as well as many other foreign city planners. James Rossant, (the planner of New Town Reston, USA) designed the city's National Capital Centre. James Rouse (the planner of Columbia New Town, USA) and a full UN team, to name just a few, came to assist with the planning process. They nestled like flies in the middle of the African savannah in an attempt to turn it into something better.

However well intentioned, it is clear that the foreign architects behind this overly ambitious project all applied their own ideas of 'progress', wrapped in western templates of 'the ideal city'. Too ideal to ever have a chance of being built. Moreover, the involvement of so many foreign parties and institutions resulted in a situation where urban development became a matter of public interest; a process almost entirely owned by non-local players who were all very far removed from reality in this part of Tanzania, of the lifestyles of (existing and future) inhabitants, of the socio-cultural and economic capital, in short, the fundamentals of the city's reason to exist.

Conceptualised as an African city, inspired by Maoist ideals, designed by Canadians and Americans, built by Europeans and Asians, paid for by many, and soon to be re-built by South Koreans this hidden place has been flooded with global interest and foreign ideologies. Trapped in a planning cycle, these master plans, all of them extensively detailed, have led to disappointing results time and time again.

However, despite the fact that it's been a largely unexecuted design project, one would

**The outcome of the rather strange partnership between the Tanzanian government and the Canadian consultants was a very western, typical New Town plan**

almost overlook the fact that Dodoma itself is also a 'normal city' that is actually performing quite successfully. Since it serves as an agricultural hub for the region, the town's economy is fairly self-reliant, which was Nyerere's original aim. The Dodoma region has for instance a considerable wine industry and has recently put Tanzania on the world's wine production map. Also, several universities and schools are housed here, among them a Rural Planning Institute, a College of Business Education and a gigantic university complex (the University of Dodoma), set to become one of the leading universities in East Africa. These institutions welcome a growing number of students every year, thereby contributing to economic growth and poverty reduction. None of these successes can be attributed to imported city templates. The reasons for their success lie rather in smaller, well-targeted projects or, in the case of the agricultural sector the city's own economy, which is not directed from above. Moreover, essential for the success of any planned project is political will; a factor that has always been (and still is) remarkably absent while building the capital city project.

Dodoma is not alone in the 'tradition of failed plans', relying on overseas urbanists and engineers, who bring along their models. In fact, it's become a fairly typical experience for African cities. Ever since the start of colonial planning, we have seen the export of master plans that are based on the values and experiences of overseas planners (mostly westerners), instead of being adequate responses to existing issues. Like the 1976 master plan for Dodoma, most of these master plans are in fact too 'ideal', and therefore of little relevance to the actual development of the city. As a result, plans for cities like Abuja (Nigeria), Addis Ababa (Ethiopia), Dar es Salaam (Tanzania), Nairobi (Kenya) and Kinshasa (Congo) have remained largely unfulfilled. In the 'best' case they have been partly executed, thereby benefitting usually a small group of higher income groups. In most cases, this has led to increasing inequalities and the growth of slums.

Today, Dodoma is neither the classless rural capital envisioned by Nyerere, nor Hancock's suburban dream. While an extravagantly designed parliament building, performing as a spaceship surrounded by empty streets, reminds us of the fact that it is a capital city after all, all ministries have stayed in Dar es Salaam. In the meantime, Dodoma has developed in its own direction. Over time, an intricate network of *dukas* (small shops), *daladalas* (buses), markets, playgrounds and pedestrian routes have bypassed its formal logic. The few planned neighbourhoods that have been built are havens for the wealthy. These occasionally realised city bits contrast sharply with the sea of self-built neighbourhoods around them. Extensive parts lack the most basic of services. Due to an enormous gap between formal and informal planning rules,

*Left:* The setup for Dodoma's communities was derived from existing model cities and then integrated on site
*Right:* Leisure facilities at large open spaces soon came to move aside the original focus on communal rural plots as the centres of collectivity

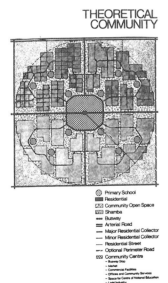

THEORETICAL COMMUNITY

- Primary School
- Residential
- Community Open Space
- Shamba
- Busway
- Arterial Road
- Major Residential Collector
- Minor Residential Collector
- Residential Street
- Optional Perimeter Road
- Community Centre
  – Busway Stop
  – Market
  – Commercial Facilities
  – Offices and Community Services
  – Space for Centre of National Education
  – Light Industry

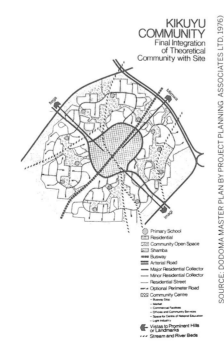

KIKUYU COMMUNITY
Final Integration of Theoretical Community with Site

- Primary School
- Residential
- Community Open Space
- Shamba
- Busway
- Arterial Road
- Major Residential Collector
- Minor Residential Collector
- Residential Street
- Optional Perimeter Road
- Community Centre
  – Busway Stop
  – Market
  – Commercial Facilities
  – Offices and Community Services
  – Space for Centre of National Education
  – Light Industry
- Vistas to Prominent Hills or Landmarks
- Stream and River Beds

SOURCE: DODOMA MASTER PLAN BY PROJECT PLANNING ASSOCIATES LTD, 1976

SOURCE: CDA ARCHIVES, DODOMA

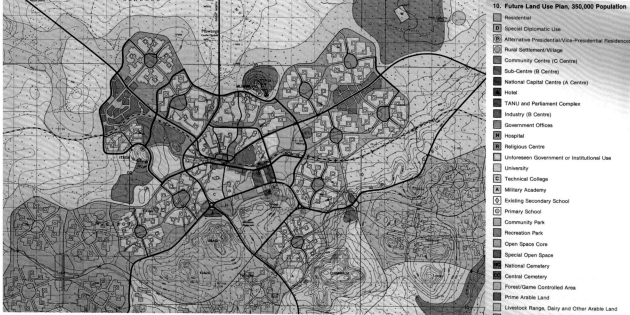

10. **Future Land Use Plan, 350,000 Population**
- Residential
- **D** Special Diplomatic Use
- Alternative Presidential/Vice-Presidential Residences
- Rural Settlement/Village
- Community Centre (C Centre)
- Sub-Centre (B Centre)
- National Capital Centre (A Centre)
- Hotel
- TANU and Parliament Complex
- Industry (B Centre)
- Government Offices
- **H** Hospital
- **R** Religious Centre
- Unforeseen Government or Institutional Use
- University
- **C** Technical College
- **A** Military Academy
- Existing Secondary School
- Primary School
- Community Park
- Recreation Park
- Open Space Core
- Special Open Space
- **NC** National Cemetery
- **CC** Central Cemetery
- Forest/Game Controlled Area
- Prime Arable Land
- Livestock Range, Dairy and Other Arable Land

SOURCE: PROJECT PLANNING ASSOCIATES, 1976

the process of city making in Africa has its own unpredictable logic.

The history of Dodoma teaches us some important lessons. First, it shows how seemingly unnoticed planners (remarkably all foreign) can turn ideologies into plans with completely different (even opposite) aims to their original intentions. Secondly, it shows how the focus on 'prestige' (in this case: a capital city) favours costly projects over urgent urban tasks. For many cities on the African continent these urgent tasks are first and foremost: running water, toilets, roads and electricity. Apart from the artificial Bunge (the National Parliament building), left unused for most of the time, Dodoma has in recent years welcomed several newly built communities to be used as *pieds-a-terre* for the government elite. Furthermore, Rossant's National Capital Centre plan has apparently been dusted off, as now Chinese contractors are finally building it. Remarkably, these ambitious projects are often built on isolated building sites far from the beating heart of town. As a result, they are disconnected and hence seem to lack reason.

At the same time, inhabitants of successful developments are sometimes evicted in favour of planned urban panoramas. An early example of this is Chang'ombe, one of Dodoma's suburbs, which developed rapidly in the 1980s along the spatial fixtures of the designated green belt. Although completely in line with the ideological aims of the master plan as a whole (communities of smallholders cultivating seasonal crops), an attempt

SOURCE: CAPITAL DEVELOPMENT AUTHORITY - BUILDING THE NATIONAL CAPITAL (1978)

*Top:* **Dodoma master plan**
*Left:* **Dodoma's CDA staff with the United Nations Environmental Program (UNEP)**

was made to relocate the settlers. As shown by Wilbard Kombe and Volker Kreibich, this effort has been largely unsuccessful due to a powerful system of local land market regulations, guided by local land managers. This informal system should not be underestimated. Again, the gap between formal and informal planning in Africa is considerable and is in fact one of the reasons why most of the 'grand urban visions' to be built in developing countries are so likely to fail in the first place.

Lastly, a city that is determined to live up to an urban dream, tends to neglect its existing qualities, as well as the essential needs and potentials of those who live in it. Besides the example of 'undesirable' urban developments like Chang'ombe, the fact that the numerous informal routes and public spaces in the city have never been incorporated in the plans also illustrates this. While European New Towns struggle with too-rigidly planned structures,

**A city that is determined to live up to an urban dream, tends to neglect its existing qualities, as well as the essential needs and potentials of those who live in it**

PHOTO: SOPHIE VAN GINNEKEN

PHOTO: ANTONI FOLKERS

PHOTO: SOPHIE VAN GINNEKEN

*Top:* **Prototype housing blocks in the Canadian neighbourhood (designed by PPAL) are now inhabited by people from the middle and higher income groups**
*Bottom Left:* **The Bunge (National Parliament)**
*Bottom Right:* **The Institute for Rural Development Planning**

African cities, and New Towns in particular, seem to struggle with the rigidity of their planners, determined to build their urban fantasies. Too often, these plans neglect existing planning processes, economic and social structures. With their forced setup and zoning of programmes, these plans cannot keep up with the actual growth and reality of its informal planning dynamics. When built, they often frustrate valid economic networks, usually located in the existing city and the dynamics that have contributed to its culture and identity in the first place. The evident path towards more flexible and resilient African cities seems, therefore, to find its roots in a more open, inclusive planning that integrates the expertise, labour and commitment of local planners, entrepreneurs and residents, while at the same time enabling informal land management systems to participate. These lessons should be kept in mind while building the numerous new city developments that are now on drawing boards throughout the African continent.

*This is a short-read version of the article for the forthcoming publication 'New Towns on the Cold War Frontier', 2015 by Crimson Architectural Historians. The author would like to thank Antoni Folkers (African Architecture Matters), the Netherlands and Matthias Nuss, Germany, Capital Development Authority Dodoma, Tanzania, Nicola Colangelo, Coastal Aviation, Tanzania for their inputs.*

# Engineering the Perfectly Pedestrian City

**Shyam Khandekar** explains how cities can be built with humans as the focus of attention

The earliest cities were pedestrian cities out of necessity really, because humans had few other means of movement: by carts, horses or mules. These cities were of a small scale; based on the scale of the human body. And while private life took place in private residences, the streets, squares and plazas were the places for a multitude of urban activities. They formed the 'open-air living-room' for all the citizens. The buildings in turn responded to the public use of urban spaces by having a suitable and friendly interface with the streets and squares.

While cities began to change with the advent of the horse-drawn carriages, the real damage to the urban spaces began once the automobile started invading the city in large numbers. Suddenly the streets and public spaces, which were the podium for urban life, had to cater to the demand of the aggressive automobile. And, consequently, streets that were meant for pedestrians – to walk, gather and to lounge – lost their function as places for urban interaction. So much of technology has gone into cars that there really is no way the pedestrianised citizen can compete with the car.

**The arched spaces in the central squares of the medieval city of Uzes in France illustrate how the buildings respond to the public space creating a magically human interface**

While the human race can walk comfortably at 5 kms/hour (and the exceptional human can for short stretches do 35 kms/hr), this is no match for the car that can travel at 300 km/hr

## Building Bye-laws

As cars have ruled the streets, the streets have simply become conduits for noisy and polluting traffic; the buildings have just turned their backs to the streets. The earlier human interface between public spaces and buildings has been destroyed. The space allotted to pedestrians has been reduced to small edges of public space such as a sidewalk for getting from point A to B. The function of urban spaces for broader human activities has been utterly lost in cities with pervasive cars.

Over the decades, building laws and byelaws have evolved, which take the car traffic as a given and the whole city design has been dictated by the needs of the car. This has resulted in massive investments in roads and parking infrastructure with the by-product of environmental (noise and air pollution) degradation and in many societies, social segregation for those without cars.

The damage to the urban fabric due to the automobile is in fact so great and growing, that drastic measures need to be taken to restore the city to its ultimate users: the pedestrians.

## Back to the Future

Our study shows how to go back to a city designed mainly for pedestrians. In fact, it shows how we can go to the future to design cities for pedestrians; the byelaws that we need to redesign and the use of latest technology to help pedestrian movement, access and general well-being.

The study shows that not only is such a city financially viable, but that it is also more affordable. That it costs less than our present cities, which are geared to the automobile. And it is healthier for its citizens, environmentally friendly and socially inclusive.

## The Case Study

The case study involves development of a part of a large city based on the present byelaws in India. The study shows the built-scenario, which we can expect if, based on the present byelaws, we build a series of plots in a city-segment of 1 km. x 1 km. For the purpose of this study all urban blocks have been taken to be 65 m. x 65 m., with a Floor Space Index (FSI or FAR) of 2.5. This means that on a plot, the total built-up area of all floors must not exceed 2.5 times the site area of the plot.

## The Present, Automobile-Dictated City

One of the biggest problems for creating a street-building interface for pedestrians is the byelaw regarding the 'setbacks'. The present byelaws (used in most Indian cities) dictate that the building has to be a certain distance away from the street and this distance is related to the height of the building. The higher the density of the city, the taller the blocks and the greater are the setbacks. In our case study where we work with an FSI of 2.5, the city we will get will be one of 10-12-storeyed towers, whereby the buildings have to be constructed (according to the byelaws) 12 to 18 metres from the street. And cars dominate the streets with pedestrians having little place to walk.

Illustrations on this page show how the present bye-laws and dominance of cars lead to tall blocks on each urban site. The aerial view shows an urban area of 500 m. x 500 m. All streets are used by cars (red arrows)

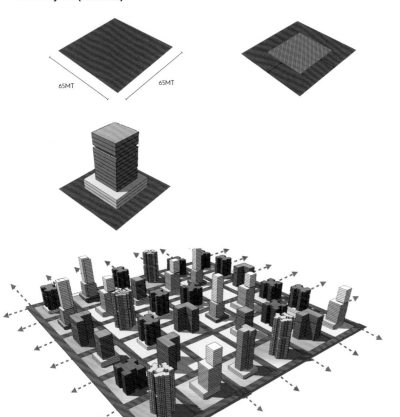

65MT     65MT

## The Pedestrian City: Designing With Renewed Bye-laws

In the Pedestrian City the bye-laws have been formulated first and foremost to take care of the well being of the pedestrian. The bye-laws not only allow, but also state that there should be excellent interface for pedestrians between the streets and the building. The buildings are pushed to the edge of the site and provide a good quality interface with the pedestrian-dominated public spaces around the building. By building along the perimeter, the built form can provide more built-up area per floor and the built-area of 2.5 FSI can be achieved in four storeys. The streets are spaces for a vast multitude of pedestrian activities for young and old, men and women, rich and poor. The limited height of the buildings results in greater interaction between those living in the buildings and the activities in the public spaces. The peripheral building block allows those residents who want the solitude of their private home, to open their units to the quiet internal courtyard within the block.

## Street Sections And Street Design: Economy Of Development

Except for incidental streets in which facilities are provided for a dedicated lane for public transportation, dedicated cycle paths and pedestrian spaces are provided throughout the Pedestrian City. The sections of 12 metres of street space can be redesigned, as the illustrations below show, from conduits for three lanes of vehicular

**Street scene of the present automobile-dictated city**

Illustrations on this page show how new bye-laws based on the well-being of pedestrians can lead to more human scaled blocks. The aerial view shows an area of 500 m. x 500 m. Light green arrows indicate streets which are exclusively pedestrian, light blue ones indicate streets where pedestrians share the space with cyclists and orange arrows indicate streets also with public transportation

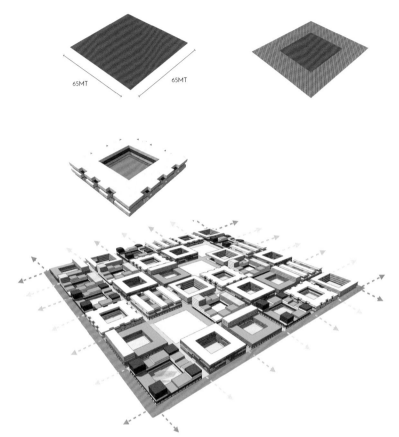

65MT    65MT

traffic to a haven for pedestrians young and old, women and men, poor and rich.

Compared to the vehicular street paved for cars, this street will be clearly more economical to build and on an average the cost of infrastructure for the Pedestrian City will be one-third less than for building vehicular roads.

## The Role of Modern Technology in the Pedestrian City

The savings achieved in building the pedestrian city infrastructure can be ploughed back into technological innovations to make the city pedestrian-friendly. These could be of two types:

**A**. Infrastructure built into the streets: Examples of these are travelators, which will assist pedestrians to walk farther and faster. The use of travelators in public streets has already been successfully demonstrated in Hong Kong and can be introduced in many of our cities. Other facilities in the public spaces could be umbrellas (with sensors), which open to shade pedestrians and diffusers that spray cool water in hot arid conditions. Solar panels could be used to shade streets, at the same time generating electricity for any lounge facilities for pedestrians. Additionally, the provision of free and ubiquitous Wi-Fi in public spaces will be a must.

**B.** Innovative appliances for aiding pedestrian propulsion: These can be categorised under two types, namely the 'wearables' and the 'non-wearables', which assist pedestrian propulsion.

**Street scene of the Pedestrian City**

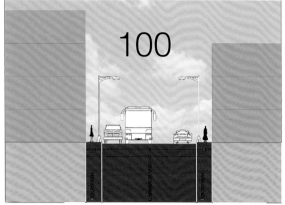

**Vehicular Road**

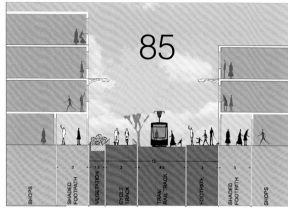

**Pedestrians + Cyclists + Tram**

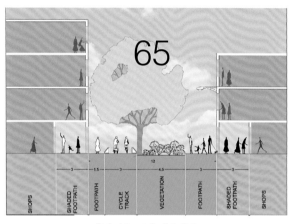

**Pedestrians + Cyclists Path**

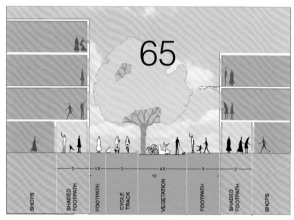

**Pedestrians + Cyclists Path**

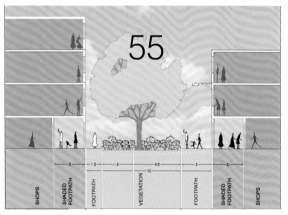

**Exclusive Pedestrian Path**

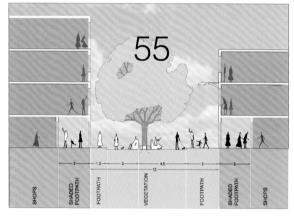

**Exclusive Pedestrian Path**

The sections above show how the same street space in an automobile dominated city (coloured red, entitled Vehicular Road) costing say 100 monetory units, can in the Pedestrian City be used for a street with public transportation (coloured brown, costing 85 monetory units), for pedestrians and cyclists (coloured dark green, costing 65 monetory units) and exclusively pedestrians (coloured light green, costing 55 monetory units)

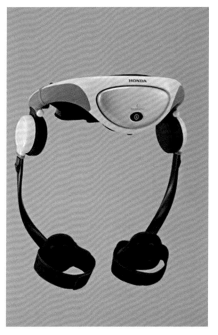

PHOTO: WORLD.HONDA.COM

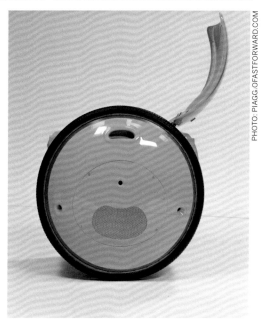

PHOTO: PIAGG.OFASTFORWARD.COM

Under the wearable category we can think of the many exoskeletons that are evolving from medical (revalidation) use and military use. But also smaller gadgets like the Honda Walking Assistance Device, which can assist walking. Under the non-wearable category we can think of devices like Piaggio's Gita, that is a device that can carry goods weighing up to 18 kgs. for the pedestrian and simply follows its 'master' via his smart phone.

## Three-Pronged Initiative

What the above study shows is that an urban settlement based primarily on pedestrian movements is not only possible, but is also more economical for governments to execute. Therefore, what will need to be done is:

**A.** To change the building bye-laws to those based on primarily pedestrian movement.

**B.** Allow for the use of new and disruptive technology to assist pedestrian movement in a

New technology to augment pedestrianisation: the Honda Walking Assistant (top) and Gita by Piaggio (below)

## The Numbers

How many people will be able to live, work and recreate in such a city?

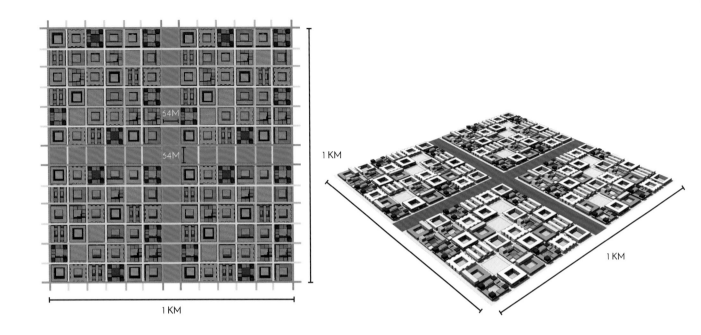

- A 1 km. x 1 km. city will contain 144 blocks.
  The total built up area of 144 blocks will be 144 x 10,500 = 1,512,000 sq.mt.
- 70% of 1,512,000 = 1,058,400 sq.mt. can be deemed to be residences. Based on an average size of 80 sq.mt. per residence and occupancy of four persons per residence, this means that 52,920 persons will live in this 1 km. x 1 km. settlement.
- 20% of 1,512,000 = 3,02,400 sq.mt. can be deemed to be for commercial office use. Based on an average occupancy of one working person per 15 sq.mt. of commercial space 20,160 persons can work in this 1 km. x 1 km. settlement.
- 10% of 1,512,000 = 1,51,200 sq.mt. can be deemed to be commercial and non-commercial amenities such as shops or clubs or creche etc. Based on occupancy of one person per 30 sq.mt. of space 5,040 persons can work in this 1 km. x 1 km. settlement.

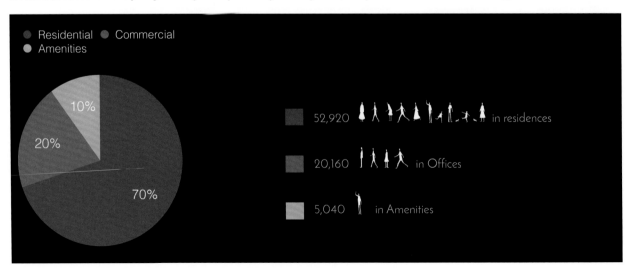

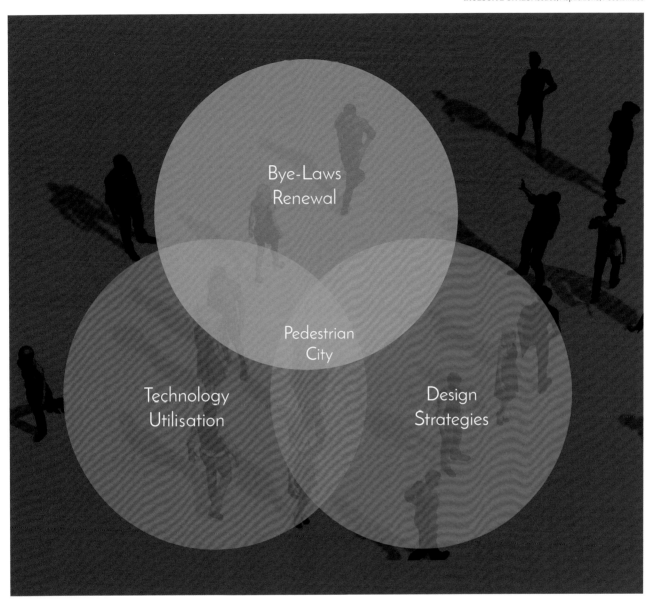

**In the Pedestrian City the bye-laws have been formulated first and foremost to take care of the well-being of the pedestrian**

way that it is simple and inclusive.

C. To redesign the network of public spaces to make them into a pedestrian paradise for all.

### Conclusion

When properly designed and executed, the impact of Pedestrian Cities will be to make our cities:

A. Socially just and inclusive, since all public spaces will be accessible to all.

B. Environmentally sustainable, since the noise and air pollution caused by cars will be absent.

C. Healthier, since better environment leading to more walking will tackle the rising problem of obesity in urban populations.

D. And economically sensible, since the government will save greatly on building such cities and the citizens will save on the expense of private cars.

E. It will also increase civic engagement and pride as more citizens meet one another in public spaces. ●

*Acknowledgement: Prajakta Gawde (inputs) and Manali Patil (illustrations)*

# Affordable Housing

## Global Perspectives, Local Realities

# Affordable Housing

## Global Perspectives, Local Realities

Vinayak Bharne & Shyam Khandekar

Affordable housing today has become nothing short of a global crisis, with an estimated 330 million households (equivalent to 1.2 billion people), currently lacking adequate shelter (World Resources Institute, 2017). A new McKinsey Global Institute (MGI) report, based on data from 2,400 metropolitan areas, finds that the affordability gap (the difference between the cost of an adequate housing unit and what households can afford, by spending no more than 30% of their income) now stands at $650 billion a year. This number is expected only to grow with urban expansion. This analysis suggests on the one hand, the crucial role affordable housing will play in mediating economic disparities in the coming future, acknowledging its pivotal role in making inclusive cities. It suggests, on the other, how affordable housing could represent a significant opportunity for the global construction and housing-finance markets, recognising its role as an economic engine and catalyst.

This section offers a focused, yet multifaceted discussion on affordable housing as a policy and community initiative, planning strategy, business model and architectural paradigm. The chapters in this section also span a range of regions, but this section's overall narrative is particularly significant for perspectives on how advanced societies – France, Russia, Singapore, United States, the Netherlands – have dealt with the affordability housing challenge in various phases of their development; how new, innovative trends of affordable housing are emerging today; and what other regions might serve to learn from them.

This section opens with a conversation with Somsook Boonyabancha, Chairperson of the Asian Coalition for Housing Rights (ACHR). In **Chapter 13: Affordable Housing for the People, by the People,** Boonyabancha notes that when communities, particularly the poorer demographic, discuss their problems, develop community organisations, negotiate for land and explore affordability models and materials, they not only develop secure housing, but also build a social support system to improve their status as citizens.

The two chapters that follow offer analysis-based principles for adequate and affordable housing. **Chapter 14: The Five Principles of Adequate Housing** develops the notion of 'housing justice' that is, housing which is available, accessible, affordable, acceptable and adaptable for all in an equitable, inclusive and sustainable way. **Chapter 15: High Rise or Low Rise?: Rethinking Affordability and Building Density** debunks the planning myth that increasing Floor Space Index (FSI) reduces the proportionate cost of land on each dwelling unit and thereby makes housing more affordable. It demonstrates why higher FSI does not make homes more affordable if the land price is not kept down.

Next, we feature commentaries on socio-cultural phenomena in two different parts of the world, as a reminder of unforeseen factors and consequences that can affect mainstream perceptions of affordable housing. **Chapter 16: Making Chandigarh Affordable Again** discusses the increasing affordability gap in India's six-decade-old, built-from-scratch state capital. State-owned government accommodation in this city has to be surrendered by the employee at retirement. With the city's increasing population, and land being a fixed commodity, there is little choice left for retired employees, even as housing supply remains a far cry from the demand. **Chapter 17: Conserving Social Housing in Moscow** discusses the case of citizen protests against a new law aimed at the renovation, demolition and rebuilding of Soviet-era housing of the 1950s and '60s. Even though residents were promised new apartments, these protests were triggered by their fear that resettlement would take away decades of social networks – an evidence that affordable housing is not just about shelter but community as well.

The next three essays focus largely on the Netherlands, a nation that has a long track record for providing social housing for a significant proportion of its citizens. **Chapter 18 – Social Housing in Amsterdam and Belgrade** offers a comparative survey of the origin and evolution of modern social housing in two European cities. It analyses why some public housing experiments, generated with the noblest of intentions, have not lived up to expectations and why apartments today may be affordable for the original dwellers, but not necessarily for the succeeding generation of residents. **Chapter 19: Who Can Afford to Live in London or Amsterdam?** overviews a range of strategies – subsidies, private client agreements, mass fabrication, integrating affordable housing with market housing – through projects by the noted Dutch architecture firm MVRDV. **Chapter 20: Dutch Social Housing Today** analyses the business model and working methods behind the successes and shortcomings of social housing corporations in the Netherlands that together own an impressive 2.4 million houses, roughly a third of the country's housing stock.

We follow with three case studies that can serve to inform the architecture and design of affordable housing in various cultural and economic circumstances. **Chapter 21: Cité Manifeste: A Unique Social Housing Project in France** is the study of a recent social rental housing project located within the former industrial site. It elaborates on the economic and social ideas behind this effort: factory workers were given access to individual houses close to their work place and, consequently, the reduction of travel time could now convert to extra working hours. **Chapter 22: Micro-Living: Affordable Housing in Unaffordable Cities** studies designs for small studio apartments, less than 35 square metres that provide compact yet comprehensive living environments for single individuals within New York's expensive real estate market. **Chapter 23: Learning from 'Chawl' Housing Typologies of Mumbai** documents 11 historic cost-effective housing projects through mediums of social space, circulation, built areas and densities to illustrate their application potential for existing, new or hybrid affordable housing models native to the Indian context. This study shows how the rich daily social life of chawls is as much a product of a specific architectural framework as the appropriations residents make to their dwellings.

**Chapter 24: Innovative Technology-Driven Affordable Housing** concludes this section with an award-winning proposal for creating an affordable neighbourhood using minimum resources. The uniqueness of this design lies in its use of an unconventional material: Styrofoam (Expanded Polystyrene or EPS) consisting of 4% petroleum-based mono-styrene and 96% air, making it fully recyclable, reasonably cheap, non-toxic, fireproof and impervious to moisture. This proposal highlights how design and construction aspects such as easy assembly, dismantling, transport and storing can lead to innovative ways of re-thinking affordable housing for the future.

# Affordable Housing for the People, by the People

In conversation with **Shyam Khandekar**, **Somsook Boonyabancha**, Chairperson, Asian Coalition for Housing Rights (ACHR), advocates a policy of community-led public development assisted by the government and developers

**How, when and why did you get involved in the issue of affordable housing?**

I have been involved in issues of affordable housing development for about 40 years. After completing my architecture education in 1975, I joined Thailand's National Housing Authority (NHA) in 1976 to help plan housing projects. As an architect with the Slum Upgrading Office, my first assignment was to design a community centre in a Bangkok slum. I organised discussions with the community members and tried to bring their ideas into the design process.

In 1981, I joined the Center for Housing and Human Settlement Studies (CHHSS), a collaborative programme between Thailand's NHA and the Institute of Housing Studies (IHS) in the Netherlands. After eight years with them, I did a brief stint with an NGO before I helped set up Thailand's first national Urban Community Development Fund (UCDF) and the Urban Community Development Office (UCDO) to manage the fund and use it to support various development activities of urban poor communities. The Fund started with a grant of about US $40 million from the Thai Government, which supported community-driven development

**Somsook Boonyabancha**

activities through cheap interest community loans across Thailand. The work grew in scale and strength.

In 2000, UCDO was merged with the Rural Development Fund to become the Community Organisations Development Institute (CODI), a public organisation supporting community-driven development activities at a national scale.

CODI now finances citywide slum housing

**The wisdom and practices by people and local communities that have sustained Asian societies for centuries have been ignored**

and upgrading projects (as well as rural housing development) in more than 300 cities throughout the country. It has a total revolving fund of about US $200 million for different kinds of community development loans with low interest rates at 3–4% per annum.

In 1988, after a regional meeting of people and NGOs involved in urban poor housing in Asian countries, the Asian Coalition for Housing Rights (ACHR) was set up to enable groups working on issues of urban poverty and housing to learn from and help each other find regional and international support for their efforts to solve eviction problems in their countries. Since inception, ACHR has developed programmes to support horizontal exchange learning, community finance systems, community-driven disaster rehabilitation and citywide housing upgradation. Between 2008 and 2014, ACHR's ACCA Programme (Asian Coalition for Community Action) supported a process of citywide slum upgrading in 215 cities in 19 countries across Asia.

## What exactly is the mission of the Asian Coalition for Housing Rights?

ACHR is a coalition of Asian professionals, NGOs and community organisations who share a commitment to find ways to make changes that are suitable for particular cultures. The collective experience of all these groups represents a huge resource of knowledge, understanding and possibilities. We have begun exploring ways of joining forces and supporting each other through joint initiatives: housing rights campaigns, fact-finding missions and community organisation training to resist eviction.

Over the years we've realised that government or private sector solutions are not the solutions for poor people. So ACHR evolved training and advisory programmes across Asian countries where good cases and experiences were identified and raised funds for extensive learning workshops, exchange visits and advisory trips.

This mutual support and sharing of ideas between Asian groups is important, because so many of the development theories, planning paradigms and urban development models which set the course in Asia – and which we are often obliged to follow – are mostly transplants from somewhere else, with knowledge, theories, technologies, international agendas mostly implemented in a top-down development culture.

*Left to Right from Facing Page:*
*- Housing in SuanPlu Community in Bangkok under CODI's Baan Mankong Programme. The slum was reconstructed after a fire*
*- Community participatory planning for upgrading the Bagmati River in Nepal by Community Architect Group*
*- ACHR supported housing project in the Philippines*
*- Community-driven housing development project in Yangon, Myanmar*
*- Participatory planning and the final result*

The wisdom and practices by people and local communities that have sustained Asian societies for centuries have been ignored and we seem to have lost confidence in our own considerable human and cultural wealth.

By being a regional coalition, many key pieces of knowledge from actual ground implementation or experiments have also been shared with the groups in the coalition.

### How did Asian cities differ from European cities in their periods of rapid growth in the last century?

Urbanisation started much earlier in Europe which is about 80% urbanised today as compared to 50% or less of Asia. However, Asia has urbanised much, much faster, in mostly unstable political situations and in different ways. Asia has a huge rural hinterland and many people are fleeing poverty, climate change and conflict. Today, Asia has more people flowing into its towns and cities in a shorter time and there's a greater disparity between the rich and the poor and unprepared urban management than in Europe.

There are also sharp differences in governance structures. While decentralisation is long established and working comparatively well in Europe, Asian countries are still very centralised, with powers concentrated mostly with the central government. When people have less political power and fewer opportunities to participate, development happens in ways that favour the upper strata of society.

One of the most visible manifestations of unbalanced power in city development is the lack of viable, affordable housing. In most Asian cities, the poor have to make their own houses and settlements on whatever possible land they can and carry on with their lives as best they can. This informal, people-built housing may be substandard, but it represents an enormous and flexible system that supplies shelter to those the public and private sectors have left out. Because their city governments give them no legitimate space, power or access to finance to solve their housing problems and most of the public and private sector housing is unaffordable for them, Asia's urban poor are forced to be illegal and informal.

When we talk about the management of cities today, there is a tendency to focus more on economic or technical aspects. Asian cities love taking up ideas from Europe or America, like 'smart cities', 'world class cities' and 'investor-friendly development'. The agenda for our city development and urban form comes more from outside Asia. Of course there are many good and successful practices in the West and we can learn from those experiences. But this outward-looking policy can become very problematic because we fail to look at, and build on, the enormous strength and development potential that exists in our cities and in our urban citizens when we try to figure out what form urban change will take. In European cities it's been a gradual democratic development and cities have long developed mechanisms and practices that balance power between the city government and the citizens, which provide more opportunities for participation. This participation

**We have to engage many different kinds of construction or delivery systems to get the housing built, but the social element should be a must**

**A housing project with support from the urban poor community by Women for the World and ACHR, ACCA Programme in 2010–2014**

*Top:* **Community-based rehabilitation in Leh, India, by Tibet Heritage Trust and ACHR; an example of rehabilitation and heritage of an old town by the community**
*Bottom Left & Right:* **Young professionals from CAN training programme support community rehabilitation after an earthquake in Nepal**

is also reflected in the city planning processes and in the provision of services to residents, which seem to be more equal than in Asian cities.

A good example of this imbalance in urban management can be found in historic preservation. European cities, both big and small, are full of beautifully preserved and shady public spaces and historic buildings even as newer quarters have been added. In Asia, we don't think it important to preserve our old towns or historic spaces; worse we demolish our built history to put up shopping malls and build parking lots. And if an area is designated a heritage site, people who live there face eviction. This is because money economics is a predominant system for the area. If Asian cities want to be truly inclusive and liveable for all their citizens, people must take an active part in the development of their city and housing is one of the best places to start.

Asia has a long tradition of public markets, canals and many forms of community housing. These Asian traditions and forms could bring many interesting and vital aspects to our urban planning, if our public and private sector developers could only move beyond just economic development or economic generation ideas, which make housing an individual commodity bought and sold by the rich.

## Could you explain your concept of community-led development for low-cost housing and its advantages compared to developer-led development?

Do we want people to be more powerful living engines with diverse energy and power to make creative changes for themselves and the cities, or just be passive followers? Community-led is the way to allow people to get together and achieve the desirable development. It is to unlock peoples' energy and potentials to help them attain affordable housing and build a healthy community system.

However, physical and affordable housing for every poor family may not be enough to make a significant change. In the conventional approach to development, we are encouraged to look at poverty as a problem, which the poor have to endure and somebody else has to fix. But in order to survive, poor people must develop strength, resilience and capability, which is the flip side of poverty. Without such strength, how could so many millions of people without money or connections or education, whose lives as poor squatters are illegal and marginal, manage to shelter themselves, earn enough to feed their families and send their kids to school? If we can understand this other side of poverty – the problem-solving side – then we'll understand what form development should take and how it can help unlock these people's energy to redevelop their lives.

This is especially true in housing. When poor communities have space and support to come together, discuss their shelter problems, develop their community organisation, explore affordable housing models and materials, plan their own solutions to their housing problems and negotiate for land, they are not only developing their own secure housing, but they are also building their social support system and ways to improve their status as citizens in the city. When people are at the centre of housing production, the final product is always invariably cheaper, better, more socially lively and culturally appropriate than the minimal, individual kind of 'housing units' favoured by developers and found in public housing.

The individual approach may work for better-off people, but not for the poor, whose position at the bottom of the economic ladder leaves them especially vulnerable when they're alone. But while the poor may be weak in financial terms, they are particularly rich in social terms. In communities of the poor, there is a social force, which can and does deal with the economic disadvantages people experience individually.

## Can the social and economic advantages of community-led development of low-cost housing be combined with the scale and speed of the developer-led model?

When people of a community design and construct their own low-income housing, it's great, because the housing development process becomes an opportunity for them to work, learn and design together, manage finance and construction and build their community organisation and strength in the process. But people-built should not be the only option; it can be mixed with other options since we have huge housing demand.

In Thailand, many of the communities developing their housing projects under CODI's Baan Mankong Programme build their own houses and bring down the costs. Others hire contractors to build all or part of their new housing while some hire contractors to lay foundations and construct reinforced concrete frames and the families finish the work, to bring down costs. The contractors hired are usually small, local businesses in the area, are part of the communities or collectives of skilled community builders. At the other end is professional developer-built housing, which can also work.

Options for the way housing is constructed should be kept open. What matters more than who actually builds is that the residents should

**People-built housing may be substandard, but it represents an enormous and flexible system that supplies shelter to those the public and private sectors have left out**

A minister in Sri Lanka is awarded the ACHR for his support to community housing activities taken up by the Women Co-ops

**Housing development by the urban poor. Activities in the Philippines supported by ACHR's ACCA Programme**

play an active role in the project. Even if the housing is to be built by developers, it should be possible for the residents to share their views, take part in the designing, planning and implementation and build as a group through the housing planning and implementation process.

But this is rarely the case in most of the developer-built housing. Hence, poverty and isolation persist even in the most solidly built housing projects. To reach the enormous scale of housing needed, we require different kinds of construction or delivery systems, but the social element should be a must.

### Which are the important issues where the governments need to play an important role in solving the problem of affordable housing in Asian cities?

**ISSUE 1 - Scale:** It's time we aimed for change of scale. We could reach the scale of citywide change in housing, if we can find ways to link all the different actors to visualise an overall picture and develop plans to solve housing problems for different groups in that particular city. It should be a programme or a package of support structures, where everybody in the city is part of the development process. Today, almost all public housing in Asia is developed on a project-by-project basis and private sector housing is scattered project-based. In many cases, even people-driven housing initiatives are project-based. Why don't we combine all these efforts into a city-scale programme that sees human settlements for all and the city's function and participation and social system more as a whole? Governments could play a role in turning that scale into policy, providing finance or making existing financial tools work better and more flexibly to support housing development on a citywide scale.

**ISSUE 2 - Flexible Finance:** It is crucial

to have financial mechanisms that are creative and flexible to support people-centred and citywide housing development programmes at scale. Conventional banks or government fiscal budgeting alone cannot do it. When you provide finance to support such a citywide process, with special funds from banks and with new institutions to provide different kinds of finance to create a flexible development system at the city scale, different cities around the country can proceed at the same time. And governments can help facilitate the setting up of these new flexible finance mechanisms.

**ISSUE 3 - Cities Solve Their Own Problems:** Allow the city to fix the problem. This relates to the planning and several other city development issues. Central governments should allow the people and the city (various actors) to develop their own comprehensive solutions, but with poor communities as the key actors. The people who will live in those new housing projects must be active. The government should provide the platform: you don't dance alone, you don't control or own the big national or city housing platforms, but you allow the actors to dance together. This is vital.

**ISSUE 4 - The World Has Changed:** People in cities all over Asia want change. They want to be part of a reasonable and active change in their lives and settlements. Our countries are urbanising rapidly and our societies are changing by leaps and bounds, but our governments are not keeping pace; they are mostly stuck in old, conservative highly top-down patterns and are very slow to change. It's time for our governments to make a new platform and allow active people who want to change things to sit together and make different teams to fix things and bring about change. This is the smart way for both the central government and the city government. Make it a more proactive process. ●

# The Five Principles of Adequate Housing

**Alonso Ayala**, **Maartje van Eerd** and **Ellen Geurts** advocate housing as a human right

## Introduction

Over the past 70 years, though many different housing policy directions have been tried out leading to a plethora of affordable housing programmes and projects, access to adequate and affordable housing remains a challenge across the world. The McKinsey Global Institute (2014) frames the housing challenge as a global affordability crisis stating that "330 million urban households around the world lack decent housing or are so financially stretched by housing costs that they forgo other basic needs, including food, health care and schooling for children" (2014, 1).

The housing enablement approach of the last decades, far from being the expected agent of change for a functional housing sector, did not improve the situation but rather worsened it. It resulted in an acute shortage of formal affordable housing for the increasing urban poor population who continued to solve the problem themselves through informal means.

Currently the housing paradigm is shifting towards recognising housing as a human right. The commitment across the globe to ensure the right everyone has to housing, together with an increased awareness regarding the contribution of housing to urban sustainability, has become the prominent angle to housing policy development. Housing as a challenge and as a complex urban development issue is now understood as 'more than a roof above your head' to include urban economic, social and environmental considerations. Housing and urban planning are therefore inextricably linked.

At the Institute for Housing and Urban Development Studies (IHS Rotterdam) we have worked on understanding what makes housing policy work by developing our own understanding of what 'adequate housing' means. Therefore, we have formulated five principles which we believe provide a strong basis for evaluating housing policies and approaches in a comprehensive manner. We call these principles the 5 As of Adequate Housing: Availability, Accessibility, Affordability,

Acceptability and Adaptability. The added value of evaluating housing polices and approaches against these principles lies in the understanding of their mutual reinforcement and complementarity, thus highlighting the complexity of the housing challenge.

Additionally, our purpose in defining these principles is also to develop the notion of 'Housing Justice' as the rational outcome of housing policies, which are designed and implemented in order to achieve these principles. As a starting point we can define Housing Justice as 'adequate housing for all', that is, housing which is available, accessible, affordable, acceptable and adaptable for all in an equitable, inclusive and sustainable way.

## The Five Principles of Adequate housing: Availability, Accessibility, Affordability, Acceptability and Adaptability

The principles of adequate housing represent a fundamental truth to understanding and evaluating the housing challenge from the point of view of availability, accessibility, affordability, acceptability

> The principles of adequate housing represent a fundamental truth to understanding and evaluating the housing challenge

**The 5 As: Principles of Adequate Housing**

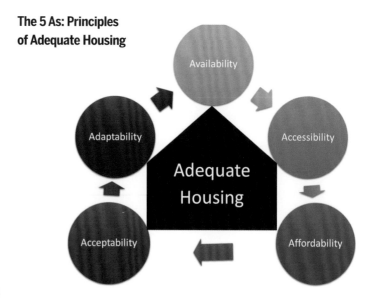

and adaptability of housing. These principles are a proposition. They aim at establishing the foundations for composing rational housing polices and approaches that lead to the notion of housing justice. The following sections explain in more detail the five principles of adequate housing.

## Availability

Availability of housing is more complex than just making houses available in the market. The principle of availability refers to the existing or newly built housing that is adequate for the intended target group in the locations where people need them. It also refers to the supply of housing finance (Ayala et al., 2014).

Availability needs to be understood as a location-specific issue in relationship to people's housing needs. Housing needs can only be met if housing policies aim at meeting people's real needs for housing. There could be a serious mismatch between where houses are located and where people can meet their housing needs. Therefore, the need for housing goes beyond the quantitative mismatch between supply and demand of housing to include the qualitative features of the available housing stock that may need to be improved, demolished or replaced (Angel, 2000).

It is important that housing policy makers have a good understanding of the relationship that exists between the supply and demand side of not only affordable housing but also the supply and demand of serviced land that is required to build affordable housing projects. Within a framework of well-planned urban extensions and densification, counteracting urban sprawl is also a matter of the available attributes of both the house and the neighbourhood. Therefore, the availability of housing typologies that consider

end-users and provide mixed-use neighbourhood developments is of paramount importance to achieve urban sustainability objectives.

In short, availability needs to be ensured not only in terms of the number of housing units, but also in terms of location, type of dwellings, appropriateness for the target group and the prevention of socio-spatial segregation and urban sprawl.

## Accessibility

Accessibility to affordable housing refers, on the one hand, to the eligibility criteria determining access to housing programmes and housing finance and, on the other, to the access households have to urban infrastructure.

The eligibility criteria for affordable housing projects need to be realistic in terms of the intended target groups and their capacity to comply with the targeted financial instrument. The identification of sub-target groups and priority-setting, as well as quota-setting for specific target groups can enhance accessibility as long as it reflects a good understanding of people's real housing needs and their financial capabilities. Accessibility to urban infrastructure refers to the physical and financial access people have to urban infrastructure, making it affordable and available in their neighbourhoods, towns and cities.

King (2016) shows the relation between quality and access and explains how a trade-off is made between those who cannot afford housing and those whose aspirations and needs cannot be satisfied because their incomes are too low. The clear distinction is that, in general, higher quality will mean that less people can access it as quality comes at a cost, thus limiting access. He places great emphasis on the relationship between incomes – or

**Spatially and socially isolated from the rest of the town with no public transport connections nearby, the Plemetina social housing project for Roma communities at the outskirts of Obiliq in Kosovo highlights the provision of housing in the wrong location**

### Availability

Number of housing units (housing stock) newly built or existing which are located in the right places

Supply of serviced land and houses in combination with the supply of housing finance

Housing needs

PHOTO: ALONSO AYALA, 2012

rather the lack of – and access to housing.

The human rights framework that we see developing for housing in many countries has put further emphasis on access to housing. It has led to an understanding that housing policies should ensure that either housing is affordable or that people have sufficient income and economic opportunities to afford a place to live. If neither of this is driven by policy, it means that housing will not be, to a large extent, accessible for many low-income households (Harris, 2015).

## Affordability

Affordability can be defined in different ways. Many scholars agree that in order for a household to afford housing, no more than 25–30% of the household income should be spent in housing related costs (i.e., mortgage or rental payments and maintenance). Housing costs should never jeopardise the attainment of other basic needs for survival such as water, food and health.

Affordability is also affected by tenure options. It may differ depending on the tenure models available and accessible to people. The very poor and higher income groups are often best served by home-ownership options, while low to middle income households can be served by for example, social rental housing provided that rent levels are more affordable than those on the market. Home ownership levels can differ from owning a sites-and-services plot with secure tenure and serviced land, to a basic starter unit or core house that can be extended, to owning a finished housing product. The higher the costs for any housing solution the more subsidy or grants are required, assuming that households can only afford subsidised rates and

not market-level prices. Therefore, affordability of housing bears a strong relation between housing costs and household income (Ayala et al., 2014).

Eligibility for bank loans is often conditional on secure, regular and formal income. Affordability needs to be also considered over time because very few households can afford a one-off purchase of a house. Hence, the monthly payments should be affordable, encompassing not only loan repayments (e.g., mortgage or subsidies) but also management and maintenance costs depending on the type of housing.

In seeking affordability for low income groups house-units have been sometimes given for free. It is important to highlight that housing given for 'free' is not a good idea because it eventually results in long-term costs for their owners, simply because housing requires maintenance and payment of a wide range of services and attributes that flow through it. For example, the costs of energy, water and sanitation, as well as the costs attached to the transportation required to access employment, goods and services. On the other hand, the market value of such housing may be limited which affects access to credit for housing improvement (Huchzermeyer, 2016).

In summary, there are different definitions of housing affordability. These include the percentage of income spent on housing, the basic quality of the housing unit and the percentage of households that are eligible to access various types of affordable housing.

## Acceptability

Acceptability by people of the housing outcome is fundamental to achieve sustainability of interventions. It relates to people's perceptions of

> **Affordability of housing bears a strong relation between housing costs and household income**

The slum of Petare Norte, home to 150,000 inhabitants, is located at the eastern fringe of Caracas and represents the lack of proper access the urban poor have to adequate housing and urban infrastructure

### Availability

### Accessibility

Double access condition to land, housing and economic infrastructure.

Eligibility criteria (Priority setting - Target groups; specific needs groups ; demand-driven models)

PHOTO: ALONSO AYALA, 2008

## Affordability

Proportion of income spent on housing (Affordability threshold)

Tenure Models: -Rental vs. ownership debate

Ownership models – Sites & Services to a finished product

The basic quality of the affordable unit: Standard unit?

Availability

Accessibility

PHOTO: ELLEN GEURTS, 2010

belongingness, identity and the cultural adequacy of the housing made available, accessible and affordable to them. Acceptability incorporates a more individual understanding of the housing process because choice and the freedom to choose becomes part of the equation regarding what people consider an acceptable quality.

Sustainability and acceptability are intrinsically related. This refers to the contribution the quality of housing has in achieving physical, social, economic and financial objectives. Physical objectives relate to the accessibility and affordability of urban infrastructure and a structurally sound and well-maintained housing stock. Social and cultural objectives are mainly attained through the attributes of house-units, which reflect the real housing needs of its occupants, and also the characteristics of the neighbourhood regarding availability of public

spaces and social infrastructure for community life and interaction, including recreational opportunities and a synergy of the built-environment with the natural environment. Economic objectives refer to the availability and accessibility of housing to employment opportunities and a convenient urban environment where daily activities requiring the exchange of goods and services can easily take place. Lastly, financial objectives refer to the acceptability that comes from the affordability to specific financial instruments that households can access to sustainably acquire, manage and maintain the available housing stock that better reflects their housing needs.

In terms of affordability, often overlooked elements include whether maintenance is affordable (long-term sustainability) or whether access to the energy sources connected to the

**The B. G. Alexander social housing project in Johannesburg provides affordable rental housing to around 1,000 tenants. It occupies an entire city block with a series of buildings designed around a central courtyard space featuring a soccer pitch, a church facility, an after-care centre, a full-catering kitchen, four recreation halls, a lecture hall and a creche**

**The Lunawa Environmental Improvement and Community Development Project in Sri Lanka is the best practice with regards to community participation and acceptability of the housing outcome by people**

## Acceptability

Quality of housing outcomes

Real housing needs

Cultural adequacy

Housing outcomes are the expression of cultural identity

Availability

Accessibility

Affordability

PHOTO: RANJITH SAMARASINGHE, 2009

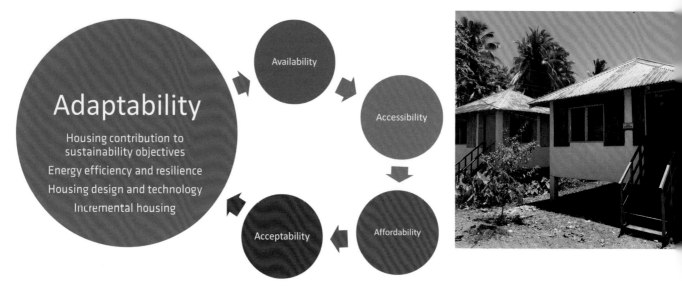

houses are affordable (e.g., do households have access to sources of energy that they can pay without falling into what is known as energy poverty?). Therefore, affordability of these aspects needs to be acceptable.

In terms of accessibility, the enrolment system for affordable housing programmes should secure or support the participation of beneficiaries in other aspects beyond acquiring a good quality house. These are for example vocational training opportunities, access to schools and health care and, generally, access to the labour market. This principle, therefore, serves to ensure a balanced, holistic, integrated and sustainable interpretation of the previously explained three principles.

## Adaptability

This principle relates both to the adaptability of housing to climate change as well as the adaptability of the housing product to the changing needs of the occupant or end user.

Regarding adaptability to climate change, the principle reflects the contribution of the housing sector to sustainability objectives and the attainment of resiliency in housing. According to several studies the most efficient way to slow down climate change is by using less energy. The contribution of housing to reducing the carbon footprint is quite important. The availability and, eventually, the affordability of technologies to reduce GHGE in terms of energy consumption in both new and existing buildings can cut it down from an estimated 30–80%, with potential net profit during the building life-span (UNEP, 2009).

Ultimately, the attainment of the housing principle of adaptability to climate change cannot be detached from an understanding on the contribution that housing can make to sustainability objectives. This is because housing construction, its further use and maintenance during its lifespan consumes large amounts of resources. Housing is on the other hand a fixed asset with a long life and it is central to quality of life thus having implications in terms of transport needs, access to health and education, employment opportunities and the creation of community life (UNEP, 2009).

Apart from adaptability to climate change, housing should also be adaptable to changing housing needs of the end users. Research has shown that, particularly for the urban poor, it is important to provide them with housing solutions that can incrementally develop as housing needs change and income increases or is made available for housing construction or renovation.

In summary, housing adaptability is a principle which refers to both technological and design considerations. This means the ability of the housing solution to adapt to changing needs in terms of space and use (i.e., incremental housing approaches), but also to climate change through mitigation (i.e., reduction of GHGE) and adaptation measures (e.g., resiliency against extreme climate events).

## Linking the 5 As to the concept of Housing Justice

After elaborating on the five principles of adequate housing the ultimate question is: How does the attainment of these principles contribute to

**In the province of Capiz, the Philippines, post-disaster recovery has led to the adaptation of housing by raising them above the ground in order to cope with the yearly occurrence of typhoons and the flooding that comes along**

**Housing injustice is determined by the city's socio-economic and political structure**

understanding the notion of housing justice?

We could argue that housing justice is a new concept. It builds on the concept of justice that has already been on the agenda for many years. Rawls (1971) in his book, *A Theory of Justice,* considers what trade-off between equality and freedom is socially just and respects individual rights and interests. According to him, inequalities and major differences in income and wealth may be justified only insofar as any disparity in wealth contributes to the greater benefit of the least well-off. So a society should allow for inequalities if, and only if, this situation maximises the life chances of those with the minimum resources. In housing this could translate in the design of targeted housing policies that benefit only those in need (e.g., social housing, housing vouchers, rental subsidies and so on). Justice is the first virtue of social institutions, as truth is of systems of thought. Accordingly, a theory must be rejected or revised if it is untrue, likewise laws and institutions must be reformed or abolished if they are unjust.

In *Social Justice and the City*, Harvey (1973) argues that urbanisation takes place because of concentrations of surplus, being largely invested in urban property, connecting capitalism, urbanisation and the resulting process of social exclusion. He criticises the capitalist mode of accumulation in which the rich accumulate their assets by displacing the poor. This trend can be observed across the globe. For instance, in cases of riverfront development projects, where often the argument of adaptation to climate change, or improving liveability and attractiveness of city centres is used to evict the poor and move them to often underdeveloped resettlement projects far from their original locations.

Urban justice, climate justice and gender justice are high on the development agenda. In the neo-liberal era where decisions are driven by money, and growth promoting policies are the mainstream, a counter-stream has stood up questioning the domination of growth oriented thinking, driven by the negative impact on both the more vulnerable in societies all over the world as inequalities have grown enormously (Piketty, 2014).

Fainstein in her book, *The Just City* (2010), aims to develop an urban theory of justice, that is built on the principles of equity, democracy and diversity. For communicative theorists the test of policy depends on who is included in its formulation, on the existence of an open, fair process and on better arguments as the deciding

factor. For *The Just City* theorists, the principal test is whether the outcome of the process is equitable.

But what about the housing justice process, should it be to stimulate redistribution? Should housing contribute to a redistribution of benefits and opportunities? Should housing policies solely target the poorest and most vulnerable because they are the ones who need the most support? What is the right balance of housing justice?

All these questions need to be answered. The last one we would like to propose is: Housing justice for whom? For those in power or those without? For those who claim it or those who don't? As Fainstein has formulated: "If the content of justice is defined by a community, and the city is made of diverse communities, whose definition should prevail, particularly if diversity, democracy, and sustainability and not just equitable material distribution, are constitutive of justice?" (2010, 16)

## Conclusion

Adequate housing is the foundation for creating sustainable communities and human settlements. It enables people to be productive, healthy and contributes to access education, all fundamental preconditions for human development.

The renewed interest in end-user's participation in the housing process, as well as the recognition of incremental housing developments as matching the way most people ultimately access housing, acknowledges the necessity to arrive at products that are more responsive to people's housing needs. The interest for these type of interventions also stems from the awareness of the global financial crisis, after which, the attention somewhat shifted to affordable housing policies aimed at achieving a kind of social and spatial justice.

Housing injustice is to our belief determined by the city's socio-economic and political structure. It is shaped by how the principles of housing affordability, availability, accessibility, acceptability and adaptability interact with one another in relationship to urban planning and land markets, manifesting in a whole range of housing conditions such as derelict city centres, peripheral and isolated housing projects, informal settlements, forced evictions and inadequate resettlement projects, gated communities and segregated enclaves of ethnic minorities and poor migrants.

Our plea is that working towards the realisation of housing justice should be a core value for all professionals working in the housing sector. ●

## HIGH RISE OR LOW RISE?

# Rethinking Affordability and Building Density

**Ashok Lall** explains why we should build low-rise instead of high-rise when constructing housing for the people who need it

The numbers put out by Niti Aayog, the present policy think tank for the Government of India, make it abundantly clear that the 'shortfall' of housing in cities is principally for those households who are at the bottom of the income pyramid. This constitutes about 60% of the population of cities. The shortfall, though, includes those existing homesteads where people are living at present, but which are considered to be unsafe and unhealthy for habitation, i.e., slums, buildings and neighbourhoods that need to be upgraded, redeveloped or relocated.

Although slums persist in many of our cities today and much of the policy space is consumed by the idea of slum eradication and slum clearance as post facto corrective measures, the discussion is about the prospective possibilities of housing policy and housing design, where slums do not occur any more.

Given that the provision of housing will, inevitably, follow three streams – 1) self-build small-scale construction; 2) medium scale low rise, high density construction in suburban areas and cities; and 3) large projects by big players – diverse strategies according to the particularities of each of the three streams are called for. The common issue is that of land: its location, its availability and its utilisation.

### Spatial Equity and Land Equity

The economic shifts toward urbanisation signal an opportunity for the processes of urban growth to be designed for distribution of wealth. Affordable homes for the majority of citizens that are legally secure, structurally and environmentally safe, located close to opportunities for employment and trade, with access to educational and health services, are at the centre of such a strategy. This objective calls for spatial equity, land equity and parcels to be reserved for homes so that one can stay close to work and to income opportunity, which means spatial equity. And land prices would be sheltered from the deleterious effects of land

> This objective calls for spatial equity and land equity so that one could stay close to work and to income opportunity

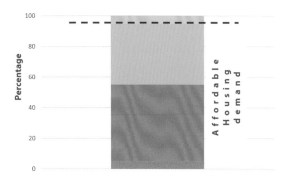

## HOUSING SHORTAGE & AFFORDABILITY

### (HOUSEHOLD INCOMES FROM Rs. 10000/MONTH TO Rs. 40000/MONTH)

Income (Rs)/month ■ 0 to 10K ■ 10 to 20K ■ 20 to 30K ■ 30 to 40K

**The bulk of shortage is for Households with incomes between Rs.10000 to Rs.30000 a month**

speculation, so that an affordable home is within reach. This is land equity.

## Land

Let us be clear about one thing, that the speculative markets of private lands and the State's penchant to ride such speculation, to capitalise on the market value of land as a revenue source, have had the opposite effect. 'Market based solutions': solutions that are driven by the current unregulated speculation on land and an artificially created scarcity of land have been the cause of greater spatial inequity and land inequity. If one has poor earnings one must live farther away and commute farther, for it is only at a great distance from the economic heart of the city that land is affordable. A good third of one's energy and earnings are dissipated on burning fuel and time in travel. No wonder the resultant is slums and unauthorised habitation in the interstices of the city.

## Singapore's success

The success of Singapore's Government in providing affordable, quality homes to about 80% of its population through its Housing Development Board (HDB) is instructive. Through farsighted legislative and fiscal measures large tracts of land were reserved for affordable housing and taken out of speculative land markets. The cost of land, being freed of speculative markets, became affordable for the state and the homebuyer. The monetisation of land as revenue for the urban development authority was done judiciously, for selected downtown sites and new reclaimed land from the sea, in a manner that did not cause speculative landholding. In sum, the priority of the island nation's land policy was to secure affordable homes for its citizens. It was necessary to regulate the land market to meet the legitimate needs of its citizens for affordable homes. It is now established that in emerging economies, where land markets are not mature and tend to be distorted, 'housing for all' requires a strong land regulation and land release policy.

## Social Housing in the Netherlands

Let's take a brief look at the success of the social housing programme of the Netherlands. This little nation has 350 non-profit Social Housing Corporations who finance housing for those at the bottom of the economic pyramid. Such corporations provide 45% of the housing stock of Amsterdam. Once again, the essential feature of affordability is that the land allocated to social housing is priced at a third of the open market price. All homes are leasehold or rental. Private area-developer projects (townships or neighbourhoods) are, by law, required to reserve 33% of the land for social housing in partnership with the Housing Corporations. Typically, in land-short Netherlands, housing is low rise up to four storeys high. The principle is twofold: to keep the city really compact with a comforting, active, humane network of streets, squares and gardens, which are inhabited by people, and to reduce the distinctions and spatial segregation between classes and communities.

## The high Floor Space Index (FSI) folly

A myth is being perpetuated that land is expensive and in short supply. On the basis of this assumption, city planning authorities are raising permissible FSI to accommodate the anticipated demand – not only in the large metros, but also in satellite towns and tier two and tier three cities. It is said that increasing FSI reduces the proportionate cost of land on each dwelling unit and thereby makes access to housing more affordable.

'Going vertical' to house more people is deemed to be the automatic and inevitable result of land shortage and land cost. In this arithmetic the permitted FSI keeps climbing from 2.5 – which calls for buildings that are about eight-storeys tall – to 4 resulting in buildings more than 16-storeys high. Now, we have seen that across most cities in India raising the FSI has not resulted in bringing down the cost of buying a home. It has, on the contrary, raised the cost of land in proportion to the amount of building you are allowed to pile on it. The higher the permitted FSI, the higher the market price of land. Higher FSI does not make homes more affordable if the land price is not kept down.

Furthermore, taller buildings are more costly to build, take longer to build and require more capital to undertake projects. It is no surprise that huge numbers of multistorey housing towers are lying incomplete today, with developers becoming insolvent and so much steel and cement hanging up in the air as locked, unproductive national wealth. Even when cross-subsidised, as in the Slum Redevelopment Authority projects of Mumbai, they are woefully inappropriate for tiny homes for people with meagre incomes. This lesson has been learnt.

## High-rise means high lifetime cost

Our research on construction costs shows that construction costs and building operation costs rise by 15% for every six-storey increase in height. The maintenance costs for the lifecycle of tall buildings, with their dependence on elaborate electro-mechanical systems for vertical transportation of people, goods and water and safety against fire, and

# BUILDING HEIGHT & AFFORDABILITY?

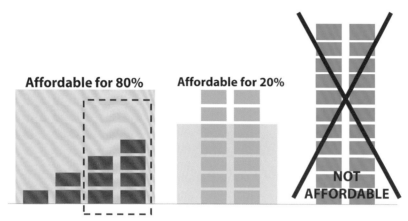

**Affordable for 80%**    **Affordable for 20%**

**NOT AFFORDABLE**

**Costs of Low Rise High Density are most Affordable**

|  |  |  |  |
|---|---|---|---|
| **Building Cost** | 900 (Rs/sqft) | 1400 (Rs/sqft) | 1700 (Rs/sqft) |
| **Maintenance Cost** | 1.5 (Rs/sqft) | 2.5 (Rs/sqft) | 3.5 (Rs/sqft) |

their exposure to weathering and vibrations, are 20% higher than costs for four-storey buildings. Affordability is not just about building construction costs, but needs to be ensured through the life of the building. As these homes are occupied, people should be able to afford their maintenance and running costs. If we are talking of affordability at our present levels of income, for 60% of our households with income below Rs.3,000 per month, we must choose to build low rise, the more economical way of living in buildings.

## Task for the designers of the Built Environment

Housing environments – places for all those who would live their lives there including children, youth and the elderly – do not drop out of arithmetic formulae. It seems that many 'stakeholders' like administrators, political bosses, financiers and bankers, municipalities, city development authorities and even speculative developers are unable to see anything beyond the quantities of floor area stacked up on some land like gunny bags full of potatoes. They tend to restrict the role of the designer, apart from her primary one of 'tarting up the elevation' to the reduction of costs of construction and to driving floor area efficiencies.

When we talk of the challenge of affordable housing we refer to the less well off 60% of our

urban population. The living condition of this 60% is what constitutes 'the quality of life of a city'. The challenge of planning and design is to develop liveable urban morphologies and building types in ways that work at the present economic threshold of affordability for the 60% and yet provide the foundation for progressively raising standards of living and improving and enriching their quality of life. Research and innovation is needed to find the answers to this objective.

## Robustness of housing typologies

Households are not a standard or a static entity. A bunch of college students can be a household; friends or cousins can be a household. Even in a typical nuclear family there will be changes over time: the young couple, with young children, their grandparents may come to stay, the children grow up, some of them leave for studies, then the son brings a bride and grandparents may have passed away. Then comes a time when it may be advantageous to rent out a room. Or one might be working from home. Confined small spaces cannot be cast in concrete forever. For optimum service and use of the small home over its 60 years of useful life, building design must promote ways of adjusting the inside arrangement of the home.

And we do expect that life will get better for everyone after they move into their home. The

*Top & Bottom:* **Brick-wall row housing of Europe**

## BUILDING HEIGHT & CARBON EMISSIONS

Low carbon city = Affordable City

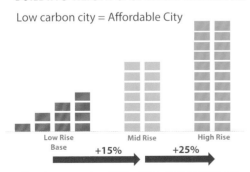

Low Rise Base  Mid Rise  High Rise

**+15%**  **+25%**

**Housing comprises 70% of the city's Built Space**

Build low rise high density for low carbon urban futures

safe, comfortable home is that essential support that enables people to devote their energies to build a better future. Some residents will move on to better places elsewhere. Others will want to enlarge their homes by buying from their adjacent neighbours. Designing for these changes and transformations over time makes sense. It means that the basic structure of the building remains useful for a long time.

### European experience

The brick-wall row housing of Europe that was built in the late 19th and early 20th centuries, with a semi basement, three floors and an attic, has proved to be a truly robust solution. They are still there, adapted and modified to meet the changing needs of changing times all made possible because the structural chassis of the buildings enables change without wholesale demolition. This is strategic design for long-term robustness and sustainability.

Contrast this with the all RCC formula gaining popularity today – all walls, internal as well as external, will be cast-in-situ RCC – in the name of economy. This is fossilising the home, fixing it forever with no possibility of adaptation or alteration. The worst kind of homes, from a standpoint of environmental sustainability, that you can build today are high rise, all RCC towers. Empirical research shows that the lifetime carbon emissions of 12-storey, all RCC buildings work out to be 30% higher per unit of floor area built compared to a four-storey row housing of RCC frame with flyash or lightweight concrete block masonry. The culprits, as you build taller and taller, are: the increased dependence on steel with its high-embodied energy and the operational energy of lifts and pumps.

### Resilience

Answer this simple question: Which of the two kinds of buildings are you safer in when there is power grid or infrastructure breakdown, an earthquake, a fire or an explosion – the 20-storey tower or the walk-up four-storey apartment? The city must choose a way of building homes that is inherently resilient and not dependent on layers and layers of complicated technologies to enable day-to-day living. Resilience of simple self-sustaining systems is a long-term insurance policy.

### Solar Cities

'Solar Cities ho!' If anyone is serious about this potential for leapfrogging into a low carbon urban life, with the promise of reversing climate change the answer is rooftop solar PV (photo voltaic) over four- or five-storey-high buildings. Thanks to plentiful sunshine across the Indian subcontinent approximately 80% of the annual electricity requirement of simple (non air-conditioned) homes can be met by rooftop installation for the four or five storeys of homes below those roofs. As you build taller this ratio declines. The taller you build the worse it gets. The Solar Cities dream becomes fiction in a high-rise city.

## Silver lining

But there is a silver lining. Let us look at two recent awards for affordable housing:

HUDCO Design Award 2016, First Prize: Affordable Housing for Rajkot Municipal Corporation, Architect: Parag & Mona Udani. NDTV Parryware Award for best Affordable Housing project 2106 – by Happinest Mahindra Lifespaces at Chennai. Architect: Ashok B. Lall Architects.

These are awards that give due recognition to the Opportunities of Collective Living – of the enhancement of the home as an active participant in the making of collective well-being. Balconies,

**Affordable Housing for Rajkot Municipal Corporation (HUDCO Design Award 2016)**

**Happinest Mahindra Lifespaces in Chennai (NDTV Parryware Award for Best Affordable Housing Project 2016)**

The compact, low carbon, affordable city is achieved in a low rise, high density solution. A humane scale of streets and gardens continue the grain of the city. Flat roofs unencumbered by services and tanks are the newfound shared ground: a community resource for community services such as solar laundry, yoga class and games, supported by temporary arrangements. An integral system of recycling organic waste enables self-sustaining organic farming and gardening on balconies and roofs

WE CAN !
OPPORTUNITIES
FOR COLLECTIVE
LIVING

Five years on, each home finds its own expression: painting, planting, shading, screening and balconies

terraces, the shared street courts and the identity of each home marking its unique presence. And most importantly, they demonstrate the value of human scale and variation of space and arrangement, which create an outdoor environment where residents find 'comfort and security' amongst their neighbours as their homes gather around and look onto the street and the court. Where homes are small, less than 50 square metres in area, and at least half the population is below the age of 15, there is need for 'habitable' common spaces adjacent or near the home.

At an FSI of 1.5, residential densities of 1,000 persons per hectare (and higher) are achieved with low-rise buildings. This is a land conserving, affordable, culturally and socially appropriate solution for the great majority of cities in India undergoing rapid urban growth and regeneration.

## Imagine

Imagine a compact city of streets and squares, quiet, safe, unpolluted, trees, birds and shaded walks with convenient connectivity to rapid transport to places that are beyond walking or cycling distance, rather than a city that has been sacrificed to the motor car; a city of small build buildings, with plenty of variety; a robust city fabric which has the ability to change and renew itself continually without the trauma of the demolition of the four-storey podium surmounted by 20-storey towers. Imagine a city in whose making and renewal, small and medium size entrepreneurs are able to participate rather than being produced by the heavy repetitive stamp of the big developer; a city whose roofs are places of recreation – flying kites, skating, yoga, dance – and of production: electricity from the sun, vegetables, herbs, solar kitchens and solar laundries. A city with the DNA of long-term sustainability where knowledge and wealth are distributed as the mechanisms for its sustenance. This is a city of the 60% first. ●

# Making Chandigarh Affordable Again

**Sangeeta Bagga** discusses how India's favourite city needs to retain its old charm and inhabitants while building affordable housing for the new generation

SOURCE: AUTHOR

SOURCE: JOSHI, KIRAN 1999. THE INDIAN ARCHITECTURE OF PIERRE JEANNERET, MAXWEL FRY AND JANE DREW. CHANDIGARH ADMINISTRATION, MAIN INDIA

Affordable housing has been the agenda for discussion in diverse forums. Affordability is also a difficult term to qualify as it would depend upon a host of parameters and vary within different economic zones in countries with cities and towns of different sizes. Broadly speaking 'affordability' would try to address the paying capacity of the individual and his or her ability to shell out from their income and savings an amount that would not only allow them to look after the needs of their family but also secure a shelter for them.

The city of Chandigarh and new housing design are synonymous. Chandigarh has many firsts to its credit such as an underground sewage disposal system and piped water supply to each house in post-Independence India. One of the salient features of the city plan was the laying of basic urban infrastructure at the right time. Tucked away underground – with due respect to the lay of the land and water table levels – was a grid comprising the supply and disposal of water as well as sewerage lines, while the city's network of roads was right above. The responsibility of laying basic urban infrastructure was undertaken by the city administration as its responsibility, so that housing and other functions could be realised thereafter.

Being a government capital city, as a counterpoint to the loss of Lahore to Pakistan in the wake of India's Partition, development of a robust housing stock was one of the key mandates of the administration. A conscious decision was taken to build 13 categories of house types on the basis of an employee's monthly salary. In return, the employee was required to pay 10% of his salary as rent every month, which would go into the government exchequer for house and precinct maintenance. The 13 categories included Type 1 as the chief minister's bungalow and Type 13 as peon and staff housing, which served the government machinery. Within the two sides of this housing matrix resided the officers, clerks and other staff. However, following the democratic and egalitarian principles of the new capital city, each house had piped water supply and a bathroom with an underground sewerage disposal system. In very small but sure ways, this was the new capital city's first embrace of modernity and contributes to the city's high quality of life, affordability and popularity index.

The 13 categories were combinations of single, double and duplex housing typologies, set in cul-de-sac garden landscapes, free from crisscrossing traffic. The commonality of building materials unified to create the Chandigarh style of architecture. Low rise, brick and plaster, painted white surfaces, courtyards and terraces, terracotta, screens and sun breakers as well as deep insert windows and projecting brick overhangs constitute the city's urban fabric and the fine grain and uniform texture of the neighbourhoods. This is easily identifiable as typical Le Corbusier: modernist, minimal and purposeful.

*Left:* **The use of local brick, sand and riverbed stones, plastered and painted surfaces, irrespective of the economic status of the inhabitants were the common idioms for generating the Chandigarh style of architecture**
*Right:* **The dictates of indigenous technology, people and materials, a harsh composite climate and a shoestring budget led to the modernist vocabulary of Chandigarh's government-owned housing stock**

In this town, affordability of state-owned housing stock brought with it beauty and aesthetics through the *'equipement rationnel'*

## Who will reside in Chandigarh if the original inhabitants leave due to ill affordability?

The housing types were designed in response to the three dictates governing the city's design. Jane Beverley Drew, the English architect who was responsible for designing many of the house types, skilfully utilised her experience of working in the hot and humid climates of Ibadan (Nigeria), Ghana and several English territories to develop self shading, courtyard and perforated screens, sun breakers and brise-soleil (an architectural feature of a building that reduces heat gain within that building by deflecting sunlight), which on the one hand tackled the climate and on the other provided the visual privacy essential to the cultural ethos of the Indian lifestyle. Together with her husband Maxwell Fry and Pierre Jeanneret (her most staunch opponent on the team), the trio brought together locals, materials and methods to arrive at a new definition of affordability in Chandigarh.

Affordability is often devoid of higher orders and sensibilities such as beauty and aesthetics. In this town, affordability of state-owned housing stock brought with it beauty and aesthetics through the '*equipement rationnel*': a term used to define the minimalist architecture of the city. The utilisation of basic building materials even in the interiors of houses of all categories through elements such as built-in furniture, lighting fixtures, fire places, chimneys, flues, vents, which were an extension of the microclimatic amelioration elements, reflects the *equipement rationnel*. Projecting bricks for sunbreaks, louvres for shade and sunray deflection and brise-soleil to mitigate heat penetration were all exterior elements lending the identifiable character to modernist housing. The aesthetics of the Chandigarh style were thus born out of the functional and the essential rather than the decorative.

The housing stock performed well as the city grew and filled in. While phase one of the city engaged in the 13 categories of housing, walkup four-storey apartments and later six-storeyed houses were seen as housing solutions for phase two of the growing capital of Chandigarh to provide affordable housing to its employees. Slowly, with the city maturing and an increase in vehicle density and population pressure, there was another challenge to be addressed. The state-owned government accommodation had to be surrendered by the employee at the age of retirement and he had to move into private housing either within Chandigarh or its two neighbouring tricity towns: Mohali and Panchkula. The first phase of the city had a mix of government houses and private plots, while phase two was more of the apartment type.

However, land is a fixed commodity here and so Chandigarh's population boom has left little for the employees to look at after retirement. Land values have increased exponentially and the real deserving citizens have been marginalised by the rich farmers of the hinterland who can afford the plots in the city. The responsibility of the state lies in providing 'affordable housing', but the supply is a far cry from the demand. Subsidised housing offered by the Chandigarh Housing Board is a weak mechanism and inflation rates leave much to be desired. By the time the housing board flat is ready for occupation, its market value is way beyond the base price and the owner finds it more lucrative to sell off and move to the outskirts.

The big question remains: who will reside in Chandigarh if the original inhabitants leave due to ill affordability? The city would lose its original character and turn into another run-of-the-mill city. The administrators need to find a solution so that the original intent of planning is not compromised and the original citizens are not marginalised by the affluent few. The laws of the land need to be revisited safeguarding the interests of the employees, who are currently being pushed to the outskirts. The solutions need to be more informed and based upon principles of egalitarian order, which was the mandate at the city's inception. As a forerunner of civic design for the country's post-Independence cities, Chandigarh's housing stock, both state-owned and privately-built and owned, must be regulated with special legislation for ownership, degree of permissible transformations, heritage guidelines and regulations. Through this the city can embrace modernity yet again and be the torchbearer for others following its path. ●

# Conserving Social Housing in Moscow

The Russian government proposed a generous multi-billion-dollar plan to demolish and replace Moscow's Soviet-era housing. The reaction of some residents, however, shows how the intangible qualities of neighbourhoods can sometimes overwhelm the desire for improved creature comforts. **Nathan Hutson** takes a look

On May 14, 2017, several thousand Muscovites protested a new law aimed at demolishing Soviet-era housing dating back to the 1950s and '60s. The majority of the buildings targeted for demolition are the so-called 'Khrushchevki' that were rapidly constructed in a massive building boom shortly after Khrushchev ascended to power. The law is entitled 'On the Status of the Capital of the Russian Federation', but colloquially referred to as the Law for Renovation. The intent, however, is not to renovate. In exchange for demolishing their existing homes, residents are promised a new apartment of similar size, generally within the same rayon (city region).

On the surface, this programme seems like a positive development for the residents of these apartments, which are often cramped and severely deteriorated. Nevertheless, the law ignores several of the peculiarities of Moscow land use and housing practices that could leave a significant minority of homeowners worse off than they were before.

One of the participants in the May 14th protest was Anna Sorokina. Anna, a former professor at the Russian State University for the Humanities, had never attended a protest rally of this nature before. She decided to attend because her five-storey home had appeared on a list of houses to be demolished. According to Anna, the pronouncements of the Moscow city government

> **"We don't just live in the apartments themselves, we live in the neighbourhood as well"**

SOURCE: A. SOROKINA

Protesters at the May 14 rally with signs that read: 'Ramenki District against the Renovation'

that everyone will be made better off once they have been transferred to a new apartment misses an essential point: "It's a neighbourhood. We don't just live in the apartments themselves, we live in the neighbourhood as well."

In Soviet/Russian planning jargon the term 'neighbourhood' typically refers to a micro-rayon or micro-region. A rayon or region, is an assemblage of micro-rayons. The legislation, as currently drafted, promises that residents would be resettled within the same region or the neighbouring region. It is important to note, however, that each Moscow region (rayon) can house more than 100,000 persons. Therefore, the promise of relocation within the rayon is not analogous to relocation within the neighbourhood. Many of the residents protesting this action fear that through resettlement they will lose access to social networks that have been built over the course of decades. In addition, a traditional Soviet micro-rayon was designed to provide residents with equivalent access to green space, schools and transit. Major roads did not enter the micro-rayon in order to provide safe refuge for children walking to school. It is unclear whether or not the replacement buildings would adhere to these standards, given the lack of appropriate building sites within Moscow.

## Evolution of the Khrushchevki

Russians are fond of the proverb "there is nothing more permanent than the temporary," and the Khrushchevki epitomise this concept. They were originally built as temporary structures to address an acute housing crisis that had long festered absent dissent during Stalin's rule. Khrushchevki were, for many Muscovites, the first modern home they had ever occupied after leaving the village. For others, they meant the first apartment that was not shared with one or more other families. Yet, while the political intent of the Khrushchevki may have been as temporary structures, their engineering suggested otherwise. Many were built of pre-stressed concrete panels. They have no elevators or other moving parts. These features have allowed the Khrushchevki to deliver a habitable – if somewhat uncomfortable – existence to their residents for half a century. Khrushchev himself admitted as much during his famous 1959 'Kitchen Debate' with Richard Nixon on the comparison of Soviet and American housing models, bragging, "We build firmly. We build for our children and grandchildren," as opposed to American homes that he claimed were only designed to last for 20 years. In the 1970s, the Soviet Union began

to transition away from standard five-storey to 9- to 16-storey buildings with larger floor plans, however, the lowest cost option remained five-storeys, which required less costly materials and less intensive capital utilisation.

The most common Khruschevka was a two-bedroom apartment with a living space of 55 sq.m. The kitchens were approximately 5–6 sq.m., and ceilings were 2.5 m. high. The early buildings were, in many cases, not merely utilitarian but inadequate as single-family housing. To begin with, the breakneck pace of construction often rendered the 'completed structures' unfinished. A Russian professor of architectural history noted his personal experience that "snow would blow in between the panels" that had not been properly sealed. Perhaps an even greater insult to Russian sentimentalities, the new structures possessed small kitchens, thereby depriving families of their traditional gathering place. They were nevertheless a significant upgrade from a communal apartment that provided no common space for family gatherings. New residents were left to their own ingenuity to

SOURCE: A. SOROKINA

SOURCE: NATALYA GARNELIS /TASS

*Top:* **Five-storey building where Anna Sorokina resides with her family near Metro Dynamo. The building appeared on a 'to be demolished' list on May 1**
*Bottom:* **Aerial view of a Moscow micro-rayon**

complete their apartments. Not knowing if and when they would ever be able to move into a larger apartment, families laboured to extract the maximum amount of liveability out of every square metre.

This process of incremental improvement only accelerated after Russia's independence. Many Khrushchevkis today are Soviet on the outside, IKEA on the inside. While some families took advantage of privatisation to upgrade to larger, more modern apartments, those who remained in their original government-issued flats often had significant disposable income to reinvest in interior renovation. Ironically, the fact that Soviet apartments required such active intervention to make them habitable is one reason the idea of abandoning these apartments to the wrecking ball is at best a bittersweet experience.

### Micro-rayons

Plans to demolish Soviet-era housing were evaluated in the Moscow General Plan (GenPlan2025), published during Moscow's housing bubble prior to the global economic recession. With the price of new modern housing hovering at $7,000/sq.m., builders salivated at the possibilities of replacing the five-storey buildings with towers of 20 or more floors. Many individual structures were demolished on an ad hoc basis. The plan indicated that the government would demolish approximately 10% of the total housing in the city, equivalent to 25 million sq.m., while constructing approximately 100 million sq.m. of new housing. This would have been a dramatic shift for a city that is already densely developed. One of the most controversial strategies was to develop new spaces on vacant land in existing neighbourhoods despite the fact that these areas were deliberately left vacant by Soviet planners to maintain a sustainable density. Significant protests and opposition arose in response to these plans.

Three concurrent events helped to put the plan on hold for a period of time. The first event was the recession, which greatly dampened enthusiasm for new construction. The second was the annexation of regions to the south of Moscow with plans to build a second downtown, dubbed 'New Moscow', to relieve the need for additional density within the city. Finally, Moscow's longtime pro-construction mayor was replaced in 2010 robbing the GenPlan of its most powerful backer.

Now it appears that the GenPlan has risen from the dead in another form. Densification is no longer the principal goal of the plan given the continued fall-off in demand due to the weak economy. Rather, the plan is being promoted as economic stimulus for the building industry that will help the local economy as well as the individuals living within Khrushchevki.

The Moscow City government is attempting to make the process of determining which buildings will be demolished more responsive to citizen concerns. As part of the process, the government is soliciting votes from residents of the Khrushchevki to determine whether or not the impacted population supports the initiative. To participate, voters use an online forum established by Mayor Sobyanin's office called Active Citizen. They must first register and affirm that they are owners and residents of a five-storey house slated for demolition. This otherwise laudable effort to directly engage citizens is significantly undermined by a decision of the Moscow government to automatically count anyone who does not vote in the forum as a supporter, as summarised by the Russian television station NTV: "If you want to vote for the demolition of your five-storey building, you can do nothing at all." Even if a high percentage of apartment owners participated and voted against, it would be unlikely that this number would outweigh the number of non-participants counted as supporters by default. While the website is entitled Active Citizen, it is likely that the passive citizens will carry this election.

Another problematic element with the online voting system is that it adds even greater uncertainty to the market. Several conflicting official and unofficial lists of houses slated for demolition have circulated. This uncertainty may significantly suppress the value of houses, whether or not they have appeared on an official list. While almost all of the media reports have thus far focused on Khrushchevki, the language of the

Commentary on the Active Citizen voting process depicting Moscow Mayor Sobyanin, with the caption: "You're going to, what, cast my vote on Active Citizen too?"

SOURCE: ALEXANDER SVERDLOV (SVESMI), THE MICRORAYON TOMORROW, 2010)

legislation is sufficiently broad that it could justify demolitions of newer, higher quality Soviet-era apartments constructed during the 1970s and 1980s, or older brick structures that emerged from the pre-Stalin constructivist era.

A society's desire to preserve architecture reflects its faith in the future intentions of developers, particularly in countries where the rule of law is selectively applied. For example, even when a society is not enamoured by its current cityscape, it may seek to conserve existing structures and/or green space out of fear that what would come in its place would be worse. This is the essential disconnect between supporters of the plan, who are understandably eager to receive a potentially upgraded living situation after so many years spent in a crammed, hastily constructed flat and opponents who believe that the government will not make good on its promises. Reticence to embrace new construction is enhanced by the fact that many residents have witnessed illegal demolitions and blatant zoning code violations in order to accommodate elite new housing that upends the integrity of existing neighbourhoods and strains municipal services.

Meanwhile, the Russian Duma has concluded that any solution to the Khruschev-era housing situation aside from demolition is futile. There are strategies under development elsewhere in the post-Communist world for improving the facades and the overall habitability of existing structures in a way that is far less expensive and socially disruptive than demolishing and rebuilding them. Riga, Latvia, is an example of a city that is currently trying to modify the layout of the micro-rayon to better serve modern conditions.

A joint Dutch-Russian project entitled SVESMI has examined strategies for reinvestment that would be based on demolishing the oldest and lowest quality buildings within the micro-rayon and selling the development rights to build a handful of modern buildings. The new revenue would be used not to demolish the remaining buildings, but rather to rehabilitate the buildings and improve the landscaping, as can be seen in the before and after artist renderings in the two sketches above.

## The Ironic Fate of the Khrushchevki

It is a great irony that the Soviet-era apartment, which had long been lampooned by critics as symbolic of the communist government's attempt to remove individuality and human aesthetics from society, is now defended as a symbol of individual rights and the right to private property. A half century ago, the City of Moscow cleared traditional wooden housing on the city's outskirts to make space for a sea of grey boxes now known as Khrushchevki. This was the future, Soviet citizens were told. Now the government is eager to erase what it feels are embarrassing remnants of an inglorious past. Despite flaws in the approach, the Russian government should be credited for voicing a principle that all citizens have a right to decent housing. From all indications, the protesters of this action are not on the street based on a shared animus towards the federal or city government. They clearly have an interest in improved housing conditions and aspire to more than 60 sq. m. of living space. Rather, their message to the government this time seems to be: don't adopt the same one-size-fits-all mentality that led to the original Khrushchevki. Don't assume that the only thing citizens seek from their neighbourhood is four walls and a nice kitchen. There are ways to systematically improve living conditions; however, for something as intimate as a living space, the burden of supermajority should be on those who seek to demolish rather than those who wish to remain. ●

*(The background for this article is taken from* Social Housing with a Human Face: Conserving Moscow's Soviet Era Housing Legacy, *in the Routledge Handbook of Global Heritage Conservation, Routledge, 2018.)*

# Social Housing in Amsterdam and Belgrade

**Mirjana Milanovic** tells us about two mass housing projects from the past in Amsterdam and Belgrade

The heritage of housing projects from the '70s is still present in European cities. In this last phase of modernism, efficient prefabricated building techniques led to mass housing plans. The amount of affordable social housing built at that time was a considerable achievement in providing healthy, comfortable living in the cities. As the alternative to low-rise, car-oriented suburbs they contributed to the consolidation of cities. On the other hand, the speed of the building process led to uniformity and non-adaptability. Building for known clients and large state companies led to the lack of social diversity which, in the following decades, led to social problems in these areas and deterioration of their physical structure.

The two examples presented in this article were built along the lines of maximum efficiency, reduction of the costs and uniformity of built and social structure. In both cities and countries they were the turning point in thinking of a city as a makeable, modernist ideal.

## POLITICS OF SOCIAL HOUSING

In their respective countries, the two projects were both part of a statewide political project.

In the Netherlands, providing social housing for the working and middle class followed basic income and basic pension for everyone. In Amsterdam, social housing started with housing corporations at the beginning of the 20th century. Social housing became the fabric of the city to the extent that in the '70s, almost 70% of all apartments in Amsterdam belonged to one of the few social housing corporations. The political scene of Amsterdam was for decades dominated by a left wing Labour Party that worked closely with housing corporations. In the '60s and '70s cultural change was strongly present in Amsterdam, with the peace movement, squatters and demonstrations for the right to housing.

In Yugoslavia, a socialist country, the new part of the capital city Belgrade, called New Belgrade, had to become a symbol of the new country. Socialistic

**In both cities and countries they were the turning point in thinking of a city as a makeable, modernist ideal**

PHOTOS: GORAN BASARIC

*Top:* **Panorama of Bezanija blocks 61 and 62 in New Belgrade in 1980**
*Bottom Left:* **Building with prefabricated systems, New Belgrade**
*Bottom Right:* **New Belgrade blocks in 1988**

PHOTO: STADSARCHIEF AMSTERDAM

PHOTO: MIRJANA MILANOVIC

*Left:* **Bijlmer under construction. Honeycomb flats in open landscape, 1970**
*Right:* **Bijlmer block Kleiburg after reconstruction, 2014**

ideal was providing housing as a basic need, but also more than that. In socialist countries modernism was embraced as the way to build both the city and a new society: transparent, modern, equally accessible for everyone. In Yugoslavia, with its specific in-between ideology and foreign policy in the '70s, socialist ideas were already accompanied with the market economy. Opening of borders from the late '60s onwards brought strong influences of other European and American thinkers and architects. In the '50s and '60s New Belgrade was experimental ground for modernistic ideas and the transition in the late '70s was stronger than in most socialist countries.

## Social Housing Projects in the '50s and '60s

Masterplans for extensions of Amsterdam and Belgrade were made before the Second World War and provided the base for housing projects in the post-war decades. Like in many other European cities, the '50s in Amsterdam and Belgrade were marked by a huge housing shortage. In Amsterdam the first parts of the Western Garden Cities were built at the same time as the first blocks of New Belgrade. In both cities, standards for dwelling were strictly regulated and state controlled. Buildings were mostly rows of medium rise slabs, with green spaces as a main quality.

During the '60s, with a better economic situation, new housing areas got more variation in block forms and architecture. In Amsterdam, in Buitenveldert, south of the city, variation of typology of blocks and children's playgrounds designed by Aldo van Eyck, achieved high living quality. In New Belgrade, blocks in the central and eastern part had a variety of large closed blocks that incorporated neighbourhood amenities. The political doctrine of self-management of that time was also applied in neighbourhoods, where the size of 5,000 people was a measure for both local democracy and structure of amenities.

## Architecture of Social Housing in the '70s

The '70s was a time of changes in economy and culture, with the economic crisis caused by the oil crisis in 1972, and first manifests on sustainability, individualisation and new local culture, opposed to the international style of modernism. The political spectrum was changing across Europe. The economic crisis led to cuts in government budgets, less investment in large state projects and in social housing. The neoliberal market economy was slowly taking over in the housing policies in Western countries.

Bijlmer in Amsterdam was built in the beginning of the '70s. The repetitive hexagonal structure had 7,000 dwellings, in 10 floors of high buildings around vast green spaces. The original plan was ambitious having public and semi-public spaces, including the covered street on the first floor. Apartments had high ceilings, spacious rooms and large terraces overlooking the green areas. Ambitions were not fully realised after budget cuts; state planning led to new towns like Almere in the vicinity of Amsterdam and a large part of first dwellers consisted of emigrants from Suriname. It all led to vacant apartments, lack of amenities and, finally, deterioration. Very early on Bijlmer was criticised by its first dwellers, and in professional circles, for its massive scale and monotonous architecture.

New Belgrade plans for blocks were chosen in open competition, providing open professional discussion about the right qualities for the new city. The plans of apartments followed the principles of 'Belgrade apartment', offering comfortable living for families in small available space.

Bezanija blocks – 18 parallel slabs with 6,000 apartments – were built on an open land at the edge of the city. Large building companies, active worldwide, took the lead, adapting the design to efficiency of the prefabricated building process. The blocks provided the much-needed housing for the Belgrade middle class, but the mass housing

**In terms of the approach to the city and city culture, they were outdated already before they were finished**

*Left:* **Open green areas in original blocks in Bijlmer, 2014**
*Right:* **New Belgrade in 2014, with illegal buildings in the foreground**

PHOTO: MRJANA MILANOVIC

PHOTO: GORAN BASARIC

development, the lack of amenities, good public space and good public transport, provoked strong critique in professional circles.

## Renewal and Reconstruction

Massive housing projects of the '70s failed the modernistic ideas of the previous period by lowering costs to the extent of diminishing quality and by putting efficiency in building above the functionality in use. In terms of the approach to the city and city culture, they were outdated already before they were finished.

In Amsterdam, Bijlmer was followed by small-scale renewals in the old city and decennia-long reluctance to start with new large-scale projects. In the '90s, several proposals, among others from OMA (Office for Metropolitan Architecture), tried to improve the Bijlmer area. The change started with new cultural and sport functions adjacent to the railway station.

Reconstruction of Bijlmer started in 2000 and was interrupted during the economic crisis in 2008. Two-thirds of the original 10-storeyed hexagonal structures were pulled down and replaced partly with new social housing and partly with family homes for the market.

Nowadays it is one of the last affordable areas in Amsterdam for the low-income groups. Not only migrants, but also students, artists and startups in the city have been rediscovering this area. City investments in public space made the area attractive. One of the last developments is the reconstruction of the block called Kleiburg that was saved from destruction by a small private company. They renovated collective areas and sold individual apartments in casco state, one, two or three units per buyer, bringing to practice the '70s theory of John Habraken, the one of common structures and different architects for separate units.

In New Belgrade, the reaction to Bezanija blocks came with the competition for a small central block, next to the congress centre built

in 1976. Sloped roofs, elevated green pedestrian streets and detailing of facades brought radical changes in the thinking of urban schemes and architectural quality. In 1986 the international competition offered a wide range of ideas for the reconstruction of New Belgrade.

The transformation of New Belgrade started with the fallout of the country and transition to a market-oriented system. Developers added illegal objects, new shopping, built green areas and business centres. Bezanija remained unchanged and many original inhabitants still live there. The apartments, originally bought by the army for its officers and their families, were sold to main dwellers for symbolic prices at the beginning of the '90s. Apartments are affordable for the remaining original dwellers, but will not be for the next generation of residents. The houses and public space are deteriorating without public investments in maintenance.

## The Future of Social Housing

After following these two examples one can ask if there is a future for social housing in European cities. Cities like London and Paris are becoming too expensive for any form of affordable housing. Amsterdam might follow, especially in the central areas. In Belgrade, the few social housing projects are being built on the outer perimeters of the city.

Whose task is social housing in the future and what are the means to realise it? Weakening of government engagement, growth of the population in cities, flexible jobs and unsteady incomes, all these trends are accompanied by the need for affordable housing.

The scale of the projects from the '70s should not be repeated again, but their aim: providing affordable housing for as many people as possible, should be an important part of city making in the future. Smaller projects, space for innovation and new collective buildings are some of the strategies that can integrate affordable housing and good living environments. ●

# Who can afford to live in London or Amsterdam?

**Jan Knikker** of MVRDV (the Netherlands-based architecture and urban design practice) tells us how to solve the affordable housing crisis that continues to paralyse urban development

Social housing has historically formed an integral part of new build investments, regeneration schemes and offerings of suitable housing for citizens. Housing issues take precedence across varied geographical contexts in Western Europe with the observable impact of the global financial crisis, worsening the case for the provision of affordable housing. On a global scale, national budgets for investing in housing schemes were drastically cut and still continue to decline. Communities have been deeply affected by this decline leading to evictions and relocations in order to make way for privatisation of the sector as historic housing complexes are knocked down to make way for 'ivory tower' apartment blocks as part of larger regeneration schemes; 'yuppification' and gentrification are a threat to many urban dwellers, now a familiar occurrence in urban centres. Affordable housing, some might argue, has had its heyday and in the not-so-distant past, exemplary schemes could be found in abundance in countries including the Netherlands, Germany, France and the United Kingdom.

Social housing policy expert and researcher Kathleen Scanlon points out that since the 1980s, in relation to social housing, "public expenditure pressures have increased, liberalisation and privatisation have become increasingly important and alternative tenures are now more readily available." She further highlights how previously, "housing was seen as part of the social contract between government and citizens, which made up the welfare state in Central and Eastern Europe, a more corporatist approach was normal and housing more tied to the organisation of production and therefore accommodated workers and their dependants where required."

Take Rotterdam's The Kiefhoek for example, a working class quarter built between 1928–1930, located in the southern part of the city and designed by Dutch architect, J.J.P. Oud. The scheme consists of 300 standardised dwellings of low-budget public housing, two round-cornered shops, a cubic ornament-less church, a hot-water station, playgrounds and small gardens that complete the estate as a densified but attractive collective community for workers and their families. Oud rejected the idea of a modern neighbourhood that was in keeping with the traditional concept of the street as an exterior room, thus designing elongated rows of standardised two-storey units that respond to their surroundings in different ways giving rise to a varied urban plan. Port Sunlight, on the other hand, located in the Northern British county Merseyside and built at the end of the 19th century, expanded social housing on a much larger scale turning it into a model village for workers employed at the nearby Lever factory. The Lever Brothers employed nearly 30 different architects to realise 800 contrasting family homes to house a population of 3,500 workers across 223 acres. The model village also included green spaces (allotments), institutions, recreation grounds and other open spaces. The brothers created a scheme for residents called Prosperity Sharing where rents paid by employees were capped at a level sufficient to cover upkeep and repair.

Sadly, bad planning occurs and large-scale developments often fall into crisis and disarray from time to time as observed with The Million Homes Programme in Sweden and Berlin's Märkisches Viertel, the first large settlement in what used to be West Berlin. Both of these social housing projects suffered from a boom in the number of residents rising faster than available infrastructure – schools, kindergartens, shops, restaurants and better access to transport links turning them into undesirable areas for inhabitants and also places with stigmatised labelling.

Paris's 'Banlieues' are well-known examples of satellite cities and the term is now used as a pejorative description for areas dominated by immigrants and colossal concrete housing projects. These developments were built during the post-war decades and originally conceived as

> **Bad planning occurs and large-scale developments often fall into crisis and disarray from time to time**

utopias for the working city dweller; today they are in the news regularly for riots. In the UK, tower blocks including Balfron, Trellick and Shepherds Court shifted the image of apartment living to a point that it made sprawl seem the more suitable alternative to single family and terraced housing, which are catastrophic for dealing with population growth, $CO_2$ emissions as well as traffic. This has contributed in the building of affordable housing coming to a halt in many countries, as it has in the Netherlands, the once top country for this initiative, with a liberal government that has abandoned the law that required 30% affordable housing in each new development.

The ongoing debate around the future of social housing in England is more active than it has been for many years. The demand for social housing and pressures on affordable housing in particular are intense and active. Previously, concerns grew over the concentration of social housing located in disadvantaged areas and about the low levels of economic activity found amongst tenants. Today,

the situation is different, sharp price rises in London, Melbourne, Sydney, Paris, Amsterdam and Barcelona mean that blue-collar workers and even essential caretakers of the city such as police officer, nurses and fire-fighters cannot afford to live here anymore; populations have been relocated from existing urban social housing schemes to continue the city's gentrification as observed with The Heygate Estate in London that was controversially sold off by Southwark Council, knocked down and the new development in its place sold to an overseas investor. The estate was once home to 3,000 people before being demolished in 2011.

If housing is not affordable it creates a dangerous situation for the future sustainability of our cities because they lack a diversity of workforce and services that might potentially lead to extreme political situations, as people have no more access to places that provide work. Social unrest arises through gentrification. Who can still afford to live in London, Berlin, Amsterdam or Paris? In Sydney, the average monthly mortgage repayment

**Silodam, 1995–2003
Amsterdam, the Netherlands**

*Top Left & Right:* **Silodam 1995–2003 (facade and interior) Amsterdam, the Netherlands**
*Bottom Left & Right:* **Parkrand 1999–2006, Geuzenveld-Amsterdam, the Netherlands**

has increased significantly since 2001 (up 42% to $1,800 across the city); an increase that has not been matched by income growth. Even affluent communities struggle to make the payments. In London, it is predicted that by 2020, first-time buyers will need to earn £64,000 per year to keep up with mortgage repayments, in a city where the annual average income of an experienced young professional is roughly £30,000.

In this way, social stability and safety are at stake and hence one might say that affordable housing is a state matter and cannot be left to the market and perhaps to avoid wasting money, public-private housing associations without profit as their main goal would be a suitable and strangely progressive step forward, considering that this is a solution from the past. But there is no perfect recipe on how to tackle this problem and the enormous challenge and pressures on creating affordable housing has grown so exponentially that one concrete solution is almost impossible, unless perhaps one takes a grand and ambitious overhaul like Sweden did in the 1960s. But look how that ended up. At present, there is so much distrust in an over caring nanny state that this would be improbable. Perhaps a possible solution then is to set the goal in quality and to set up a combination

of different small and large-scale private-public but non-profit initiatives regulated through a national or municipal coordinator to facilitate the necessary building constructions. Here are some examples:

## Inclusive Mix

If a mandatory inclusion of a proportion of affordable housing into larger developmental projects in the city is introduced, this allows for integration rather than separation of users, as opposed to separating residents.

In Parkrand, 35 social apartments were 'gentrified' and interwoven into the larger mass of 240 apartments so that inhabitants behaved cordially and under the watch of a concierge. In Silodam, residents didn't share communal stairs so, as an alternative, the social flats all received fabulous bridges to townhouse style entrances that separated the commercial and affordable inhabitants but didn't alienate and exclude residents of the affordable accommodations. Also, in Silodam, elderly tenants lived inside communities and shared communal entrances, which allowed for unity. In London, the number of newly built homes has increased 6% in the past year and if a percentage is allocated for affordable units, these problems would subside drastically.

## Subsidies

City councils and developers must work together to create solutions to demands for and costs incurred in new housing developments. In our master plan for Bordeaux Bastide Niel, the city allocates land use to developers for less cost with the objective for them to provide rental houses at a certain percentage that is below the market value or to sell them to people within a certain profile (services, longer lasting low incomes). This, of course, comes at a price, but in this model, the city has no investment, dictates the conditions, but has less profit income. On the bright side, it provides homes for the young, professionals and families. Mirador and Celosia in Madrid are two examples of such subsidised housing. The problem here, however, was that due to demand, the waiting list did not allow people to refuse without penalty, so this demand meant the architect had to build for as large a group as possible.

## Ditch the Developer

In a classic case of foregoing or doing away with the developer, an urban plan was designed in Leiden, Netherlands, of 670 dwellings with half of its new housing developed within the framework of private client agreements and the rest as social housing. The urban plan set out strict parameters to ensure the relative cohesive context of the urban grid, but at the same time offered enough flexibility for consumer-driven developments. MVRDV engaged for 10 years in the project and people were able to build their own individual homes on a communal parking garage, helped and guided by the city.

## Small Scale

Instead of colossal scale developments such as The Million Programme, it would also be possible to develop many smaller initiatives within different parts of a city to avoid the ghettoisation of certain

*Top Left & Right:*
**New Leyden, 2005–2013,
Leiden, the Netherlands**
*Bottom Left & Right:*
**Ypenburg, 1998–2005,
The Hague, the Netherlands**

PHOTO: © LAURA NOVO

PHOTOS: © ROB 'T HART

*Left:* **Floriade 2022**
**2012–2022**
**Almere, the Netherlands**
*Right:* **Ravel Plaza 2015+**
**Amsterdam, the Netherlands**

**In London, by 2020, first-time buyers will need to earn £64,000 per year to keep up with mortgage repayments ... the annual average income of an experienced young professional is roughly £30,000**

areas and diversify the inhabitants that will form these new communal dwellings. In Spijkenisse town centre, 42 apartments were designed that feature 27 different housing types to create a micro-neighbourhood for lower income individuals, but at the same time also create a fantastic demographic mix of senior citizens, small and large families and younger citizens. Just imagine hundreds of these projects to be realised every year; it would lead to a multitude of housing types and a varied and specific urban area.

## Customised Mass Housing

Affordable housing needs to be cheaply produced, so mass fabrication is crucial and logical. In Ypenburg we made a neighbourhood with around 900 homes in groups of eight to 120 units that each had a totally different character. The setback-terraced housing provided a neighbourhood for families with kids overlooking each other's garden for perfect social control. The precision of how this project fosters different lifestyles makes it highly successful.

## Building Communities

Almere Oosterwold is an example of how a city saves money by not providing services and how individuals and groups get the chance to realise their homes without a developer, who would make it more expensive. This only works, however, for well-organised citizens who make decisions about how they live through constant democratic decisions and continued dialogue.

## New Software

MVRDV has been on a quest to bring the suburban

qualities of light, individualism and green outdoor space into apartment living, from the very first project to the latest: Ravel Plaza, a high-end apartment in Amsterdam's Zuidas district. The current software advances will make it feasible to realise fully customised flats for sale. This software can be used by collective private initiatives to make the now often slow and emotional process fast and efficient. The development corporation and its 30% profit margin can be avoided. Obviously, there is a maximum size to this and developers act as risk takers making more reliable partners for cities.

## Conclusion

All of what is suggested above demonstrates that a combination of approaches is required to solve the larger issues of social housing. This calls for an ongoing exploration of architecture as both a critical and practical response to our spatial, social and environmental crisis that needs to be in the form of a series of locally specific, tailor-made solutions. It is evident that the housing issue is more critical than it has ever been before. Housing shortages continue to rise and populist parties thrive on social exclusion and problems in society. Architects, designers and urbanists must then focus on changes of behaviour, technology, territory or look for options to extend. We need to stimulate a change in attitudes worldwide by providing exemplary solutions, inspiring others and sharing knowledge, to contribute to understanding, testing and providing progressive responses. Let's find ways to provide more affordable homes. ●

# Dutch Social Housing Today

**Siddharth Khandekar** explains how the Dutch organise social housing in the hope it inspires social entrepreneurs in other countries

## A Little History

Can you imagine a country where the well off and the less fortunate live in the same neighbourhoods, send their children to the same schools and buy groceries from the same shops? A place where families with a low income can feel confident that their house is well maintained and that the landlord charges them a rent that covers the costs, but no more than that? This may sound like a socialist utopia (and maybe it is) but it's a pretty accurate description of the way the Dutch organise social housing. The groundworks of this system were laid roughly 100 years ago. And, surprising as it may seem, there are actually some similarities between the early 20th-century Netherlands and some other countries today such as a fast changing society, farmers leaving their villages to look for work in the cities, slums notorious for overcrowding, unsanitary and squalid living conditions and poor families living crammed in single-room accommodations without sanitation. The more privileged members of Dutch society found these miserable housing conditions hard to ignore in those years.

Several initiatives were taken around the year 1900 to address the housing situations of the poor; not only by the government but also by diverse factions of Dutch civic society. The churches started some initiatives, others originated from the labour movement and yet others from wealthy citizens and rich industrialists. But all these initiatives came down to one thing: using local funds to develop simple but decent housing for the working class. These social housing organisations were neither controlled by the state nor profit-driven. They aimed to provide decent housing at affordable prices.

## Dutch Social Housing Today

Fast forward to 2015. The Dutch social housing corporations have stood the test of time. Together

> The Dutch social housing corporations have stood the test of time

**Early 20th-century Dutch social housing in Amsterdam**

Housing project in Nijmegen, the Netherlands. The seven-storey buildings at the back are social housing, the low rise buildings in the front are owner-occupied. The public green area is common to both.
Architect: Architectuurstudio Herman Herzberger

PHOTO: PATRICK FRANSSEN

they own 2.4 million houses, which is roughly one third of the total Dutch housing stock. Some social housing corporations are small entities with less than 100 houses. However, the largest of them all provides housing to well over 75,000 households. Typically they have their focus on a specific city or region and local monopolies are not common. The city of Amsterdam, for instance, has nine active social housing corporations within its territory.

Most social housing corporations are foundations. The statutory objective of these foundations may have changed over time but the essence is still the same: to provide decent and affordable housing for those in need. They are non-profit entities and are managed by an executive board with an independent non-executive board. The social housing corporations don't receive any direct subsidy from the government. They themselves are responsible to keep their finances in check. As with any (profit driven) real estate company, that means collecting enough rent to cover all costs like maintenance, salaries, taxes and financing.

## Business Model

How do they manage without subsidies? What's the business model? Three factors provide the answers. First of all, the social housing corporations set up a scheme that functions like a non-profit mutual credit insurance company, ultimately backed-up by the Dutch national government. Loans that social housing corporations close with the bank are typically guaranteed by this scheme. If

one social housing corporation goes bust, the others are responsible for repaying the loans. Since this scheme is considered very credit-worthy (current rating with Moody's: AAA), banks charge low risk premiums. This results in low interest rates on the loans of social housing corporations, currently as little as 1.5% for a 10-year loan. Because of the low financing costs, social housing corporations can keep the rents low. The gains add up to roughly € 22 (US$ 25) per household, per month.

The second factor is less a matter of sophisticated design and more of lucky chance. Dutch housing prices have risen considerably in the last couple of decades. During the period 1995–2015, residential real estate prices rose 4.5% per year, easily outpacing inflation at 2.3%. As the happy owners of one-third of the Dutch housing stock, social housing corporations thus made a very decent indirect return on their assets. The third factor involves the price of building plots. Local governments charge social housing corporations less for building plots than they charge commercial real estate developers.

## Good Housing, Mixed Neighbourhoods

The way in which the Dutch organise social housing has some obvious advantages, especially for the tenants. They get a decently-maintained house at an affordable price. It is also nice to have a landlord who, if and when required, works together with the municipal social workers. And there's more. Social housing corporations are an important factor to keep spatial segregation at bay. To give an example, Amsterdam-South is one of the

**The way the Dutch organise social housing has some obvious advantages, especially for the tenants**

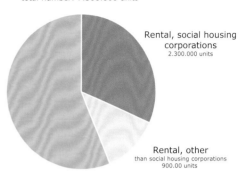

**Dutch housing stock**
total number: 7.300.000 units

Rental, social housing corporations
2.300.000 units

Owner occupied
4.100.000 units

Rental, other
than social housing corporations
900.00 units

most popular residential areas in the Netherlands but it still has 30% social housing. Rich and poor live in the same neighbourhood. And as social housing is quite common it doesn't come with a social stigma as in some Anglo-Saxon countries. Sometimes it's hard to tell the difference between social and 'normal' housing. Just look at the picture above; can you tell which is which?

Another advantage becomes apparent when a neighbourhood is in danger of impoverishment. If every single property is owned by individual investors, it's difficult to break the negative spiral until it hits rock bottom. Some owners might be prepared to invest in their property, but only if they know that other owners will follow suit. Otherwise the investment will probably not deliver enough returns. In the Netherlands, social housing corporations are an effective bulwark against this mechanism. They typically own a large share of the properties in such neighbourhoods, have a long-term commitment, the necessary funds and the organisation to turn things around. Or at least make a very serious effort. Social housing corporations are thus an important reason that less popular neighbourhoods in the Netherlands are not nearly as bad as the ones you might find in the US or UK.

## Perfect System

Sounds like a perfect system, right? But there are drawbacks. Drawbacks serious enough for the Dutch government to bring about some changes in the social housing sector. An important disadvantage is that the dynamics of the housing market get disrupted. Tenants have a decently maintained house at a low rent and thus have

little financial incentive to move, especially if they happen to live in a popular neighbourhood. Earlier in this article the posh neighbourhood Amsterdam-South has already been mentioned. In such areas, the difference between free market rents and the prices of social housing is significant. Households that managed to find themselves a social house in that area are hesitant to move. They might stay put even though the house becomes too small as the family grows or after old age has made it difficult to climb the stairs. Another drawback, though less tangible, is very real still. Together the Dutch social housing corporations have more than € 140 billion (US $156 billion) worth of real estate. Economists would say that this capital doesn't give as much financial return as it would with some proper old-fashioned market discipline. And they are probably right. The big question however is how the social returns measure up to the lower financial returns. It's a question easier asked than answered, but also a crucial question in the current debate in the Netherlands about the future of the Dutch social housing sector.

## Inspiration to Social Entrepreneurs

Social housing corporations started off in the Netherlands in the early 20th century when the country was characterised by rapid urbanisation and squalid living conditions for the masses. The Dutch social housing corporations initiated bottom-up, formed by religious groups, wealthy citizens and industrialists. That's more than 100 years ago but it has proved to be a durable system. And it might give some inspiration to social entrepreneurs in other countries. ●

## CITÉ MANIFESTE

# A Unique Social Housing Project in France

How do you lift social housing to a new level of recognition for the city and its inhabitants? **Hélène Leriche** provides answers with this case study

Inaugurated in 2005, the 'Cité Manifeste' is a housing project of 61 social rental dwellings in Mulhouse, France. It is located in the former Muller industrial site owned by Somco, a social housing developer. The Muller neighbourhood, founded in 1853, was at the time the first of its kind: it had clear economical and social purposes. Travelling time was avoided and the time saved could turn into extra working hours since the workers were close to the factory. And, for the first time, the workers had access to individual houses in a safe and healthy environment.

One hundred and fifty years later, in the early 2000s, Somco decided to celebrate its special anniversary by once again launching an ambitious social housing operation. The goal was to bridge the gap between the wishes of the people and the usual production system in the field of social housing.

Pierre Zemp, director of Somco, wanted to bring in something new and inspiring to counter the declining and bureaucratic housing architecture and to upgrade the image of social housing. He also wanted to open social housing to new customers, as the middle classes continued to abandon it. The Cité Manifeste would be built on the former Muller factory for people who were not workers. The project is typical for the city of Mulhouse, which has a tradition of social, technical and cultural innovation. It takes into account the evolution of the city, the society and the lifestyles of its inhabitants.

To make this happen, the company director asked the architect, Jean Nouvel, to take up the challenge. He agreed and suggested that they work with four other design teams: Poitevin & Reynaud, Lewis and Potin-Block, Lacaton & Vassal, Shigeru Ban and de Gastines. During the discussion that followed, three main themes were defined:
1. The residents should have a central and active role. They should have the ability to own their environment. This meant the architects would have to make proposals on how the personal and common areas inside and the private and public spaces outside could be integrated with each other.
2. The neighbourhood should be social and give a congenial feeling to the residents. Hence, the hierarchy of the spaces would create usability.
3. There should be a good balance between the

## The goal was to bridge the gap between the wishes of the people and the usual production system

*Left:* **The project site (top right corner in the picture) located in the formal workers quarter, the Cité Muller founded in 1853**

*Right:* **Site plan with the proposals of the five architects. Lacaton & Vassal office in red**

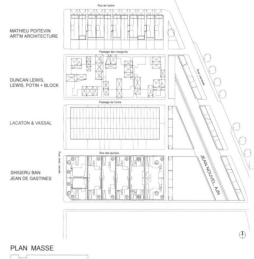

MATHIEU POITEVIN ART'M ARCHITECTURE

DUNCAN LEWIS, LEWIS, POTIN + BLOCK

LACATON & VASSAL

SHIGERU BAN JEAN DE GASTINES

JEAN NOUVEL AN

PLAN MASSE

**The way the
intermediate
open spaces,
the alleys and
passageways
are organised,
enable the
inhabitants
to meet and
interact easily**

accommodation, the garden and the greenery as Emile Muller had defined in 1853.

The proposals resulting from these requirements present an exemplary character by their innovative approach in different registers:

•**Urban design:** The new quarter is adjacent to the Cité Muller and, therefore, the project offers the opportunity to improve the status of this historical neighbourhood. This is ensured by the extension of the alleys of the former workers' housing quarters and the use of the same template of its building blocks. A template based on the 'Mulhouse Square' – a typology of four grouped houses surrounded by a garden. There is more than cohabitation between the existing and the new quarters and a morphological continuity between them. The way the intermediate open spaces, the alleys and passageways are organised enable the inhabitants to meet and interact easily, in a very natural way.

•**Process:** The architects have a dominant position in the way of working. They have been using some principles of freedom to arrange the volumes of the houses. The free plan is the key theme shared by the five designers; not 'free' in the sense of structural constraints like during the Modern architecture period, but 'free' from the habits of the contractors just as how calculation of the rent is related to the dwelling surface.

•**Volumes and Surfaces:** The result of this way of working can be seen for example in the size of the dwellings. Lacaton & Vassal designed

accommodations twice as large as normally expected for social housing. The other designers also managed to exceed the standard of +30 to +50%. But bigger houses are more than a question of size. It is a matter of perception of the inhabitant, his or her need to be able to construct a living space, to furnish it more freely and with more fluidity. That is what the architects achieved in the Cité Manifeste; they improved the quality of use of space by increasing the capacity of housing and facilities for the inhabitants.

•**Organisation and New Spaces:** For Lacaton & Vassal, the greenhouse on the top floor is the multifunctional space of the house. Its structure is made of galvanised steel and transparent polycarbonate walls. A part of the greenhouse is heated and insulated; the other part has a well-ventilated roof and facade, so it can be used as a winter garden.

**Lacaton & Vassal developed the concept of a horticultural greenhouse. The structure of their houses is a cheap and simple envelope, which defines, on the loft principle, a maximum surface area and volume. This results in quality houses that are, for the same price, considerably larger than in the standardised social housing**

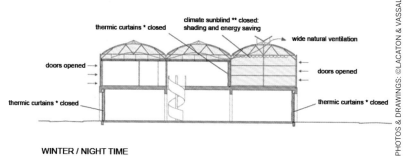

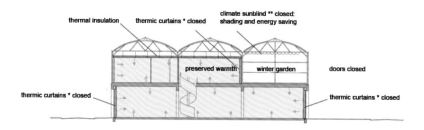

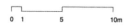

*thermic opaque curtains: reflective aluminized on the exterior side + thin wool layer + fabric on the interior side

** mobile screen made of light aluminum striped fabric: overshadows during the day, retains warmth overnight

0  1        5          10m

project: **Cité manifeste, Mulhouse**
comment: bioclimatic functioning
credit: © Lacaton & Vassal

PHOTOS & DRAWINGS: ©LACATON & VASSAL

*Top & Middle:* **The winter garden is the multifunctional space of the house and is, like the rest of the house, composed of unusual materials: the frame is made of galvanised steel and the walls of transparent polycarbonate**
*Bottom:* **A part of the (green) house is isolated and heated while the other one, the winter garden, is largely ventilated via the roof and the facade**

Another example from Poitevin & Reynaud: the garage is one of the centerpieces of the project and provides flexible spaces for various uses. It is oversized (30m²) and its door (occupying the entire width of the garage) is provided with small windows ensuring minimal natural light. It's directly connected with the living spaces on the ground floor, in particular the kitchen, for which this is a potential extension.

•**Image and Materials:** In the architects' search for a new image in the field of social housing, they implemented an expanded material library, apart from industrial ones such as concrete and steel and even unusual ones, as Lacaton & Vassal did with the polycarbonate walls of their greenhouses. Unexpectedly, most of the future residents validated the use of those materials, proving that the desire of breaking with the ordinary was more than an architectural concept. The 12% difference between the estimated budget and final accounts is still limited, given the exceptional nature of the architecture and the additional surfaces supplied by the architects. The risk of experimentation probably lies more in management costs than in construction costs.

The Cité Manifeste is one of the three most significant housing operations in France between 2000 and 2010. This is because of the ambitious nature of the project, the exceptional quality of the team (client, architects and contractors) and because of the fact that it brought about a response to a series of issues at that time, in terms of process, programme and approach in the production of housing.

It is the convergence of the three degrees (of demand: the client, of design; realisation: the architects and contractors, and of use: the future residents) that validates the success of the Cité Manifeste and the identification of a majority of people to its architecture as a result of involvement and educational process. This could be an important lesson for many (social) housing projects in France and abroad. ●

# MICRO-LIVING
# Affordable Housing in Unaffordable Cities

**Amit Arya** and **Buvana Murali** tell us about the new big idea for small, liveable spaces

The biggest challenges facing housing in the urbanised world today are accessibility and affordability of a house for all. Cities around the world have delved into the idea of affordable living for decades with varied levels of urgency, focusing on different aspects of the problem and constructing solutions to address growing challenges of density.

Designers in South America have focused on affordability, unit type repeatability and onsite rehabilitation solutions for migrant populations living in the city. In Asia, examples have focused on large-scale rehabilitation in intensely populated and dense mega-cities in the form of site and service schemes as well as subsidised housing strategies funded by government grants to address the lack of formalised housing settlements.

However, in most of the western world, the housing challenge has been plagued by the concern to keep housing in cities affordable for all. Cities like New York, London, San Francisco, Los Angeles and Chicago have seen a constant rise in the housing markets forcing people out to the suburbs by way of constant gentrification making downtown and inner city neighbourhoods unaffordable for most of the population. While these cities have seen a constant rise in the price of housing, it has not deterred the steady increase of migration of highly-skilled, working-class individuals seeking employment opportunities in the cities. The skilled working-class population is represented by the single male/female between 25–35 years of age looking for an affordable housing solution without an excessive demand for space. This user type represents close to 52% of the total population in need of housing in urbanised areas of the city (Graham Hill, founder of the small-living site *LifeEdited.com*).

Thus, an urban dichotomy of an increasing demand for affordable living within steadily rising unaffordable cities requires 'out of the box' solutions. One such growing experiment in American cities like New York is the idea of 'micro-living': a relatively inexpensive idea to provide a compact yet comprehensive living environment for the single individual in a desirable and well-connected neighbourhood of the city.

There are multiple reasons why micro-living experiments are considered as popular living models for the future. Continuous economic uncertainty and job instability are leading many urban individuals who could afford larger residences not to part with their hard-earned money for high rents. There is a desire to live at a walkable distance from work and in urban cores and neighbourhoods with a strong social life. Finally, young single professionals yearn to live alone.

An interest in smaller spaces, apart from being a practical solution, is also a reflection of the changing demographic of the apartment dweller in the 21st century. A growing trend of delayed household formation, an increase in single-person households, a decrease in car ownership and an overall tendency to accumulate fewer belongings and participate in the sharing economy has contributed to the rising demand for smaller affordable living solutions and amongst all examples of this the most radical is the idea of micro-units.

## What is a micro-unit?

A working definition of a micro-unit is a small studio apartment, typically less than 350 square feet, with a fully functioning and accessibility compliant kitchen and bathroom. However, different cities have different sizes of apartments that, as per the state's norms, qualify as micro-unit apartments. But the main restrictions applied on such developments come from the Zoning for Quality and Affordability norms, which encourage a variety of apartment types within a development thus restricting a developer to build an entire development comprising only of micro-units. However, legal restrictions notwithstanding,

> In most of the western world the housing challenge has been plagued by the concern to keep housing in cities affordable for all

PHOTOS: AMIT ARYA

developers have shown a keen interest in micro-living and it promises to be the next big typology to become a ubiquitous phenomenon in cities around the world.

There are reasons for this:

• Micro-units are known to outperform conventional units in the marketplace. They are able to achieve higher occupancy rates and garner significant rental premiums (rent per square foot) compared to conventional units.

• Developers who have experimented with micro-units acknowledge that rental apartment communities that have a higher percentage of micro-units are more expensive to build since more units are placed on offer on the same property but a rent per square foot logic more than compensates for the added cost.

• Micro-units provide the possibility of living in relatively inexpensive units in highly desirable or expensive neighbourhoods close to work and social life.

Micro-units have displayed flexibility in the form of becoming solutions that have been adapted both for the single, working-class communities in cities like New York and Seattle, as well as ideas for state/city sponsored schemes for the homeless and the impoverished population of cities like San Francisco. Two recent examples of micro-unit developments illustrate this flexibility.

**Carmel Place, NYC:** A total of 55 Residential units ranging from 260–360 square feet each are housed in this building. The construction used pre-fabricated technology of steel frame modules with concrete slabs manufactured offsite over a period of nine months and assembled onsite over a span of four weeks

## Carmel Place, NYC by nArchitects

As per nArchitects, Carmel Place provides a 'systemic new paradigm' for providing affordable housing in cities, which face such challenges. More than 60% of all New York households comprise one or two people, yet there is scarcity of studio and small-sized one-bedroom apartments in the city. In the 1980s, zoning laws were introduced in New York that prevented apartments from being smaller than 400 sq. ft.; a recent amendment to that law has allowed for smaller apartments to be re-introduced into the market. Carmel Place was a pilot project for this zoning amendment and was the winner of an open architectural competition for micro-dwellings organised in 2012 by then mayor Michael Bloomberg in order to serve as a new

model for affordable housing for single and two-person households. The project comprises 55 units, which range in size from 260–360 square feet. This tall, narrow nine storey building is composed of four slender stepped volumes and was pre-fabricated offsite with the possibility of quick onsite assembly, thus reducing the construction cycle and, therefore, the overall construction budget for the project. The success of the project lies in its compact yet efficient space planning that allows the dwelling unit to convert from a living room by day into a bedroom by night. Another equally important feature is that within a compact footprint the designers prioritised the feeling of a large volume with all units getting equal light, air and views of the surrounding neighbourhood.

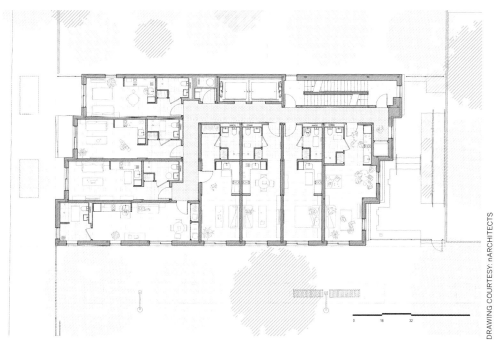

*Left:* **Carmel Place, floor plan**
*Bottom Left & Right:* **Interiors of Carmel Place**

DRAWING COURTESY: nARCHITECTS

PHOTO COURTESY: PABLO ENRIQUEZ / nARCHITECTS

**Micro-units have displayed flexibility in the form of becoming solutions that have been adapted for the single, working-class communities**

PHOTO COURTESY: PANORAMIC INTERESTS

Interiors of Micro Pad

### Micro Pad, San Francisco by Panoramic Interests

The Micro Pad is designed as a housing solution for homeless people in San Francisco and other cities of North America. It is deployed in a fast and quick construction cycle of prefabricated, affordable dwelling units on underutilised city-owned lots or other forms of government designated land. Each compact dwelling unit measures 160 square feet and comes fully furnished with a private bathroom, kitchenette, armoire, desk and bed. This solution reduces construction costs dramatically since the modules have been designed to be fabricated offsite in four weeks and the onsite construction process takes between four to six months to finish. The manufacturing company, Panoramic Interests, funds the project entirely and offers local authorities to rent out the modules on behalf of homeless people. Alternatively, the company offers a sale option where the local city authorities can eventually purchase the building.

Within growing urban challenges of increasing population and increasing inequality around the world there is an urgent need to find creative solutions for density and affordability. There are many compelling arguments presented by the idea of micro-living and micro-units in particular:

• The possibility of re-densifying our cities while maintaining focus on ideas of affordability.
• Providing housing solutions for those who cannot afford ever-increasing market rates.
• Proposing ultra-compact living solutions as affordable ideas to the city authorities in order to address problems of homelessness.
• Building more with less, condensing population and minimising our liveable footprint within a smaller area is a resourceful and sustainable way of perceiving the future.

The world is rapidly urbanising and densifying without a clear thought for the future. Micro-apartments are ideas that promise a large-scale positive impact on our urban challenges. It is an idea that is demographically inclusive, economically viable and designed for a sustainable future. ●

# Learning from 'Chawl' Housing Typologies of Mumbai

**Sameep Padora**, architect and founder of sP+a Mumbai, explains to **Prajakta Gawde** how researching and learning from historic examples of housing can help architects and planners devise creative solutions to housing typologies

**In the last couple of years your studio has researched the design and structure of several old housing (and mixed-use) urban projects. What can we learn from this study?**

Our research project, In the Name of Housing, attempts to provide a framework to question the top-down quantitative prescription of policy as an approach to the creation of housing. This has led to the setting up of models like the Slum Rehabilitation Authority (SRA), which on paper offers parity of space for residents, but actually results in inhuman and apathetic living conditions.

Our research sifted through the fabric of Mumbai, excavating historical and current models of affordable housing tucked deep within the city. The research compares 11 housing projects through mediums of open space, social space, circulation space, built areas and densities using drawings, sketches and models to highlight and illustrate their projective capacities. Our focus was to document the potential of existing and emergent architectural types native to our context,

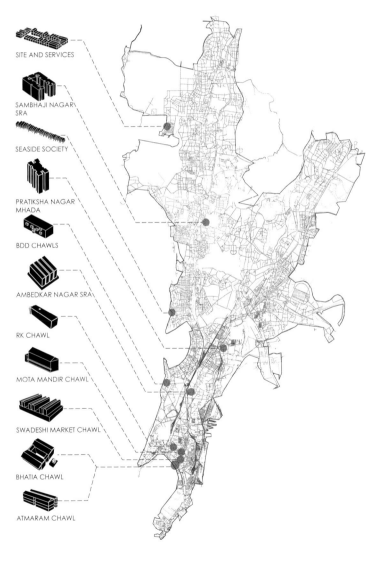

SITE AND SERVICES

SAMBHAJI NAGAR SRA

SEASIDE SOCIETY

PRATIKSHA NAGAR MHADA

BDD CHAWLS

AMBEDKAR NAGAR SRA

RK CHAWL

MOTA MANDIR CHAWL

SWADESHI MARKET CHAWL

BHATIA CHAWL

ATMARAM CHAWL

Sameep Padora

as a means to inform new or hybrid models for the design of affordable housing. We are, in a sense, arguing for architectural proclivity to inform regulatory mechanisms, which in turn would then feed into policy frameworks along with considerations of tenure, occupancy and equitable allocation. As a result, a desired built and spatial form then influences the framing of a housing policy from the bottom up, rather than the other way round.

The data for this study was collected through fieldwork that entailed measured drawings, interviews with residents and observations at each of the sites. The format of the exhibition that preceded the publication allowed for each project to be compared across ten factors: location, building form, circulation, programme, tenure, community, floor plans, envelope, unit plans and analysis. In a departure from the structure of the exhibition, our book presents the research of the projects as individual case studies.

In the Name of Housing initially started as research into the architecture of affordable housing types as background material for a design project in our studio. While we found that there were many narratives that described the socio-cultural life, there was very little quantification of the architecture that enabled this fabric to exist. Our biggest learning was that the much-eulogised social life was a product of a specific architectural framework as much as it was the other way round. Appropriations that people made transformed particular types of habitations creating new hybrid configurations of the old and new.

### During your research, did you discover any specific common factors among the areas you focused on?

The more time we spent in the field looking specifically at the form of these projects, the more instructive they became, both through the breadth of their variations, as well as the depth of their spatial and formal engagements. The analytical diagrams and drawings in the book further galvanised our belief that these frameworks, however unique, still seem to gravitate around certain emergent commonalities like:

• Networks
• Systemic Openness
• Shared Space
• Extended Domesticity
• Detail

### NETWORKS

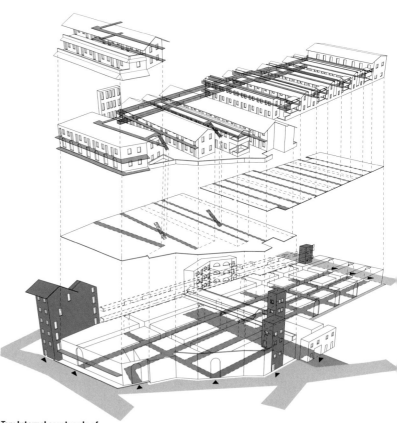

*Top:* **Internal courtyards of Swadeshi Market Chawl**
*Bottom:* **Circulation network within the Swadeshi Market Chawl**

### *Swadeshi Market Chawl (Kalbadevi)*

The responsiveness of architecture to the streets and vice-versa is integral in the formation of a symbiotic housing system, further enriching the economics and the quality of lifestyle of the residents.

Swadeshi Market Chawl is one example of efficient networks within the city fabric. The red lines (*see facing page*) are indicative of the circulation through the *chawl*. The grid of internal streets within a mixed-use development plot and its connectivity to the main external roads proves to be efficient within a rapidly evolving city fabric.

The double-height street accommodates traders on the ground level and a staircase connects the structure to upper levels, which is used for resting or storage.

The upper levels overlook courtyards and bridges connect one part of the *chawl* to another, allowing the residential block to co-exist above the commercial segment, forming a liveable example of a mixed-use development.

## SYSTEMIC OPENESS
### *RK Chawl + Atmaram Chawl*

The transformation of a grid in a residential block allows for the creation of social spaces, room for growing families and sometimes is a means of revenue. This is evident from the

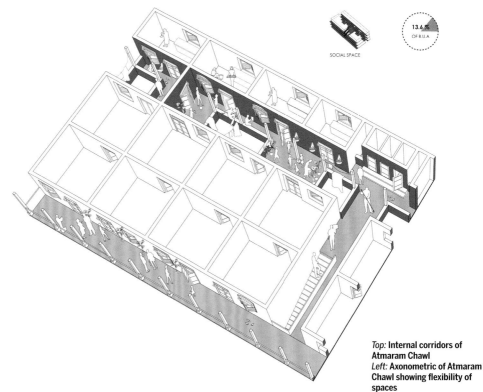

SOCIAL SPACE

**13.6 %** OF B.U.A

**The architecture of low income affordable housing whether state-built or state-enabled developer housing lacks imagination**

*Top:* Internal corridors of Atmaram Chawl
*Left:* Axonometric of Atmaram Chawl showing flexibility of spaces

openness of spaces created in RK Chawl and Atmaram Chawl.

The significant feature of the Atmaram Chawl is the separation of the kitchen from the house across a corridor. This has brought about better neighbourhoods with the creation of social spaces.

Over time, such a plan has allowed space for change. The residents have moved the kitchen within the layout of their house and created a means of revenue by renting out the former kitchen space.

The remarkable thing about the open system in these structures is that the quality of spaces is retained despite the change of functions.

In the RK Chawl, the ground level has a doubly loaded corridor juxtaposed to the upper floor plan, which pushes the corridors on the outside. This sort of grid creates four sizes of units allowing the possibility for different permutations and combinations of rooms, further making space for bigger rooms for community gatherings. This grid system allows for the creation of larger units, which enables people of all economic classes to live together in the same block and be a part of a diverse community.

## SHARED SPACE
### Bhatia Chawl + Charkop

For a socio-cultural fabric to exist, it is integral for the architectural built form to have a proportion that enables the creation of flexible and amiable shared spaces.

A typical courtyard-type *chawl* has an intimate height-to-width ratio, which acts as the social connect within the community. The shared corridors facing inwards towards the courtyard allow easy communication amongst the residents. In such spaces, the simple element of a door can transform a corridor into a more private study and the fellow residents adapt to such changes for the betterment of the community.

Another example of shared spaces is the site and services project in Charkop. It is a combination of 40-square-metre and 25-square-metre plots, some facing the main road, some flanking the three-metre-wide road and some lined up near an extended courtyard. Originally, they were all ground-storey structures, but as the community acquired a diverse character over the years, some of the individual owners expanded vertically with the addition of a first floor, considering the height restriction of about 14 feet.

Even after so many years, the shared space of the three-metre-wide road and the extended

**Appropriations that people made transformed particular types of habitations and created new hybrid configurations of the old and new**

Internal courtyards of Bhatia Chawl

courtyard is free of encroachment and is still used collectively.

## EXTENDED DOMESTICITY
### BDD Chawl

The extended home is a prerequisite to multi-generational families for liveability.

Each *chawl* building is a rectangular block with a spacious corridor running across its length, houses flanking on both sides and a shared toilet block at the far end. The tendency of domestic expansion has been noticed in these *chawls* owing to the growth of families in most cases.

The simple three- to four-foot extension outside the building line, the addition of a loft within the house or conversion of the *mori* (drain trap) into a bathroom not only adds to the existing space, but also uplifts the quality of life of residents. More than the change itself, it instills a sense of pride amongst the residents that they have their own washrooms over a shared one or the extension of the house to form an additional room.

It is commendable that the residents have maintained their corridor space, free of any encroachment and are respectful of their prime shared space.

## DETAIL
### Swadeshi+ Bhatia Chawl

The simplicity and the ingenuity of the construction details that have been incorporated in the simple architectural elements such as windows, bridges and the weather shades (*chajja*) are crucial to the lifespan of these *chawls*.

The tripartite windows are of aesthetic and functional value. The simple idea of dividing the windows in three parts to allow better airflow, visual connect and privacy enhances the liveability of the high densities in these spaces.

Most of the *chawls* are interconnected with bridges and the use of simple wire mesh or ventilators to cover them allows for light and air to filter through making the interiors easy to maintain.

The *chawls* are old structures, which are generally supported by cast iron columns and the beam edge detail is essential to fitting a weather shade, in turn protecting the internal corridors.

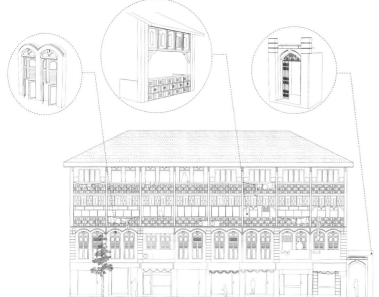

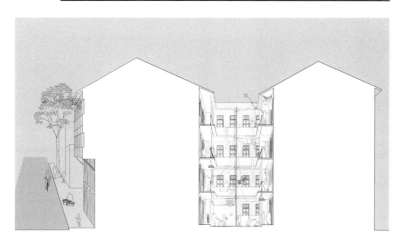

*Top:* **Details of Bhatia Chawl**
*Middle & Bottom:* **Illustrations showing quality and scale of shared spaces in Bhatia Chawl**

*Above:* **Elevation of BDD Chawl**
*Top Left:* **Illustrations showing extensions of houses in BDD Chawl**
*Bottom Left:* **Details of Swadeshi Chawl**

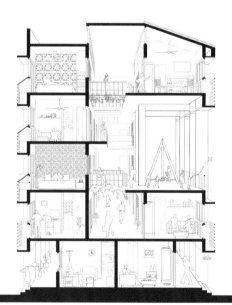

## How has this learning process led to more innovative design? Can you give us an example of a recent project?

In most cases, the architecture of low income affordable housing whether state-built or state-enabled developer housing lacks imagination and is usually just a mathematical exercise to maximise real estate profits. The previously mentioned five points are but a few of the many paradigms that can inform the design of affordable housing since, at present, the things that such design needs to consider, like expandability, systemic openness, live-work scenarios and sociocultural space, are largely absent. Our design project in Navi Mumbai though removed from the geographical and economic constraints of our field of investigation was fertile ground for the studio to test the relevance of our learnings in a real context.

The site lies on the outskirts of Mumbai city, within walking distance from a new railway line connecting to Mumbai city via the new proposed international airport site. In a departure from the client's initial brief we modified his mandate of designing separate buildings for one-room studios and one-bedroom units and instead consolidated them within a singular structure with interspaced, covered community terraces as social spaces with a variety of shared programmes. The ground-plus-four building is structured around a double-loaded corridor that staggers in plan every alternate floor, creating a continuous central sectional volume allowing for natural ventilation with hot air escaping

**Exterior and interior views of the plan**

from the corridor's clearstory ventilators. Plus, unit walls along the corridor are punctuated by a secondary system of ventilators and windows. These secondary openings also allow for the possibility of residents from units communicating with others across the corridor as well as across floors should they choose to do so.

While our current research direction also investigates auto-construction as a means to build affordable housing, the pre-cast concrete construction system for the project was selected due to the client's allied capacity of a precast company vertical. The construction system is a modified version of 3D precast concrete wet pods (kitchen and bathrooms) acting as structure with hollow core concrete slabs spanning across articulating living and sleeping spaces. Based on the learnings from the documented research projects we have anticipated the spatial and liveability needs of the residents, but the success of these strategies or their spatial and formal modifications over time will be hugely instructive only post-occupancy. ●

# Innovative Technology-Driven Affordable Housing

Architect **Rene van Zuuk** explains the background and content of his prize-winning design entitled 'RE-SETTLE', in which he uses innovative construction technology

## The Context

In the middle of 2016, when Europe was confronted by the prospect of housing large numbers of asylum-seekers from Syria and surrounding countries, two organisations in the Netherlands decided to hold a competition to seek and promote innovation in housing design for the new migrants. While the first initiative for the move came from the COA (the Dutch organisation responsible for taking care of asylum-seekers), the Government of Netherlands, through its Chief Architect, Floris van Alkemade, decided to broaden the scope of the competition to include not only international migrants, but also to seek innovative solutions for other migrants (like students, young professionals and elderly people) coming to the Dutch cities. What all migrants generally have in common is that they are seeking affordable accommodation. The problem is compounded by the fact that the number of migrants is difficult to predict and when the need occurs, large numbers of housing units are required in a very short time. The main requirement for the designs was therefore to come up with innovative, flexible solutions to meet the constantly fluctuating demand from the urban migrants.

## The Competition: A Home Away From Home

The competition launched under the name 'A Home Away From Home', organised in 2016, was

> **What all migrants generally have in common is that they are seeking affordable accommodation**

*Below & Facing Page:*
**Digital renderings of the design**

judged over two rounds by an eminent jury under the chairmanship of Floris van Alkemade.

The interest in taking part in the competition was overwhelming. Three hundred and sixty-six teams participated in the first round showcasing a wide variety of approaches. The diversity of suggestions was great: from modular housing units, building kits and do-it-yourself building systems to proposals for innovatively using or reusing specific building types such as green-houses, factories or office buildings as well as from social strategies to innovative building technologies.

Out of the multitude of entries, the jury selected six, including mine, called RE-SETTLE. The jury praised RE-SETTLE for its use of radically different and innovative building technology.

The six winning teams were each given an amount of prize-money so that they could create a full-scale (1:1) prototype of their project. These prototypes were shown later in the year at the Dutch Design Week exhibition held in October 2016 in Eindhoven.

## Design Idea behind RE-SETTLE

The existing experience with asylum-seekers indicates that a vast majority of them find the lack of privacy to be a major issue in the normal housing allotted to them. That is why the basic idea behind RE-SETTLE is to create a neighbourhood, almost a village-like environment, using a minimum amount of resources in which future inhabitants can feel safe and have the possibility to live independently either as single individuals or with their families.

## Innovative Construction Technology

The uniqueness of the design lies in its use of an unconventional material for construction and a creative way of cutting an assembly. The basic material used is Styrofoam (Expanded Polystyrene or EPS) and a unique cutting method has been developed in the last two years at our studio in the Netherlands.

EPS is a material that is produced with minimal use of resources. It consists of only 4% petroleum-based, mono-styrene and constitutes 96% air. As a single material, it is 100% recyclable. EPS is also reasonably cheap, dimensionally stable, non-toxic and fireproof. It is impervious to moisture and mould and has unique

**The model build up**

**Diagram showing the step by step model build up**

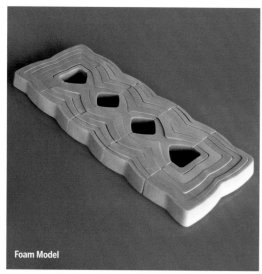

**Foam Model**

ETFE film

PVC tent

EPS material

Soft fabric [fire blanket]

Plastic Panel

Spot lights

**Detailed drawing of the build up**

properties in terms of insulation.

The design is based on modular elements cut from a single, rectangular block of EPS with the dimensions of 4.8 metres x 2.4 metres x 1.0 metre. Using the unique cutting method developed in our studio, a computer-guided cutting wire, with an adjustable angle, is used to cut a series of rings out of the solid block of EPS. Once cut, the series of rings fit together into one another like a nesting doll or a series of beach buckets. The brilliance of the applied method lies in the cutting technique itself.

Once the exterior face of the bottom (largest) ring is cut, the interior face of the one nesting above it is cut as well. This design/construction reduces the number of cuts by 50%.

Furthermore, an EPS block measuring 4.8 x 2.4 x 1.0 m. (one unit) can be cut into the needed components in just two hours. Finally, Velcro-fastener serves as 'adhesive' to join subsequent rings to one another, forming a complete housing unit.

The core of the design is a residential module with an interior structure similar to a hotel room. Each module contains basic utilities such as a shower, a sink and a toilet and is additionally furnished with a wardrobe, a table with chairs and a bed placed on the mezzanine. The modules

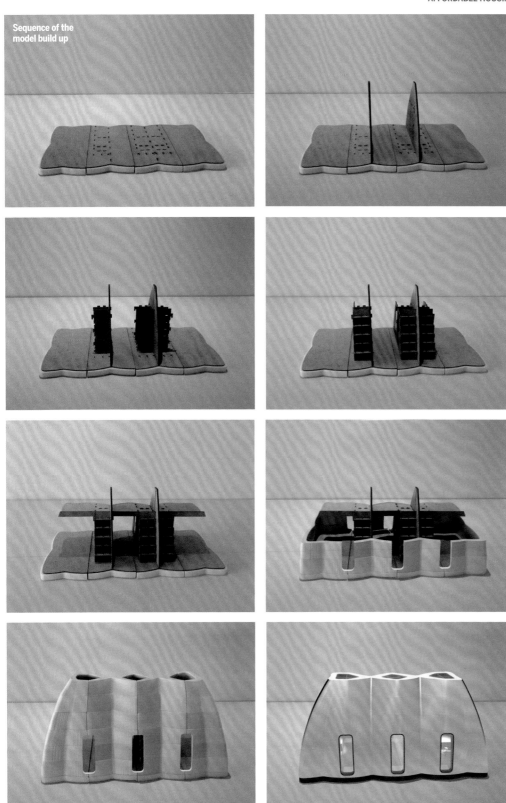

Sequence of the model build up

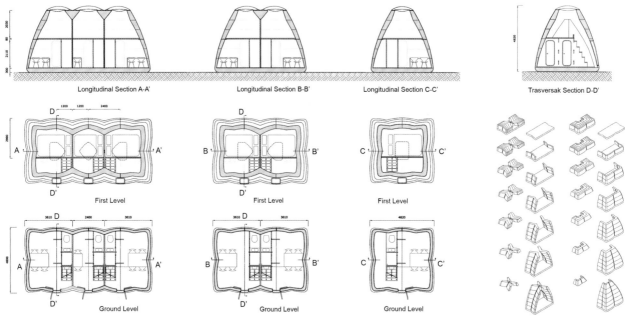

Longitudinal Section A-A'  Longitudinal Section B-B'  Longitudinal Section C-C'  Trasversak Section D-D'

First Level  First Level  First Level

Ground Level  Ground Level  Ground Level

**Section Plans**

**Prototype of the model**

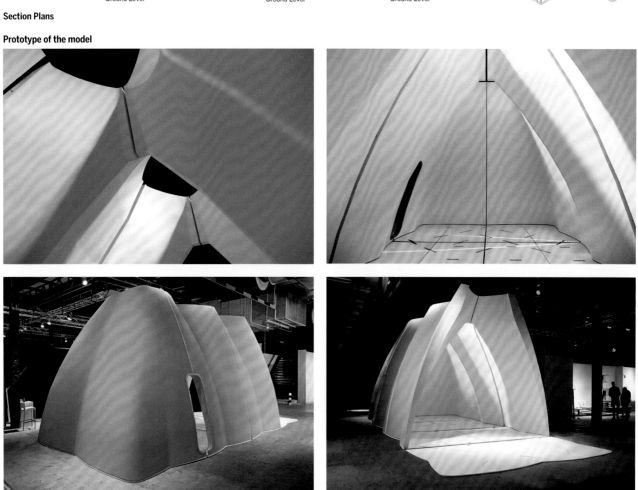

**Due to the modularity of the solution and the lightweight construction, each type of unit can be relatively easily transformed or extended**

Interior view

are placed next to one another in short rows. This means that there are basically two types of units, namely the ones forming the end segments of such rows and those forming the middle segments.

Combining modules with one another enables the creation of three types of housing units: a one-person unit of 15 sq. m., a two-person unit of 20.7 sq. m. and a detached 3–4 person unit of 26.5 sq. m. Due to the modularity of the solution and the lightweight construction, each type of unit can be relatively easily transformed or extended even after it has been built. The design and technology also allows the combination of several units to create larger clusters, which can be used for bigger families or groups or for specific communal activities.

The actual process of construction on site starts by placing a layer of water-proofing on the plot and covering it with an EPS floor. Slotted cardboard surface placed on it finishes the flooring, setting up the basis for interior walls. The interior partitions are made of 40 mm. thick cardboard panels designed to snap into one another. Then they are fixed onto the cardboard base. The unit's exterior walls have been designed as pressure-arches, wherein EPS functions as the compressed material.

The inner side of the exterior wall is lined with a fire-blanket attached to the foam-construction using Velcro-fasteners. The final result is a compact and seamless structure. All the components of a single unit, including both the EPS shell and the cardboard interior, are supplied on the site as a single do-it-yourself package.

When fully assembled, the arch-shaped unit has a size of 2.4 metres x 4.8 metres x 4.5 metres. Nonetheless, the unit is easy to disassemble back into single rings. Once dismantled, the rings fit into one another so that the whole module fits back into a package of 2.4 metres x 4.8 metres x 1.0 mctrc. As a result, six such packets can fit into a single lorry. Due the lightness of the used material, six persons on the building site can handle one packet, without using any heavy equipment.

Besides, the special features of the material used means that when after many cycles of usage, the final dismantling is necessary, the volume of EPS shrinks upon melting to just 4%, resulting in transporting 59 units in a single lorry.

## Conclusion

The uniqueness of the design lies in the combination of fast cutting technology, the nesting-method of component design, easy transportation and low-cost construction method, which optimally use the unique qualities of this unconventional building material. The proposal is perfect for an emergency, offering a short-term housing solution to large numbers of urban migrants. The units provide its users private spaces for all basic activities such as living, eating, bathing and sleeping, while waiting for a long-term permanent solution. The used design and construction technology has a unique quality: dismantling, transport and storing can be done with great ease and efficiency, without the need for heavy construction equipment. ●

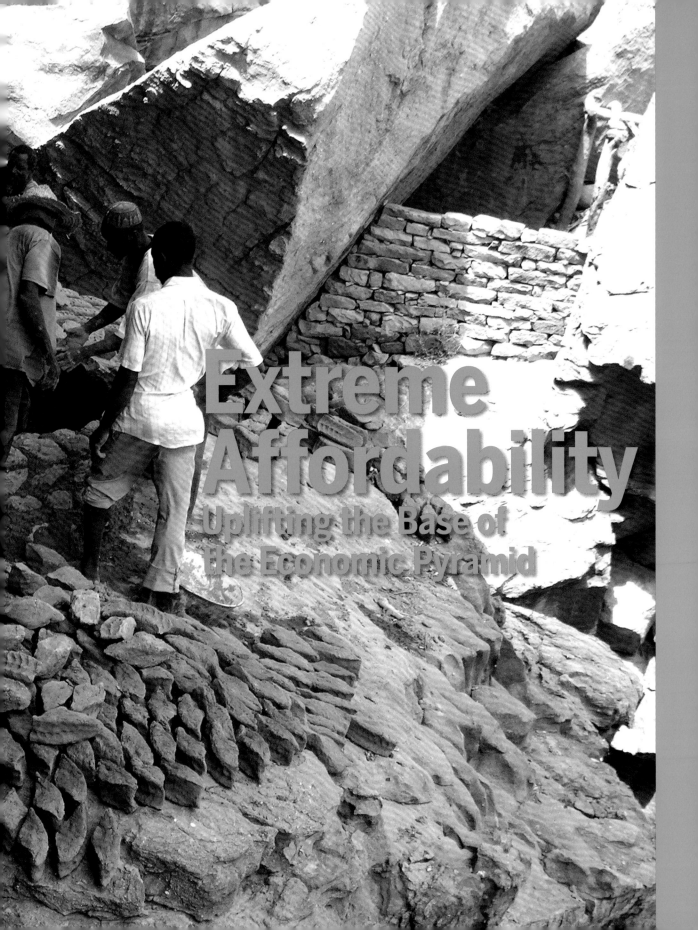

# Extreme Affordability
### Uplifting the Base of the Economic Pyramid

# Extreme Affordability

## Uplifting the Base of the Economic Pyramid

Vinayak Bharne & Shyam Khandekar

The most difficult aspect of urban affordability is the extreme inequity at the base of the economic pyramid, an extreme represented by more than 900 million people across the world, who live in slums (UN Habitat, 2006). Across less-developed nations, even as migration trends from rural areas into cities continue, the ongoing pace of urban population growth far exceeds the rate at which cities can respond to their housing needs. Consequently, people are pushed to the urban edge into poorly serviced areas, giving rise to desperate, unplanned communities. What makes these settlements different is not just their lack of conscious planning and fundamental infrastructure but, more importantly, their property ownership rights. Occupants of such insecure housing have no rights to their dwellings and face a high risk of eviction. Residents cannot confidently invest in upgrading their homes, while the government does not systematically provide public services. This phenomenon is particularly stark in developing societies – that today constitute a majority of the urban world – where one in three urban residents lives in such insecure, vulnerable habitats.

The gravity of issues underlying this socio-economic injustice far outweighs that faced by affluent regions. We feel it is unfair to conveniently mingle discussions on extreme affordability with broader discussions on urban inequity and inclusiveness. Any discussion on the base of the economic pyramid deserves its own space, because it demands readings, approaches and strategies that are significantly different, and even contradictory, to formal and policy-driven means and methods of urban transformation. This third section represents a consciously delineated space within this volume to focus on a dimension of inclusiveness and affordability that is neither easy to grasp, nor engage with and transform. In contrast to the second section that offers commentaries on more affluent nations such as the United States and the Netherlands, we present, in this section, observations and case studies from comparatively less developed regions such as Bangladesh, Brazil, Chile, India, Mali, Myanmar and Venezuela.

We begin with a conversation with Alfredo Brillembourg, a founding member of the interdisciplinary design studio, Urban Think Tank (UTT) that has, among other things, spent years documenting the famous vertical barrio, Torre David, in Caracas. In Chapter 25: Affordability through Public Participation, Brillembourg talks about why *favelas* and shanties offer invaluable lessons on how people live with few means and why a layer of informality will always pervade 21st-century cities, because people have found extremely resilient ways to live in urban conditions. Rather than invent new solutions, he argues, we must embrace informality and provide initiatives to formalise them by way of micro-loans and infrastructure strategies.

The next thee chapters offer scholarly readings on informal housing and habitats. Chapter 26: Informal Housing in Venezuela overviews extreme affordability in one of the fastest growing regions of Latin America. It observes why the poor settle in the city's informal establishments and how the lack of access to services and opportunities, exacerbates their poverty further. How long processes of consolidation and social cohesion have made these barrios an enmeshed part of the city despite their unclear legal status and incomplete socio-political recognition. Chapter 27: Re-housing Slums As If People Matter overviews the insecure housing condition in India and gauges to what degree the informal can thrive under the control of a formal planning apparatus. It critiques ongoing slum settlement schemes that offer imaginations of "compact, pedestrian-friendly and mixed-use liveable neighbourhoods," and argues why such concepts deserve a far more reflective and nuanced approach when it comes to the design of informal communities. In Chapter 28: Spontaneous Slums: Interfacing Planning & Emergence, the authors study five slums in India, and argue that the most seemingly spontaneous, informal habitats are actually being shaped by elements of leadership and planning. They posit that if informal settlements are allowed to develop over time to reach a 'climax state', some may grow into a form of urbanism similar to the older parts of our modern cities.

Three case studies of slum upgradation strategies follow. Chapter 29: Empowering Migrant Communities to Secure Housing discusses how migrant households in Yangon, Myanmar, were supported by a local non-government organisation, Women for the World (WFW), to save money for housing, procure land and work with young architects to generate their own incremental housing solutions at a fraction of the cost compared to public housing efforts in the country. Chapter 30: Housing Transformation in Resettlement Sites focuses on two cases: the Mandartola resettlement site in Gopalgonj, Bangladesh, and the Bhim Nagar resettlement site, in Chennai, India. This study is significant for its observations on how former slum dwellers cope with new living environments. It stresses the importance of providing not just shelter, but opportunities for restoring livelihoods and creating assets for those affected. Chapter 31: A Flexible Approach to Upgrade Informal Housing analyses the Baan Mankong (meaning 'secure housing') Programme, the first in Thailand to officially recognise slum inhabitants as developers of housing – representing a bridging of top-down and bottom-up practices. It elaborates on how the national government, besides offering loans to slum dwellers, also successfully negotiated with local actors – from non-government organisations to construction workers – to create a support system for slum upgradation.

The next three narratives focus on the role of architecture and art as catalysts for slum transformation. Chapter 32: Half of a Good House overviews the incremental low-cost housing of noted Chilean architecture and urbanism firm, Elemental, whose founder, Alejandro Aravena received the 2016 Pritzker Prize for Architecture. Chapter 33: Building the Dogon Way discusses how the Dutch architecture practice LEVS Architecten has revived traditional mud-brick building techniques of the Dogon tribe to build new school facilities for an under-developed community in Mali, Africa. Chapter 34: The Artistic Rebirth of a Neglected Community looks at the famous Favela Painting project of Dutch artists Jeroen Koolhaas and Dre Urhahn, also known as Haas&Hahn. It focuses on the Praça Cantão, the artistic painting of 34 houses in the Santa Monica *favela* in Rio, Brazil, that has transformed the identity of this informal habitat.

We end with two propository narratives. Chapter 35: Streets as Drivers for the Transformation and Inclusion of Slums calls for a re-thinking of slums as islands of poverty, to deprived neighbourhoods. It argues that creating and improving streets and public spaces in existing slum settlements can catalyse significant improvements in livelihoods, living conditions and social interactions. Finally, Chapter 36: Climate Adaptive Housing posits that Climate Change can lead to new insights for the future of slum development. It offers propositions on how adaptive housing might be amalgamated with issues of floor mitigation, bio-diversity protection and food production, leading to new directions for the future of insecure housing.

# Affordability Through Public Participation

**Amit Arya** and **Buvana Murali** in conversation with **Alfredo Brillembourg**, founder, Urban Think Tank

The 21st century is experiencing an unprecedented challenge on mega-cities to provide equitable and affordable forms of social living. Affordability as an idea is slowly becoming a cliché with an ever-expanding inventory of gated communities and extravagant developments becoming the hallmark of every city. In the midst of global capitalist tendencies and the constant barrage of slum tourism packages, our sensibility to distinguish 'the haves' from 'the have-nots' has diminished.

Alongside increasing adversities, the resilience for survival in the informal sector has led to new models and typologies of habitation. The occupation of Torre David in the city of Caracas, Venezuela, was one such event. It captured the world's imagination and became a symbol of a community's resolve to take control of circumstances, come together and, in the process, invent a new pattern of adaptability in the form of a vertical barrio (district).

We spoke to Alfredo Brillembourg, founding member of Urban Think Tank (UTT), who has spent years documenting the phenomenon of Torre David. The UTT team has performed an urban and

*Left:* **The Torre David facade showing the additions implemented by the residents to complete an incomplete tower**
*Right:* **View of the entire development showing incremental additions to the floor levels**

PHOTO: DANIEL SCHWARTZ, U-TT, ETH

ethnographic study, both to campaign for the validity of such an occupation as well as initiate global dialogue on lessons learnt from this exercise. Their approach posits a compelling paradigm to address the challenge of growing inequality in the Global South where they see the role of the architect as an aggressive lobbyist for affordable housing.

**Amit Arya (AA) - What is the significance of the occupation and appropriation of Torre David for our contemporary urban condition?**

**Alfredo Brillembourg (AB) -** Once we have established the fact that 50% of the world's population is living on less than two dollars a day and that less than 1% of the world's population controls 50% of the world's GDP while the other 99% has control over the rest, then we can say that it is a significant amount to work with but it has to be efficiently distributed amongst the 99%. While we say that capitalism and market forces are the only way to go, we have seen that this new age of technological advancements has demonstrated a manifold increase in the unequal distribution of wealth and has further disenfranchised the lower spectrum of the world's population from the growth of nations. Therefore, it is necessary to find a new way to create a 'common ground' and address the growing problem of scarcity in the world, which is a human-made fact.

The key is to incentivise the market to address the issues of bringing more equity to those who do not have adequate resources. Torre David was one such attempt; it is a storey of a fabricated scarcity, it is a symbol of the boom and the bust of a city: Caracas. It is not only a symbol of the economic capital that builds such kind of buildings but also a symbol of tragedy, the breaking of the economic market, the bankruptcy of a country, the rioting and the revolution of a disenfranchised population.

The economical breakdown of Venezuela left the tower empty for 17 years while simultaneously the country grew poorer and more people found themselves homeless.

In the city of Caracas, in a sheer moment of desperation 3,500 of them started squatting in the empty tower to escape the terrible monsoon floods. They inhabited the tower and kept moving up floor by floor as the population grew and created a cooperative in order to pay their electricity bills. Then they invited UTT inside to show them how people with their limited micro-incomes are completing the unfinished tower. So we approached the government with the idea that Torre David

could become a perfect example of a Private/Public partnership with a small amount of micro-loans to create a new model of social housing. It could be finished by bringing in an elevator company and using the existing tower as a place for installing energy efficient interventions, which would make the development a sustainable model by generating power autonomously, thus attaining a 30% off the grid status. In essence, Torre David is a significant example of taking a ruin and converting it into a model project of appropriation. The future of cities depends on our efficiency to build the new on top of the old, by reutilising vacant buildings and underserved assets in the city to avoid sprawl and contain the existing footprint of our cities by reprogramming them in innovative ways.

**Buvana Murali (BM) - Describe the affordable city of the 21st century.**

**AB -** The fastest way out of poverty is to migrate and since the Western colonial powers had not invested enough into their former colonies you see a migration to the places of power from the Global South to the Global North. In countries like China and India there is massive migration to urban areas; if we do not anticipate and act with imagination, their cities will become hell and start looking like Caracas waiting to enter a revolution.

Sprawling cities require costly infrastructure and the appropriation of agricultural land, which is not a sustainable model. For example, India's proposal for 'smart' new cities of the future is not a good idea because I believe that the smartest city is not a technologically loaded one but a very efficient low-tech city. Dharavi is one of the smartest cities or urban villages, which generates millions of dollars in revenue each year despite its limited resources.

Though *favelas* and shanties are not the perfect urban conditions, they tell us how people want to live with few means and an economic push towards basic infrastructure by the government. The 21st-century city is not about building the 'perfect' solution, because what is 'perfect' for society? Not what China is doing by demolishing the Hutongs and their human scale and pushing that population into fast paced, badly built 40-storey tall towers on the outskirts of Shanghai. This is a repeat of the mistakes of Pruitt-Igeo in St. Louis, Missouri. The fact is we are living in a formal and an informal city at the same time. A layer of informality will remain in our cities in the 21st century because people have found extremely resilient ways to live in cities. Rather than invent new solutions in our heads we must look at how people are living in cities today, embrace the informality and provide

**The key is to incentivise the market to address the issues of bringing more equity to those who do not have adequate resources**

149

*Left:* **The Grotao Community Centre is a proposal for providing the public space amenity within a dense** *favela* **community in Sao Paulo**
*Right:* **The Metro Cable project in Caracas by night with the cable car station positioned on top of the neighbourhood development**

solutions to formalise them by way of micro-loans and infrastructural ideas. Encourage a do-it-yourself attitude like Aravena did in Chile or what UTT did in Caracas with the 'Growing House' project where we learnt from the Favela of Caracas and their 25 year house building cycle, where they built room after room and floor after floor. Then they started providing some schools and kindergartens for the community on the ground floors as they kept moving their houses to the upper floors.

Therefore, for the 21st-century city we have to move away from the mono-functional city models. The 21st-century affordable city has to be a dense pedestrian city of one-mile radius with multiple modes of transportation and a population cap of one million inhabitants. This prototype can be multiplied as patchwork between our agricultural lands similar to what we proposed in the Parangole project.

**AA - You have referenced the work of Archigram, a relevant albeit utopian example created to generate an urban polemic but not to get it built. However, your work is far more contextually responsive to the urban challenges of Caracas and other similar urban conditions with a strong intent to build these ideas. How does one get such ideas built?**

*AB* - You have to lobby government. The architect must inhabit the public realm and must re-engage with politics. He/she should come into the city, see something existing and discover its potential rather than working on making the 'ideal' city. It is all about adding new layers to old cities by plugging into the existing. We think UTT is successful in that. We built the cable car project in Caracas and recently convinced the mayor of Mar del Plata in Argentina to build his new city hall in the poorest area of the city in order to valorise that piece of land.

**BM - Your projects are new typologies for the problems they identify and the final manifestation usually takes the form of an economically sensitive infrastructural innovation ...**

*AB* - We only do prototypes since we see ourselves as a laboratory. Our approach has always been to identify a relevant social problem and an innovative solution; we then work with governments to implement them. Sometimes we succeed, sometimes we don't. For example, we are trying to do a cable car project in Kohima, India, but we do not know if we will succeed, so we propose and move on to other challenges like the 'Empower Shack' project in Cape Town, South Africa, where we are building solutions for the problem of low-cost housing by building 100 units in a village typology. What we try to do is invent a 'Toolbox' and we are aware that our first prototypes will be just as deficient as the first Walkman or the first iPhone but then there will be others who will take it forward and perfect it.

**BM - You have mentioned that "in an infinitely unstable environment, architects must throw away their Ruskin - 'when we build, let us think that we build forever' - in favour of new goals: resilience, adaptability and transformability."**

*AB* - It is about embracing the unstable present and being contextual but not in a postmodern way. Referencing Frederic Jameson in whose words the context of postmodernity is a 'fragmented heterotopia'; at UTT we acknowledge these heterotopias by building our ideas into it and by joining more pieces together in order to create new models. It is not about making money but making a good society and the architect has to take his/her role seriously because if not then there will be no mediation. ●

# Informal Housing in Venezuela

**Alonso Ayala** takes a look at the *barrios* that have become part of the housing landscape of Caracas

The main elements of the transformation process of the modern Latin American city should be understood as the influence of European urban ideas that in general were transferred in a *sui generis* fashion to the Latin American metropolises at the end of the 19th century and at the beginning of the 20th century (Almandoz 1999). Venezuela shares a similar history to other Latin American countries, where the prevailing settlement pattern and culture was the result of the widespread Spanish colonisation process. However, the case of Venezuela differs regarding its urbanisation process because of the accelerated urban growth rates mainly triggered by the discovery of oil in 1917.

Urban population growth in Venezuela is considered to be amongst one of the most rapid in Latin America. Much of this growth took place in the capital city of Caracas. Two main factors were responsible for the urban transition: the first being the drastic change in the economic base of the country from agricultural production to mining and oil exploration. The second reason was the subsequent need to develop the service sector in order to sustain the new oil industry.

Rapid urbanisation brought about urban poverty and a steady deterioration of urban living conditions for a majority of people. The urban growth of the valley of Caracas during the 20th century led to the densification of informal settlements which, according to Harms (1997) can be explained by a number of interrelated factors: (a) the difficult topography of the valley restricting access to urban land; (b) the global city effect highlighting the demand for office space, which in turn increased the value of land thus having a negative impact on land development for residential purposes; (c) the modernisation process along the lines of development in North American cities, which led to social and spatial segregation within metropolitan areas; and (d) the changes in the relationship between the centre-periphery, in which urban sprawl increasingly outstretched the periphery from the centre, thus creating new

centres around which informal settlements grew and consolidated.

By the end of the 20th century, 40.7% of the total population of the country (8,738,000 inhabitants) was living in informal settlements, known in Venezuela as *barrios*. Such figures give a clear indication of the scale of the problem since it is in *barrios* where poverty concentrates and inequalities are most evident. In Caracas, 55% of the population lives in *barrios* occupying 33.5% of the city's area (UN-Habitat 2006). Currently, the situation has not changed much and informal urbanisation continues expanding due to natural population growth and rampant poverty.

## Poverty, social exclusion and spatial segregation of *barrios*

Geographical segregation is an extremely powerful mechanism of exclusion with significance that exceeds material deficiencies. The *barrios* in Caracas offer a socio-spatial laboratory of exclusion and segregation. Characteristic of the exclusionary process experienced by the poor in Venezuelan

**A great number of households in Venezuela are affected by exclusion**

*Figure 1*: **The Inner Metropolitan Area of Caracas**

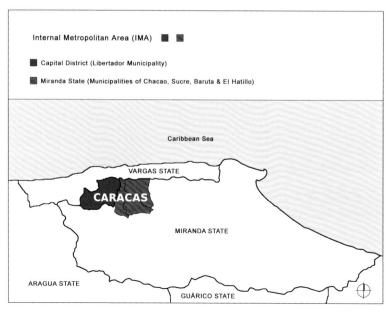

Internal Metropolitan Area (IMA) ■ ■

■ Capital District (Libertador Municipality)

■ Miranda State (Municipalities of Chacao, Sucre, Baruta & El Hatillo)

Caribbean Sea

VARGAS STATE

CARACAS

MIRANDA STATE

ARAGUA STATE

GUÁRICO STATE

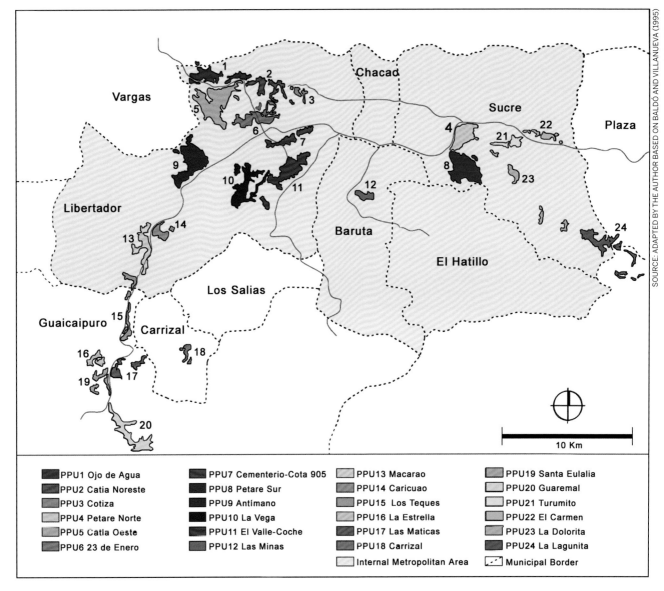

SOURCE: ADAPTED BY THE AUTHOR BASED ON BALDÓ AND VILLANUEVA (1995)

Legend:

PPU1 Ojo de Agua
PPU2 Catia Noreste
PPU3 Cotiza
PPU4 Petare Norte
PPU5 Catia Oeste
PPU6 23 de Enero
PPU7 Cementerio-Cota 905
PPU8 Petare Sur
PPU9 Antímano
PPU10 La Vega
PPU11 El Valle-Coche
PPU12 Las Minas
PPU13 Macarao
PPU14 Caricuao
PPU15 Los Teques
PPU16 La Estrella
PPU17 Las Maticas
PPU18 Carrizal
PPU19 Santa Eulalia
PPU20 Guaremal
PPU21 Turumito
PPU22 El Carmen
PPU23 La Dolorita
PPU24 La Lagunita
Internal Metropolitan Area
Municipal Border

The Metropolitan Area of Caracas and its *barrio* zones. There are 144 *barrios* in the metropolitan area of Caracas. For urban upgrading purposes, these *barrio* conglomerations have been divided into 24 Physical Planning Units (PPUs) and 206 Urban Design Units (UDUs) of diverse sizes and characteristics. These conglomerations occupy 4,616 hectares representing roughly 30% of the city's area and 55% of its total population

society is their low self-esteem, which emphasises the difficulties of carrying out self-help projects. Moreover, low self-esteem forms a powerful barrier to social organisation. In this way, the State is able to continue exercising its paternalistic approach to social development (Barroso 1997).

A great number of households in Venezuela are affected by exclusion. Between one quarter and one third of the population suffers from an extreme degree of exclusion concerning their right to education and health. These access rights to the social entitlements of education and health, as well as the preservation of individual rights, are strongly related to space, as the link to geographical segregation is very strong. Only about a quarter

SOURCE: AYALA 2012

**Housing conditions in *Barrio* La Silsa Moran, Caracas**

of the homes where the poor live are adequate in the sense of having minimum space and service connections meeting national legal standards (Cartaya 2007).

A household whose situation might lead to escaping poverty is strongly inhibited by being part of these segregated spaces. Venezuela is characterised by a gap between what the Constitution defines as social rights and what its constituencies experience in their everyday lives.

## Barrio: definition, formation and consolidation process

The origins of *barrios* in Venezuela date back to the beginning of the 20th century. They were not only the result of uncontrolled rapid urbanisation processes that arose following extensive rural-urban migration, but they were also the consequence of an incompetent public housing sector. The first barrio was already being settled in 1917.

There is universal agreement that poverty is related to the lack of or a precarious access to basic needs, poor economic opportunities and subsistence livelihoods. Considering that poverty is widespread in informal settlements, these can be defined as precarious residential areas with poor access to basic needs, formed by households living under acute economic constraints, with people experiencing social exclusion to varying degrees and spatially concentrated in distinct parts of the city, which are environmentally vulnerable and not suitable for housing purposes. Several other forces

influence their already negative socio-economic and spatial conditions. These are mainly social stigmatisation by outsiders, ambiguous citizenship underlying weak political participation and an illegal status stemming from occupying land they do not own (Ayala 2012).

*Barrios* are commonly built on public land through organised 'land invasions', which is a common feature of informal settlement processes in Latin America. They evolve through a gradual appropriation of land and incremental shelter growth. In many instances, *barrio* formation has been supported by political proselytism and the patronising structure of government institutions, which has a clear goal of gaining votes through a permissive attitude towards informal land occupation.

The *rancho* is the name given to the initial shelter structure built in *barrios* that a pioneering settler or newcomer to the *barrio* is able to afford. As the household's socio-economic conditions improve, so does the original dwelling unit until it is transformed into a solid, permanent structure. The consolidated house results from the adoption and interpretation of the widespread building technology of the city (i.e., reinforced concrete structures with brick walls) and the culture of the *barrio* inhabitant (reinterpretation of some architectural elements of rural houses). The use of the aforementioned building technology, irrespective of its structural integrity, is indicative of the consolidation of a *barrio*. The higher the number of shelters transformed into solid concrete

> **The *barrios* of Caracas are ... too large, well settled and consolidated to be dismissed as marginal**

SOURCE: AYALA 2012

**View from *Barrio* La Vega. Informal urban growth has taken over the space around a former social housing project**

and brick houses, the greater is the consolidation of the *barrio*. Housing structures built this way can sometimes reach up to six storeys.

Following long processes of consolidation and social cohesion, *barrios* have become part and parcel of urban life, interacting with the city despite their unclear legal status and their incomplete socio-political and spatial recognition. The *barrios* of Caracas are strikingly visible, constituting a major feature of the city's landscape. They are too large, well settled and consolidated to be dismissed as marginal, or as an exception to the rule.

Table 1 shows the social agents, steps and mechanisms involved in the production of *barrios*, highlighting the different stages of the consolidation process.

In sum, Venezuela's poor tend to settle in the only areas available to them, the city's informal settlements. Once they become inhabitants of these areas, they experience a structural lack of access to the services and opportunities needed to improve their lives. Under these conditions, geographically concentrated poverty continues to grow in Venezuela's urban areas, acting as both the driver and the outcome of *barrio* formation and consolidation (Ayala 2012).

*The incremental process of house construction:* Innovative ways of dealing with house construction and consolidation. *Top Left:* Shows the initial temporary shelter structure made of make-shift materials, which is gradually surrounded by the permanent structure. *Top Right:* Shows the more permanent structure built next to the shack. Once the permanent structure is finished and the family moves in, the shack is not demolished, but rented out to a newcomer or household in need of shelter

### Table 1: The consolidation process of *barrios*

| **Agents:** Social agents producing *barrios*. | **Steps:** Sequence of phases that can be interrupted temporarily or definitively. | **Mechanisms:** Modes and practices which the families looking for homes have found to secure the production of houses. |
|---|---|---|
| Inhabitants:<br>-*Barrio* community organisations<br>-Families:<br>•house owners*<br>•tenants<br>•relatives<br><br>Land owners<br><br>Government institutions<br><br>Constructors and builders<br>-construction enterprises<br>-*barrio* builders<br>-*barrio* dwellers<br><br>* *Not necessarily owner of land (frequently not)* | Land occupation and construction of shacks (ranchos).<br><br>Precarious furbishing of the land and transformation of shacks into solid houses.<br><br>Infrastructure provision (roads, electricity, drainage). Progressive transformation of the houses into multi-storey buildings.<br><br>Continuation of the upgrading process. Extension of occupied land together with the transformation and upgrading of the house. | Illegal occupation of public or private land.<br><br>Furbishing the land and constructing the houses with self-help.<br><br>Asking the government for roads and services. The government provides the materials and the settlers the manual labour, occasionally also building materials through self-financing.<br><br>Construction of houses not according to a preconceived plan; money comes whenever it is available, not regularly; every house tells a unique story, reflecting the families occupying it; building is done by the owners with self-help and family managed small contractors. |

*Source: Bolivar 1997:185*

## Expanding the meaning of *barrio*:
## Legality vs. illegality

At this point, it is important to discuss the current legal standing of *barrios* in Venezuela, as they sit at the nexus of two opposing forces: one focusing on their status as illegal settlements and the other focusing on their economic and political contributions to the city, leading to the creation of legal frameworks for their integration, regularisation and upgrade. These opposing forces are visible throughout Latin America, as it is common for settlements established on illegally settled land – through land invasion or infiltration, for example – to gain tacit approval from the state, often for political reasons.

To reprise the discussions made thus far on *barrio* illegality, they are located in areas of the city that have not been developed by the formal public or private sectors, often due to conditions such as steep slopes and environmental hazards. Their illegality stems from the fact that the underlying lands have been occupied without the benefit of legal titles and without legal permits to do so. The condition of illegality extends to the status of the residents themselves, many who do not have clear citizenship and several who work in the informal economy outside the scope of regulation and taxation. In some of Venezuela's *barrios*, the residents are faced with overt threats of eviction and eradication of their homes, or they are faced with more subtle threats such as the long-term denial of services. At the same time, the residents of other *barrios* in Venezuela feel relatively secure, given the advanced state of consolidation where they live and the possession of semi-legal documents stating that they own the physical structures they have built atop the illegally settled *barrio* lands. These semi-legal documents formed the base for renting out and selling houses in the informal market.

The reality is that *barrios* make positive contributions to the city in Venezuela: they provide a source of low-income housing as well as additional producers and consumers for goods and services. They function to complete the urbanisation process, developing communities on the last vestiges of urban lands that have been left undeveloped by others. *Barrios* also contribute political capital to

***Barrios* are commonly built on public land through organised 'land invasions'**

***Barrio* density and the 'never-ending' incremental construction process**

**The young generation's hope for better housing conditions remains a dream in the context of widespread urban housing informality**

SOURCE: AYALA 2012

candidates who may pander to the plight of *barrio* residents in order to win additional votes and support for their political campaigns.

While legal frameworks and initiatives to improve the living conditions of *barrio* inhabitants have been tried throughout the urban history of the city, they have not resulted in significant improvements in the quality of everyday life on the ground. Overall, it is clear that a mosaic pattern exists today, encompassing steps toward legality for some 'suitable' *barrios*, alongside the continuation of illegality for other 'high-risk' *barrios*, as well as steps toward legal inclusion, alongside the continuation of social and economic exclusion.

The urban transformation of Venezuela, epitomised by the drastic demographic change of the once provincial city of Caracas into an emerging modern metropolis at the beginning of the 1950s, represents a unique example of rapid urbanisation in Latin America. Urban Venezuela is the result of the discovery of oil, which eventually cursed the country as an oil-fed and oil-dependent economy and society. The gradual decay of Caracas coincided with a dramatic process of rapid urbanisation under poverty. As a result, Caracas is characterised by fragmentation and the segregated settlement patterns of its social groups.

The conflicting political situation over the last 20 years has created an additional urban burden on previously unsolved problems. Today, political autocracy and social polarisation exacerbates social exclusion processes and the negative effects of spatial segregation. The rise in inequality indices, increasing impoverishment of the middle class, rampant poverty levels and spatial consolidation of social exclusion in *barrios* is a distortion of what should be urban development. This is an issue that needs urgent intervention. The case seems to be of an inability to learn from past experiences. Before the establishment of the current dictatorship that has sunk the country into a socio-economic and humanitarian crisis, previous governments drew up poverty reduction strategies with short-term perspectives. Interventions were punctual, often manipulative and in many cases full of vested economic and political interests. They frequently aimed to mitigate the negative outcomes of poverty rather than address the root causes. Therefore, compensatory programmes persisted, political fraternities reigned and populism and paternalism were the order of the day, with no sound structural changes being foreseen.

As the middle classes suffer from downward mobility and tend to disappear, thus joining the poor, so also does polarisation and inequality in the country increase, resulting in a society made up of an extremely rich minority and an extensive heterogeneous poor sector. This distorted situation poses a threat to the development process of the society as a whole. ●

# Re-Housing Slums as if People Matter

**Sudeshna Chatterjee** looks at the lessons learnt from the BSUP/JNNURM's slum redevelopment and affordable housing projects

The urban crisis in India is often equated with rapid urbanisation that has far outpaced infrastructure development. This resulted in the proliferation of slums, growing urban poverty and crime, as well as pollution and ecological damage. As a result, India's first flagship mission on urbanisation, the Jawaharlal Nehru National Urban Renewal Mission (JNNURM), was created in 2005 for investing in infrastructure, guiding planned development and repackaging existing Indian cities as world class cities for playing larger roles in global economies. The mission asserted that all citizens should equally benefit from national economic growth and thus poverty reduction goals were married to urban development agendas to create a large, affordable housing programme under the Basic Services to the Urban Poor (BSUP) to replace and redevelop slum sites.

According to the Census of India 2011, 38% of households in India's million-plus large cities live in slums, whereas in other cities it's 61.9%. BSUP had to provide basic services (including water supply and sanitation), security of tenure and improved housing at affordable prices through provision of new *pucca* (permament) dwelling units. They also needed to ensure delivery of social services like education, health and social security to the urban poor by empowering the Urban Local Bodies (ULBs). However, BSUP evaluations have shown that the ULBs typically focused on timely delivery of a large number of *pucca* housing units by using two predominant approaches to in-situ redevelopment:
**a)** Total redevelopment of the site in apartment blocks and
**b)** Selective infill houses of built-up area 250 square feet on any plot configuration to replace the semi-permanent slum hutments.

As per the ULB's own admission, their only aim

> **Are these privately developed enclaves simply going to produce planned slums inside high-end developments?**

**Image 1: BSUP flats in Jattrodi, Nagpur**

**Award winning BSUP flats in Karimadom, Trivandrum**

was to reduce the cost of construction. This left little scope for customising houses as per each family's needs, addressing critical environmental issues linked to inadequate drainage and sanitation at the overall site level or convergence of physical and social development initiatives with BSUP.

Even though the development literature acknowledges that selective infill houses in place of semi-permanent slum hutments is a better option for continuity of community life, livelihood and social networks, ULBs across India preferred total redevelopment of the site in apartment blocks (see image 1). This approach completely erases the existing fabric of the slum and results in forced evictions. However, it is an approach that architects, planners and government functionaries are more comfortable with as it fits their idea of 'planned urban development', to bring order to existing slums. The new flats are seen as a way out of poverty and as a more acceptable way of living in the middle of the prime real estate of the city.

The 12th Five Year Plan (2012–2017) recommends that every effort should be made to economise on land use through higher FSI (Floor Space Index) in prime urban areas. It goes on to emphasise that it is also vital to involve the community in designing slum rehabilitation. The Plan seeks to promote various types of public-private partnerships for realising the goal of 'Affordable Housing for All' with special emphasis on the urban poor. This paves the way for unlocking the potential of slum real estate by bringing the informal under the control of the formal planning apparatus. But does this mean that the redeveloped high-rise, denser slum will be seen at par with the other components of the new development, which will occupy the freed up ground space? Or are these privately developed enclaves simply going to produce planned slums inside high-end developments?

What can we learn from slum urbanism for future affordable housing projects? Under the current moral, political and economic imperatives of promoting sustainable cities, the key urban theories such as sustainable urbanism and new urbanism propose high-density, walkable, diverse and multi-use, car-free and transit-oriented developments. These conditions exist by default in informally developed slum settlements as they also do in medieval cities that persist even today. Despite these qualities, why are slums not considered viable planning models worthy of emulating in formal development processes instead of being a metaphor for underdevelopment?

How does the slum compare with new urbanist imaginations of livable neighbourhoods on three of the key dimensions of being compact, pedestrian friendly and mixed-use?

## Compact and High Density

Why is density good in a new urbanist community but not in a slum? To a large extent the numbers describing the density of slums defy formal imagination. In Pune, the density in slums is about 2,19,048 (persons/sq km) compared to 8,234 (persons/sq km) in non-slum areas. This no doubt conjures images of overcrowding, ill-health, shortages and conflicts over resources in the government's mind. In Pune this resulted in planning a large scale resettlement programme under the JNNURM in off-site flatted development even though the total declared slum population of Pune occupies only 2.34% of the city's land. This planning strategy for affordable housing for slum dwellers failed however because, unlike the planners, the communities did not see density as a deterrent. The perception of liveability is shaped by many factors such as proximity to work, schools, healthcare, family and community networks. A significant participatory process involving

**Why is density good in a new urbanist community but not in a slum?**

| 0 | 100 | 200 | | 400 | | 600 | | 800 | |
|---|---|---|---|---|---|---|---|---|---|

FEET

| 0 | | 50 | | 100 | | 150 | | 200 | | 300 |
|---|---|---|---|---|---|---|---|---|---|---|

METERS

| 0 | 100 | 200 | | 400 | | 600 | | 800 | | 1000 | | 1200 |
|---|---|---|---|---|---|---|---|---|---|---|---|---|

FEET

| 0 | | 50 | | 100 | | 150 | | 200 | | 300 | | 400 |
|---|---|---|---|---|---|---|---|---|---|---|---|---|

METERS

**Image 2: Two walkable slums, one in Pune and the other in Nagpur**

local communities, NGOs, architects, planners, engineers and elected representatives led to customised infill housing where each house had a unique design based on its footprint. This ground-up pcople-centred process in selected slums in Pune resulted in some of the most successful in-situ incremental housing projects under BSUP.

## Pedestrian-Friendly and Walkable

Being pedestrian-friendly is considered the most significant criterion for achieving low-carbon cities. Most slum settlements in India follow the new urbanist mantra of being pedestrian friendly (see image 2), where most things can be reached within a five-minute walk from home. New urbanist walkable neighbourhoods enjoy an interconnected street grid network that disperses traffic and eases walking through a hierarchy of narrow streets, boulevards and alleys whose high quality pedestrian environment and public realm make walking a pleasure. On the other hand, streets and common spaces in slums are not only used for walking but also for social interactions, playing and household work like washing, cooking, bathing and storage.

## Mixed-Use Neighbourhoods

New urban neighbourhoods ideally comprise a broad range of housing types and price levels to attract people of diverse ages, races and incomes. They promote concentrations of civic, institutional and commercial activity in the area. Schools are sized and located to enable children

to walk or bicycle to them and a range of parks and other open spaces are distributed within the neighbourhood. Indian slums, where the urban poor reside due to the acute shortage of affordable housing in cities, naturally attract migrant labour, marginalised and backward classes. Despite ambiguous tenure securities, slum houses are typically incrementally and opportunistically made and expanded by residents to incorporate domestic as well as transactional needs (such as home-based work, small-scale businesses, subletting etc.). As by their very nature of being affordable and opportunistic housing, slums develop in the cracks of the ordered city on vacant land near employment sources, schools, healthcare facilities and markets. This is particularly true of inner city slums. Most slums have daily needs shops, *anganwadis* (courtyard shelter) and, if they are lucky, some community facility within their shared spaces. Slums, are a model of mixed-use development where the scale and mix of the uses do not overwhelm the residential environment, but make the everyday viable for people living in the margins.

Informal planning by poor people often succeeds where formal planning fails. The municipality of Kalyani in the Kolkata Metropolitan Area, for BSUP, decided to only include families who had land titles from an earlier refugee resettlement initiative, which gave relatively large plots of land of 4–5 *katahs* (*katah* = 720 sq. ft.). In implementing BSUP, the municipality decided to provide new houses by household so that large families benefit but imposed the condition that only those households will qualify for a new house who have at least one *katah* of land after division of the property among legal heirs. No doubt this mandate stems from the fear of density/congestion. This rule would impose fixing a density of 74,738 persons/sq. km in Kalyani. As per the ACE study (2012), many families were left out of BSUP because of this plot area cut off criterion. However, people designed informal ways of sharing the plot between many households, which proved in many ways to be superior to the planned order of the BSUP houses that only followed a rigid two-room typology with one variation (see box 1).

The ACE study also showed that the infill slum redevelopments, which secured strong participation from beneficiary families and had good professional teams working on the design of houses (in both flatted and in-situ incremental housing typologies) were more acceptable to people. Not surprisingly, such new houses were a source of pride for the residents as in the case of Pune and a source of disappointment where people were not involved in design and professional expertise in housing delivery was questionable. The most common complaint of dissatisfied beneficiaries of BSUP housing was climate and cultural insensitivity of the designs and the lack of flexibility of internal spaces (see box 2).

## The Need to Focus on Common Space

The size of a redeveloped house is never adequate for accommodating the needs of most families and particularly the needs of children and young people whose spontaneous behaviour includes play and recreation within local areas. Whenever slum redevelopment projects are planned and designed with people in mind, typically the discussion is focused on the design of the individual house with limited or no references to community facilities.

The design templates rarely include open spaces at all levels of the settlement as a networked system that works together with the house to create the housing. The premise of urban design is not the house but the settlement as a whole, yet many urban designers employed by the state or NGOs are made to produce only house type plans and a site plan locating each house. If house designs included a pattern book of common spaces found in informal settlements, beneficiaries of slum redevelopment are unlikely to oppose their inclusion. However, the

### BOX 1

### KONGAR NAGAR FAMILY LOSES OUT BECAUSE OF BSUP LOGIC

The Sarkar family comprising a widowed mother and three adult married sons living on a three *katah* plot as an extended family of 13 members. They have managed to add to and upgrade their home as per the evolving needs. Each household has a habitable room, a kitchen and share two common toilets and multiple courtyards. This family will be one of the higher income families in the Kongar Nagar-I settlement; the sons run their own businesses and are able to afford the BSUP houses. However, the BSUP logic of beneficiary selection prevented this family from enjoying the benefits of a new BSUP home as the plot when divided by four households is less than one *katah* per household (*Source: ACE 2013*).

Self-built, flexible home of the Sarkar family in Kalyani even as BSUP failed them

### BOX 2

### A FAMILY'S PERCEPTION OF THE NEW DEVELOPMENT IN NAYAPALLI, BHUBANESWAR

The Naik family has a thatched, mud house comprising two rooms, a verandah and kitchen. They received two BSUP houses in the name of their two sons. Despite this, the family continues to stay in the old thatched house, which has 280 sq. ft. floor space. According to the matriarch of the family, the old house is more suited to their needs and is convenient for everyone. They have a separate semi-outdoor kitchen in the corner of the verandah; the BSUP house proposed a kitchen in the corner of one of the rooms, which was unacceptable to them. The lack of water supply and a working toilet in the BSUP house despite being part of the proposal has disappointed them. Moreover, the family had sought a design change in the house layout that they did not get; they wanted the toilet to be accessible from the verandah outside and not from inside the rooms. The eldest married son believed the *pucca* house is a good investment for his daughter's future and a safe place to store some furniture. But he did not think it was comfortable (*see images 4 and 5*).

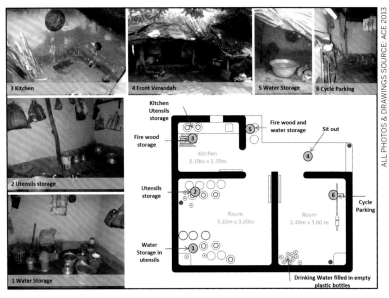

ALL PHOTOS & DRAWINGS SOURCE: ACE 2013

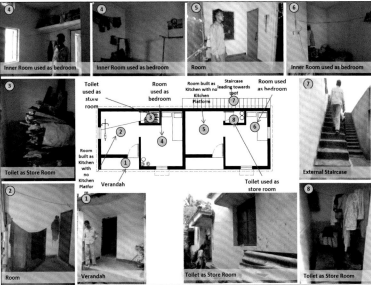

*Top:* Image 4 - Mrs. Naik's old house where the family prefers to stay instead of the new BSUP house in Nayapalli, Bhubaneswar
*Bottom:* Image 5 - Mrs. Naik's new BSUP house which the family feel is uncomfortable for living

# Being pedestrian-friendly is considered the most significant criterion for achieving low-carbon cities

question of their maintenance and supervision are potential problem areas, which need to be resolved through dialogue between neighbours and neighbourhood women's and other community groups.

BSUP, in spite of its focus on individual houses or dwelling units, failed to provide for mixed-use housing or different typologies based on family types and transactional needs. Since all units are essentially the same, with no house level open space, people in ground floor dwelling units encroached on leftover common space to make their houses more habitable. The apartment typologies provided were typically unsuitable for home-based work that generates income (e.g., banana/jackfruit chips making/cooking for large-scale catering orders). Such activities also generate garbage whose disposal continues to be a problem in every BSUP housing unit. If a truly participatory process that involved women, children and men was followed in evolving the flat and building types as per community needs, the new housing could have improved living conditions and would have removed the hardships related to home-based work.

The lessons to be drawn for design professionals include innovating spatial types for different cultural, climatological and morphological contexts, to allow for internal flexibility and adaptation for the diverse domestic and home-based income-generating activities of the family and for different life-stage needs. This would mean:
**a)** Improving the community feedback loops of built projects
**b)** Providing opportunities and institutional spaces for citizen participation in design and planning
**c)** Building the capacity of local architects as well as ULBs to work with families in a participatory manner to develop not only diverse house designs but also sustainable community designs.

The example of such a process-oriented project that custom-designed each family's infill house (though common spaces were left out of the participatory design process), is to be found in the work of architect Prasanna Desai and the Alliance comprising SPARC-Mahila Milan and National Slum Dwellers Federation in the context of BSUP housing in Pune. Lessons can also be learnt from the innovative and adaptive informal practices of house building by slum dwellers who understand the reuse potential of everyday materials and the creative use of every inch of space for storage, spiritual and aesthetic needs. •

## SPONTANEOUS SLUMS

# Interfacing Planning and Emergence

**Shruti Hemani** and **David Rudlin** argue that the most seemingly spontaneous, informal habitats are actually being shaped by elements of leadership and planning

**Residents' aspirations as reflected in the decor of informal settlements**

Humans have the innate ability to build cities. As a social species, it is hardwired into us. Up until the modern age, we used this ability to create some of the most beautiful settlements – mostly without the help of planners or architects and indeed without any clear plan of what it was we were creating – but not anymore. Today, settlements are more likely to be the self-referential towers of Dubai or the exclusive gated suburbs of America. They are increasingly dominated by the world-class global capital, which takes less interest in place or community and sees buildings as investment instruments sold to the highest bidder.

We must use the analogy of climax vegetation to explore the way humans traditionally created cities and how this might be harnessed to create an alternative to such approaches. According to this analogy, in every ecosystem, land that is left undisturbed will develop into a state of mature broad-leaf woodland, rainforest or grassland and will stay that way until conditions change. Similarly, climax states of human settlements emerge across the world to suit local climatic and social conditions through a very human process of incremental change, spontaneity and negotiation. If true, this process has been severely undermined by the well-meaning agency of the planning system and overwhelmed by the power of the market. There is, however, a place where it can

still be studied: in the development of informal settlements that accounts for a third of the worldwide annual production of housing.

One must be careful, however, not to romanticise these slums since, in the worst of them, the living conditions are truly miserable. Yet they are examples of human resilience where their residents see them as places of opportunity where they can get a toehold in the city. This is as true of Dharavi in Mumbai, Rocinha in Rio or Makoko in Lagos as it was for Little Ireland in the Manchester of the 1930s or the Rookeries of Victorian London. We, therefore, go beyond the politics of land occupation and seeming disorder to ask whether the way in which slums are being built in the developing world is so different to the way that London and Paris were developed in the 17th century or the industrial cities in the 19th century. Is what we currently witness in the slums not some modern aberration but the centuries old, messy, unpleasant business of city building? Our studies (compiled in the book *Climax City*) reveal that the form and structure of historic cities is similar to modern slums. Give the latter a few centuries and maybe they will also become beautiful, functional towns and cities. This, of course, is not inevitable (some slums never improve) and this can take many years, but it is an age-old process. Rather than lament or idealise urban informality, perhaps

**The residents see these slums as places of opportunity where they can get a toehold in the city**

we need to understand the process by which it takes place.

Informal settlements are complex urban forms that are gradually changing and evolving to meet the needs of their communities through several interlinked processes of self-organisation. They are human habitats created not through planning or design but through the interplay of relatively simple rules and forces. Small differences of culture, climate or local circumstances can change these rules and lead to different outcomes, but the world settlements created this way are more similar than they are different. Rather than being planned, they are the result of millions of decisions taken by individuals and families to make themselves more secure and safe, to improve their lives, to protect their privacy, to sell their goods, to flaunt their achievements, indeed to express all manner of human needs and desires. On one level this is similar to a termite mound and science can teach us much about how these self-organising systems function. However, even settlements that are entirely unplanned are the result of human interaction, something infinitely more complex than the handful of pheromone signals used by insects.

## Observing Five Slums in Guwahati

To understand this process, we studied the formation and evolution of five slums in Guwahati, capital of the Assam province in Northeast India. Combining morphological analysis with personal interviews and community group discussions illuminates important findings. It was clear that, unlike termite colonies, humans form community organisations that are able to exert a degree of control over the settlement and to shape the way that it is occupied, built and improved. While it may be a stretch to call what they do as town planning, they are usually able to envisage a future vision for their settlement that is better than what they currently have and also work towards it.

These settlements are not, therefore, solely emergent structures that are the blind result of individual decisions. There is an element of planning, however informal and inadequate this may be. There is also a strong element of complexity at play because their residents have limited control over what happens, which accounts for the similarities between different slums and between slums and traditional urban areas. Informal settlements are therefore rather a combination of emergent behaviour and human cooperation. It is this unique mix that creates human settlements. Through reviewing the case studies in Guwahati we were able to break this process down into a series of stages:

## Occupation

The most fundamental decision is the location of the slum because, of course, somebody initially had to decide to occupy the land. Each of the case study areas had survived for some time (one for 150 years) so by that test, at least, they were in a good location. Talking to residents it was clear that the 'best' locations were not necessarily the most advantageous places because on those one risked being thrown out by developers. Ideally, one wanted land close to work opportunities that no one else was concerned about or which could not be developed due to difficult site conditions or conflicted ownership or designation. Many slums are founded in

**Stages of growth GUWAHATI:** The gradual, overlapping and assertive stages of growth of the informal spontaneous settlements can be marked out as: occupation, appropriation, transformation, consolidation and saturation

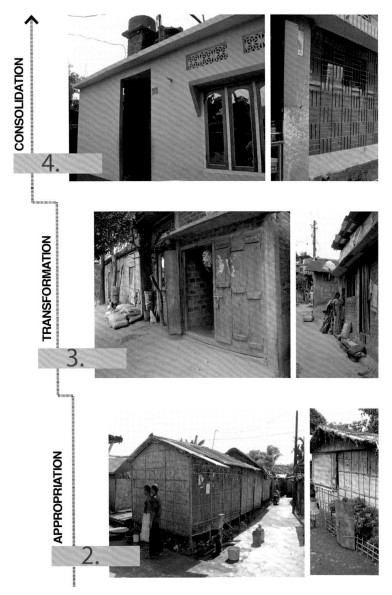

CONSOLIDATION

4.

TRANSFORMATION

3.

APPROPRIATION

2.

peripheral locations where the pressures on space are less intense. However, even these may soon become engulfed in the expanding city and appropriated for development. This is a complex process because, while someone at some point will have made a decision to found each slum, there will at any time be thousands of people looking for an opportunity to squeeze them out. The established slums are therefore a self-selecting group.

## Appropriation

Having found a suitable site, the next step involves the appropriation of the land to establish the slum. The oral histories of the slum dwellers revealed that an important part of the process concerns 'founder families'. Most slums have a small number of larger plots in the best locations. The families who first established the slum and who retain a leadership role in the community occupy them. These families often control who is allowed to settle in the slum and which plots they are allocated. They become the leaders of the community association, sometimes collecting rent and even dispensing justice. This process of allocating plots and regulating what can be built determines the physical form of the settlement. The main streets tend to be the original pathways that crossed the site but the way in which each new structure is fitted in and the way that it relates to these public routes and to its neighbours is controlled by the founder family and through traditional customs. In this way, the larger settlements develop a labyrinthine but complex street network with a hierarchy that any urban designer would recognise.

## Transformation

These slums are the result of constant change. They are never finished and never stay the same for long. The driver for this incremental process of change tends to be the individual home. Houses start off as a single flexible space, similar to a rural dwelling, in which all of the family's activities take place. As the family's fortunes wax or wane, the space evolves. Hard times might see spaces subdivided and sublet, while improving fortunes will see temporary materials replaced with more permanent ones and spaces extended upwards, perhaps allowing the ground floor to be turned into a shop. As the family prospers, they will increasingly be able to divide private functions from public areas and to appropriate the public realm outside their home to express their status and increased sense of ownership. Collectively, all individual changes to the home feed into the evolution of the neighbourhood.

As with the homes, the external spaces are never finished. There is a constant trade-off between internal space and the public realm, the limits being imposed by custom or shared agreement. This includes boundaries beyond which no one would extend their home (which becomes a common building line), or the location of the community courtyards and even spaces for refuse. This is linked to infrastructure works such as lighting and sanitation and to public facilities such as a community hall or even a school. Everything will develop and evolve through a process of incremental change, constantly working towards a position where everything is optimised even though this point will never be reached.

## Consolidation/Saturation

For many slums, the process of gradual transformation leads to their consolidation if tenure becomes available to residents. It gives households a sense of security and also allows them to invest in their home and in the settlement as a whole. Over time, the process of consolidation will turn the slum into 'respectable' neighbourhoods, indistinguishable from many other parts of Indian cities and tend to resemble the 'natural towns'. However, not all slums are fortunate enough to consolidate. Some never manage to achieve tenure and exist in a state of perpetual uncertainty. This lack of security prevents the process of consolidation. Other slums are the victims of their own success because they attract more and more people and reach a point of saturation. In one of the case studies the population density exceeded 1,500 persons per hectare, which puts huge pressure on basic services and utilities as well as community ties. However, it is probably misleading to use the word saturation because it implies a point when the slum cannot absorb any more people whereas in reality there is no way to stop more people from arriving. This process of saturation also makes it very difficult for slums to consolidate.

## Spontaneous Settlements as Emergent Systems

The above study gives an insight into the contradiction that even the most spontaneous settlements are shaped by leadership and planning while also being complex and emergent systems. This interaction between planning and emergence we believe to be at work, not only in the slums, but in all human settlements including the great cities of the developed world.

Cities may be built one building at a time, but the people deciding where and what to build do so with

**Other slums are the victims of their own success because they attract more and more people and reach a point of saturation**

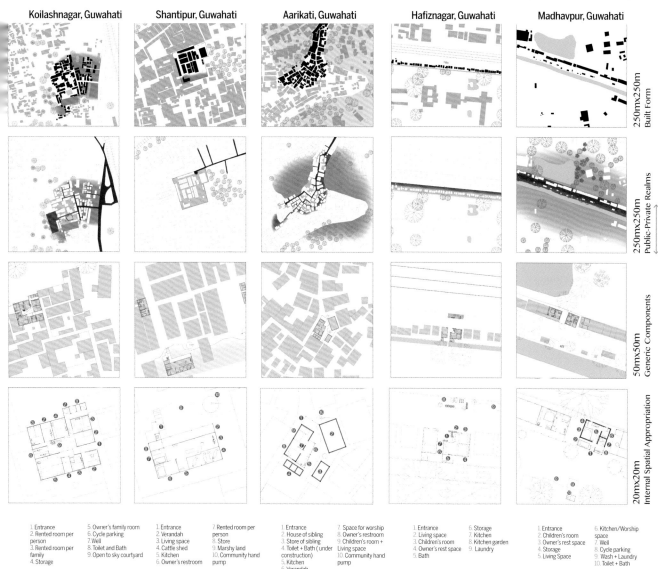

Koilashnagar, Guwahati | Shantipur, Guwahati | Aarikati, Guwahati | Hafiznagar, Guwahati | Madhavpur, Guwahati

250m×250m Built Form
250m×250m Public-Private Realms
50m×50m Generic Components
20m×20m Internal Spatial Appropriation

1. Entrance
2. Rented room per person
3. Rented room per family
4. Storage
5. Owner's family room
6. Cycle parking
7. Well
8. Toilet and Bath
9. Open to sky courtyard

1. Entrance
2. Verandah
3. Living space
4. Cattle shed
5. Kitchen
6. Owner's restroom
7. Rented room per person
8. Store
9. Marshy land
10. Community hand pump

1. Entrance
2. House of sibling
3. Store of sibling
4. Toilet + Bath (under construction)
5. Kitchen
6. Verandah
7. Space for worship
8. Owner's restroom
9. Children's room + Living space
10. Community hand pump

1. Entrance
2. Living space
3. Children's room
4. Owner's rest space
5. Bath
6. Storage
7. Kitchen
8. Kitchen garden
9. Laundry

1. Entrance
2. Children's room
3. Owner's rest space
4. Storage
5. Living Space
6. Kitchen/Worship space
7. Well
8. Cycle parking
9. Wash + Laundry
10. Toilet + Bath

a social framework that requires negotiation with others. In the formal city this may mean obtaining a building permit or planning permission. In an informal settlement it means getting the permission of the community leaders or just negotiating with the neighbours. In interceding these 'permissions' the authorities and the community will apply future concepts of how they would like the settlement to be. These might be idealised utopias or just a desire to avoid deterioration and decline. If informal settlements were allowed to develop for many years to reach a climax state, some of the slums that we have studied may grow into a form of urbanism very similar to the older parts of our modern cities. It is true that the climax city process has given us some of the most beautiful towns and cities in the world

but this is far from being the inevitable outcome.

We cannot leave the city to its own devices because the climax state of modern capitalism is not something that we should accept. At the same time we should not delude ourselves that we can devise a perfect alternative because all of our experience tells us that the task is impossible. We therefore need to look more closely at the interaction between planning and natural urban growth and rethink the way that we plan cities to shape rather than seize climax city process. Planning can set the parameters and conditions for complex urban growth to produce more benign outcomes. This was perhaps recognised in the past but has been lost in the modern planning systems. It is a vital art that we need to rediscover. ●

*(From the forthcoming book* Climax City: Master planning and the Complexity of Urban Growth. *Publisher: RIBA Publishing. Authors: David Rudlin & Shruti Hemani)*

# Empowering Migrant Communities to Secure Housing

**Banashree Banerjee** and **Maartje van Eerd** take a look at how women's savings groups helped migrants resettle in better homes

Community groups in Yangon, Myanmar, have been instrumental in the setting up of pilot housing projects. The projects themselves are small, but they represent a different way of solving the housing problem for poor urban migrants in a country that is grappling with very rapid socio-political changes and economic liberalisation simultaneously. Above all, the projects stand out for demonstration of a down-to-earth collaborative approach, in which migrant households are supported by a local NGO, Women for the World (WFW), to save for housing and procure land collectively. They then work with young architects to generate their own settlement designs and incremental housing solutions with a fraction of the cost incurred in public housing for the poor in Myanmar. This initiative, to be better understood, needs to be placed in the wider context of city development, migration, poverty and housing options in Yangon.

## Promises and challenges of housing poor migrants in Yangon

"We will establish, as quickly as possible, a programme for the rehousing of homeless migrants, who have moved to the cities as a result of natural disasters, economic opportunities and land confiscation." This is one of the promises made by the National League for Democracy (NLD) in its 2015 election manifesto. In one sentence, the manifesto sums up the development issues in Myanmar and its resolve to address the most pressing need in cities: housing thousands of migrants. Yangon, the largest city,

PHOTO: BANASHREE BANERJEE

PHOTO: BANASHREE BANERJEE

PHOTO: MAARTJE VAN EERD

*Clockwise, starting from Left:*
- **A typical family in North Okkalpa project**
- **Htantapin project**
- **Children in Htantapin project**

PHOTOS: MAARTJE VAN EERD

the erstwhile national capital and business and industrial centre of Myanmar, has always attracted its share of migrants, but events in the last decade have stimulated a huge upsurge of migration. It began with Cyclone Nargis, which devastated the Ayeyarwady Delta region in 2008. Yangon was the obvious destination for thousands of people who lost their homes and livelihoods. And then came the withdrawal of military rule in 2011 after five decades and the opening up of the country to private and foreign investment at breakneck speed. Industries, trade and commerce, resurgence of education and the accompanying construction, centred mostly in and around Yangon, continue to generate job opportunities, attracting migrants from all over Myanmar.

But the one thing that Yangon does not offer its steady stream of poor migrants is housing that they can afford with their low wages and escalating land prices. The growing number of people living in informal, insecure and environmentally precarious situations is testimony to the lack of formal housing options. The military regime had tried to cope with the problem by evicting squatters

and relocating some of them to the city's fringes. Even when public housing was constructed by the Department of Urban and Housing Development (DUHD), it was never sufficient in relation to the numbers. So, the NLD's election manifesto obviously caught the attention of voters by flagging the importance of housing for migrants. The NLD came into power with a thumping majority in the December 2015 national elections and formed the government in March 2016.

What is the new government doing about housing migrants in Yangon? Soon after taking office, the new Yangon Region Chief Minister gave an interview to *Mizzima Weekly* (April 28, 2016) in which he expressed great concern for "people who have nowhere to live and nothing to eat." He emphasised that it is important to "compile reliable information on homeless and jobless people in order to help those people." He also expressed concern that building huts informally for migrants has become a business, creating additional difficulties to finding a solution. Finally, he expressed the determination of his government to solve the problems. As a starting point, there seems

*Clockwise, starting from Top Left :*
- **Children in Htantapin project**
- **Bead embroidery in North Okkalapa project**
- **Fire-fighting preparedness in Htantapin project**

to be an understanding that evictions will not take place unless people can be resettled. The new government has continued the already committed task of the previous government of building affordable housing directly and through various PPP (puplic private partnership) arrangements in the old top-down supply-driven model. The pace of projects has been stepped up, but the scale is still nowhere near the need and, more importantly, the housing being produced is, by the government's own admission, much beyond the affordability of a vast majority of the city's population. The Construction and Housing Development Bank (CHDB) was set up to make housing affordable to the poor through credit schemes. But the poor do not fulfil the loan eligibility criteria set by the bank.

In the meantime, informal housing continues to grow rapidly in Yangon. According to DUHD, there were 153 slum settlements in Yangon in 2010. A 2016 slum mapping exercise of UN-Habitat identified 423 settlements with a population of about 364,315. This is considered a conservative figure in comparison with the estimate of Yangon City Development Committee (YCDC) of 400,000 persons living in informal settlements without basic services. Most of these settlements are in the peripheral townships, inhabited either by migrants or evictees from the city centre. A typical settlement consists of shacks made of bamboo mats and recycled material built on stilts on swampy, low-lying land with a variety of tenure conditions like insecure renting and migrants who live in floodable settlements on the banks of rivers, creeks and drains.

In spite of growing job opportunities in Yangon and particularly in the suburban townships, the poverty level is 34% (World Bank). Many of the poor, particularly migrants, are not counted or included for government programmes for housing, health and education, as they are not registered as residents where they live. Further, a Save the Children study in three townships (Lives on Loan, 2016) found, among other vulnerability indicators, a high level of indebtedness even for day-to-day survival as well as a large number of households headed by women.

## WFW and the community housing process

In 2004 WFW, the Yangon based NGO, had already found that squatter communities were crippled with informal debts, with interest rates as high as 20%. Many were on the verge of eviction, having fallen behind on the relatively high rents demanded by landlords. WFW convinced slum women from Hlaing Thar Yar township to counter

PHOTO: MAARTJE VAN EERD

**International trainees from an IHS course with the community in North Okkalapa project**

this exploitation by developing their own savings groups with small daily savings of 100 to 200 MMK (1,000 Myanmar Kyats or MMK = US $0.73). Soon, these women had enough to start distributing low-interest loans to members of their savings collective, first towards paying off outstanding debts and then to buy sewing machines or livestock, or to make small upgrades to their homes. The number of savings groups increased and spread to two other townships.

Then WFW took up the work of rehabilitating a network of 15 villages devastated by Cyclone Nargis in 2008 with support from the Asian Coalition for Community Action (ACCA) project. The experience gained in those villages in setting up women's savings groups, establishing rice banks and rebuilding destroyed houses, roads and bridges with village communities was the precursor to taking the leap from supporting savings groups to land and housing in Yangon.

Again, with the assistance of the ACCA project, WFW acquired the skills to work with the tools used all over Asia by Asian Coalition for Housing Rights (ACHR), which implemented ACCA in 150 cities in 15 Asian countries to support community groups to find their own housing solutions. The process starts with community mapping and forming savings groups. When the groups have saved enough, they set up a housing committee, look for land and buy it and build their own houses. Daw Van Lizar, the co-founder of WFW asserts that, "Mapping is a tool for building a community's understanding of where they live and for people to come together and understand – by working together – what their possibilities are for building a better community. Group savings are an effective tool to improve leadership skills, financial management … it builds trust within the community, it contributes to team building, consensus decision making, teamwork, transparency, accountability, literacy, problem solving, self-reliance and confidence of marginalised and vulnerable women at the grass-roots level." WFW uses a peer learning approach to multiply savings groups as an essential step towards social and financial empowerment and then secure housing. Those who wish to join the housing committee have to save regularly for a year. To be eligible, they should be poor and not own land anywhere. The next step is to look for cheap land, buy it and start building on it.

WFW used ACCA funding to create the Yangon City Fund, from which groups could borrow money on the strength of their own savings to buy land and build houses. The ACCA link has also enabled WFW to build the capacity of savings group members through exchange visits to countries like Thailand and Sri Lanka. So far WFW has supported three community housing projects in Yangon since 2010: 20 families in Hlaing Thar Yar Township, 30 families in North Okkalapa Township and 48 families in Htantapin Township as well as another project in Mandalay.

## Zooming in on two projects:
### Pyit Taing Htaung housing project in Yoe Lay Ward, Hlaing Thar Yar Township
The community in Pyit Taing Htaung in Hlaing Thar Yar Township moved to Yangon after Cyclone Nargis in the Ayeyarwady Delta. They first moved into Ale Yaw Ward as squatters, where they were eventually fed up of repeated demolitions. Forming the savings group helped them come together and look for cheap land. They finally found a suitable piece of agricultural land nearby (just 6,600 sq. ft.) after a year of surveying and negotiating with the landowner. A loan from the newly set up Yangon City Fund helped them purchase the land, which was enough for 20 families. Then, with help from WFW and design support from community architects from ACHR, the women designed their new community's layout plan and simple inexpensive bamboo and thatch houses, which they could build with a loan of 700,000 MMK (US $833 at that time). It took them three months to build the houses and put in pathways and toilets with shared sceptic tanks. The houses are 15 x 35 sq. ft. each in size and continue to be improved incrementally by the owners.

### PanTha Zin housing project in Hta Won Bae Ward, North Okkalapa Township
North Okkalapa Township was one of the satellite towns established in 1959 in the eastern part of Yangon. Hta Won Bae Ward consisted of farmland, located outside the city limits, isolated from it and with underdeveloped infrastructure. In 1962, 250 evicted squatter families from Downtown Yangon were able to negotiate with the government to get farmlands in the ward as part of a relocation package. They then subdivided the land into smaller plots and sold it informally or built rooms that they rented out. Later, the government

PHOTOS: VAN LIZAR

*Clockwise, starting from Top Left:*
**Hlaing Tar Yar Township**
- **Mapping vacant land**
- **Household survey by savings group**
- **Community workshop facilitated by young architects**
- **Land purchased for the project**

PHOTO: BANASHREE BANERJEE

PHOTO: VAN LIZAR

included Hta Won Bae ward in the urban area and changed its zoning from farmland to residential. With the expansion of the city more people started moving into this area and infrastructure improved with access to electricity, water and sewerage.

The women's savings group in the township consisted of renters living in different wards. After saving for a year, they got together to form the housing committee, which was able to find 20,000 sq. ft. (100 x 200) of agricultural land and despite rising prices, paid only 11 million MMK (US $13,095), with a loan from the City Fund. The committee selected the poorest households for the project. Awn Ra, a master's student from IHS, found in her research in 2016 that these households are all from the same ethnic background; the household size is between four to six, many are daily wage earners, with household income ranging between 150,000 to 300,000 MMK. Indebtedness used to be a big problem till they formed the savings groups. The women indicated that collective savings had strengthened them, although managing the group was not easy. At a certain stage accounting mistakes and disagreements almost brought the group to a standstill. But they managed to learn from their mistakes and moved on with encouragement and training from WFW.

The community organised a workshop to plan the layout of the new area and the design of their new houses with help from community architects from ACHR. Other squatter communities, villagers, architects and engineers also attended the workshop, having seen and heard about the Pyit Taing Htaung project. The houses were built with a loan of 700,000 MMK (US$ 883 at that time) from the City Fund. There are 30 houses in the project site, which are all 10 x 18 sq. ft. in size arranged in clusters of six houses facing small lanes and a community hall. All structures are built with wooden posts and trusses with bamboo mat or plastic sheet walls and corrugated iron roofs. Each house has a toilet behind the house, with three houses sharing a septic tank. The houses are built on stilts as the land is floodable, like in the rest of the ward and most other places where the poor live. Now the community, among the poorest in Yangon, is negotiating with the Cooperative Department of the township for co-operative tenure and is being helped by the ward councillor in the process. It is an upwardly mobile community with homes, jobs and home-based economic activities.

## Learning lessons

There is no doubt that these first community-planned and community-built urban poor housing projects demonstrate a new model of collective secure housing for the poorest landless migrants in Yangon's peripheral slums. They materialised because the women's savings groups managed to buy inexpensive land on the city's periphery when prices were still relatively low and build three small projects, with the support of WFW and ACCA. But since then, land prices have escalated many times and as of now it has become impossible for the poor to buy land in the same way. Can this initiative then provide a way forward for the vast numbers of the poor who need secure housing? Perhaps not in the same way, but there are many lessons here that can provide a way forward.

Collective savings are a good starting point for communities to build confidence and ability to invest in housing and deal with local authorities

*Left:* **Slum in North Okkalapa Township**
*Right:* **Building houses in Hlaing Tar Yar project**

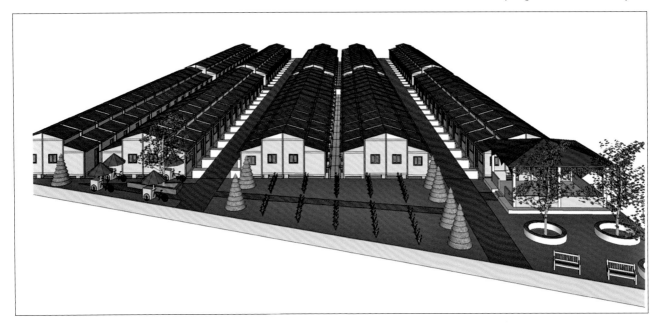

*Clockwise from Top:*
**North Okkalapa project**
**- Community's layout drawn**
  **by architects**
**- Water harvesting**
**- Carpenter at work**

to acquire services and secure tenure. Awn Ra found that the projects provide tenure security through collective land ownership and this provided them with opportunities to invest in their houses. This is in line with literature that states that collective land tenure also strengthens community processes that can help households to make the challenging transition from informal to formal and provides protection against market forces (Boonyabancha, 2009).

Small innovations made by people in their houses are also worth noting for their contribution to improving the quality of life. For instance, windows are placed for the comfort of people sitting or sleeping on the floor and empty plastic bottles are recycled for making water harvesting arrangements.

And of course, the most important consideration is production of liveable housing for a fraction of the amount invested in public housing.

Most remarkable is the collaboration between the community, architects and the NGO to evolve affordable housing solutions. This is what now brings architecture students to these projects from institutions in Myanmar and other countries to learn how to work with poor community groups to evolve design solutions.

With the coming of the new government in Myanmar, there is an interest in looking at such housing solutions for the poor and an acknowledgement that working with community groups may be a move in the right direction towards greater housing sufficiency. ●

# Housing Transformation in Resettlement Sites

**Imran Hossain Foishal** and **Maartje van Eerd** present evidence from Bangladesh and India on the importance of placing livelihoods at the centre of resettlement planning and to provide opportunities for incremental development

Worldwide urban development, and particularly infrastructure construction, is the principal cause for development-induced displacement. The number of people affected is increasing, impacting the poorest and most marginalised groups like those living in inner city slums without any form of security of tenure, leaving many of them even poorer than before.

One of the biggest challenges in resettlement is the fact that people are moved far from their original location, and cannot continue with their jobs, with women being even more severely affected than men. In addition, when they do continue with their original jobs, travel costs go up, which is an extra burden. One of the ways to deal with the loss of income is through transforming the house in order to create income-earning opportunities and to restore some of the lost income.

This article deals with the extremes of affordability and discusses how former slum dwellers cope with their new living environment in resettlement sites. It will present evidence on the importance of providing opportunities for incremental development for restoring livelihoods and creating assets for those affected by zooming in on two cases: one from Bangladesh and one from India.

## Housing transformation and its importance for livelihoods

When resettlement does not consider livelihood restoration, resettlers struggle to cope with inadequate service provisions and lack of access

> One of the biggest challenges in resettlement is the fact that people are moved far from their original location, so that they cannot continue with their jobs

Housing units in Chennai

to jobs. In such cases they react in different ways: adaptation, transformation and mobility. The case studies show the interventions people make to adjust their housing to their needs and how that contributes to the restoration of their livelihoods. Also, it discusses the moving out of early resettlers due to their inability to cope with the loss of access to employment and also the assets that are eventually created for those that managed to survive in the resettlement site.

### Case 1: Mandartola resettlement site, Gopalgonj, Bangladesh

The resettlers of the Mandartola resettlement site originated from a slum at Gopalganj Sadar comprising of 1,935 people and 387 households. In October 2009, the slum dwellers were forcibly evicted and rendered homeless. Houses were destroyed, many people lost their social networks, access to services and some lost their jobs and sources of income. After living on the streets for more than five years, 138 of the affected households were resettled on the Mandartola resettlement site in 2014. The site is located at the periphery of the city and around 10 kilometres from their previous settlement, physically isolated from other settlements by the Dhaka-Gopalganj highway. Every resettler was given a 35-square-metre housing unit with the facilities of one bedroom, one living/dining room, one kitchen, one toilet and an open veranda. Each building block has two separate units, constructed on a raised concrete platform with a brick wall and corrugated iron sheet roofing. No utility services such as drinking water and electricity are available at the location.

### Economic impact of resettlement

More than half of the respondents became jobless and lost their source of income after resettlement (56%), and half of them (54%), mostly women (77%), were still jobless after four years. Before resettlement, in many families, both husband and wife worked and contributed towards the monthly household income. Many women worked as domestic workers, but had to give up those jobs because of the remoteness of the new location and the time and money it would cost to commute. As a result, the monthly household income of 62% of the respondents had decreased. In addition to this, their daily commuting cost to social amenities such as the bazaar, hospital and school increased. Compared to their previous settlement where the majority (70%) of the respondents did not spend any money on daily commuting, after resettlement more than half (60%) of the respondents had to spend 36–50 BDT (Bangladeshi Takas) a day (figures 1 & 2). As a result, those households fell further into impoverishment.

### The social impact of resettlement

Because many of the resettlers (62%) were relocated together, their social networks were less affected. For those who were not resettled together with their neighbours, their social ties were negatively impacted. Also, due to the isolated location at the periphery of the city, 56% of respondents did not have any relatives and friends

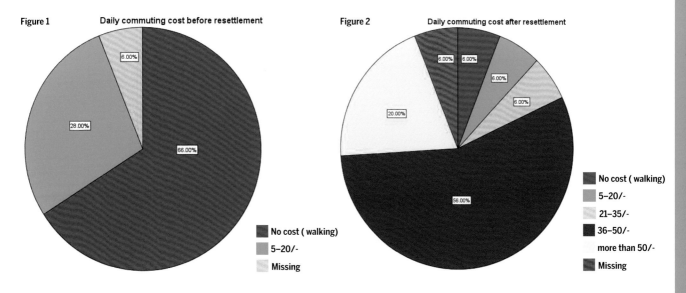

Figure 1 — Daily commuting cost before resettlement

- No cost ( walking)
- 5–20/-
- Missing

Figure 2 — Daily commuting cost after resettlement

- No cost ( walking)
- 5–20/-
- 21–35/-
- 36–50/-
- more than 50/-
- Missing

nearby the resettlement site, so they had no one to fall back on in times of need. Moreover, people became more marginalised in terms of lower socio-economic status in the new location due to joblessness and income loss.

### Spatial transformation of housing to restore livelihoods

As income after resettlement had decreased, one of the strategies resettlers developed to minimise their income loss was to transform their housing units in order to generate some extra income through home-based economic activities, as well as to reduce expenditure. Resettlers who transformed their housing are more involved in additional home-based economic activities and expenditure reduction activities. Not only did a reduction in household income lead people to transform their house, people

**Culture and lifestyle also play a role in the need to make changes to the public space in the area**

174

who were already struggling to make ends meet also seemed to have been more inclined to this option to enhance their income. For instance, 36% of the resettlers transformed their verandas into income-generating spaces such as retail shops and working space for producing paper packets.

On the other hand, to minimise income loss, some transformations also took place at a settlement level such as the construction of outdoor kitchens, cattle sheds and the planting of vegetation for consumption. Those transformations helped them to reduce their expenditure in order to meet their monthly spending. About 66% of households have been involved in this type of activity. Women in Mandartola are the main actors of these home-based economic activities. As women were more affected by the loss of income, these activities helped them to partially restore their livelihoods.

## Spatial transformation of housing to meet social needs

Transformations are also driven by social needs. In Mandartola, 44% of the resettlers constructed additional rooms for expanding families or separate bedrooms as their children grew up. About 60% of respondents functionally changed their housing units, which ranged from changing living rooms,

kitchens and verandas into bedrooms.

Social needs also influence people to initiate transformations collectively at the settlement level. Examples of these collective initiatives are the construction of a mosque, a temple, a school and tube-wells for water provisions. Culture and lifestyle also play a role in the need to make changes to the public space in the area. Open spaces within the settlement are types of resources that contribute to the creation of social capital. Resettlers use their outdoor space for household domestic work such as drying of laundry, drying of spices, communal space for sitting and chatting, as areas for children to play and for the organisation of social events like marriages, religious festivals, funerals and after death rituals.

*Case 2: Bhim Nagar resettlement site, Chennai, India*

Bhim Nagar is a resettlement site in Chennai. In the late 1980s about 15,000 slum and pavement dwellers were relocated to the site from many different localities in the city centre. They were rehoused 15 kilometres away, outside the Chennai Corporation border, on a site that used to be part of a lake, which was partly filled up by the Chennai Corporation, but flooded during the rains.

*Left:* Functional changes in housing
*Right:* Social infrastructure constructed by the resettlers

The Tamil Nadu State Government and the Government of India financed the project and the Tamil Nadu Slum Clearance Board (TNSCB) was the implementing agency. Development of the site and construction units was carried out in four phases between the late 1980s and early 1990s. The site was still under construction when the first resettlers moved into the area. At the time of moving in, the roads were unpaved and would flood during the monsoons, which made it impossible for water trucks to enter. As no waste was being collected, the inhabitants used to throw their waste in the neighbouring lake or burn it. Several communities from different localities were relocated in the same site, which led to tension and conflict between the various groups. And their local leaders were in conflict over who was in charge of Bhim Nagar. Also, there was a lively trade in drugs and liquor.

Every family was given a house of 4.5 by 5.5 metres. They had to pay Rs. 66 as land cost and Rs. 10 for maintenance per month over 21 years, after which they would receive a title deed.

### Plot transfers in 1989–1990

A survey conducted in 1989–1999 revealed that there was an active trade in plots. Seventy-six percent of the respondents in the random survey were original allottees, 19% had bought a plot and 5% were tenants. In some parts of the resettlement site, the transfer of plots was even as high as 36%, possibly because of the particularly active involvement in the 'plot business' of the local leaders.

Many of the original allottees generally left Bhim Nagar due to lack of access to employment and proper transportation facilities. People were working as informal daily labourers in construction and as coolies at train stations, often requiring proximity to the city centre. Others were working as fishermen and used to live in slums close to the seaside. Women were also heavily impacted. Many of them used to work as domestic workers close to their homes in the slums. Later, because of the distance, they had to abandon their jobs as it was impossible to combine them with their household responsibilities. Those who were unable to find alternative employment moved back to the city and sold or rented out their plot on the site.

On the other hand, buyers came to Bhim Nagar because they realised that over time the area would improve and land prices would rise, as the area would be integrated in the city. Some only bought a plot as an investment and rented it out to others. Some moved in a bit later when it was more developed and still others only bought it to rent it out. As tenants were ineligible to resettlement, they

Veranda converted into bedroom and open space in front of the house used for household work in Bangladesh

**Original allottee's house
without transformations**

had no other option than to rent a place in Bhim Nagar when their settlements were demolished.

Several local leaders in Bhim Nagar played a mediating role in the trade of plots, which was a profitable business. They were involved in reconstruction and selling of houses and plots and the contractual arrangements between buyers and sellers.

## Housing transformation in 2017

Another survey was conducted in Bhim Nagar in 2017 with households who were living at the same address since 1999–2000. By now the area had transformed immensely. Although there were some households that were still experiencing the same conditions they had in 1999, overall the outlook of the area and the quality of housing had totally changed. Many houses were expanded to several floors, some were merged into bigger ones, verandas and rooftops were constructed and roads were paved.

The survey revealed that the number of original allottees had decreased considerably when compared to 1989–1999 from about 30% as compared to 76%. The number of tenants had also decreased, although less drastically, from 5% to 0.5%, which presumably is not totally correct as observations revealed the number of rooms has gone up considerably. It is suspected that respondents are hiding the true number of tenants. There is also a discrepancy between original allottees and new tenants who were using the same door numbers. The number of buyers has gone up drastically from 19% in 1998–1999 to about 70% in 2017.

Only 4% of the original allottees have paid

off their full instalment. In those cases, people are entitled to receive an allotment order handed out by the Tamil Nadu Slum Clearance Board. In reality, only seven respondents received an official document. Most respondents are unaware of the procedures and the fact that they are entitled to receiving this document upon full payment. However, even without official ownership documents, 37% of the original allottees transformed their house.

More than half of the buyers (61%) transformed their house, mostly because the quality of the house was considered poor and too small. Roofs were changed, houses were plastered, extra floors and verandas were added, bathrooms were constructed and internal designs altered. Most transformations are made either to accommodate a growing family or for renting out rooms. There are for instance a substantial number of people from Manipur who work in the neighbouring malls and parlours and rent rooms in Bhim Nagar. That way the transformation provides for extra income-earning opportunities, creating assets for people who never had any earlier. So this is a means to move out of poverty for those who managed to survive the very tough early years after resettlement.

## Conclusion

As research has shown, resettlement often leads to impoverishment for the overall majority of those affected; this should be minimised as much as possible. When there is no other choice, people should be moved as close as possible to their original homes as access to jobs is of crucial importance. In cases when that is not possible, livelihood restoration is the most crucial element.

The two cases presented have shown that affected communities are very creative in adjusting their houses and public spaces incrementally to their needs; either through moving out whenever there is no other way possible or adjusting their housing and public space with the little means they have in order to restore some of their lost income. It shows the importance for affected communities to be involved in the design of their houses and in providing them with the possibility to incrementally adjust their housing to their needs and life stages. This can happen through extensions, readjustments of internal designs, by adding extra floors and verandas. Thereby opportunities are created to build up financial assets that in the end can provide poor resettlers with the opportunity to move out of poverty. ●

# A Flexible Approach to Upgrade Informal Housing

**Alessia Guardo, Lucia Valenzuela, Dhruv Bahl, Revathi Konduru** and **Samidha Patil** analyse the Baan Mankong Programme

## Thailand's Encounter with Rapid Urbanisation and Informality

Thailand, like many Asian countries, has been facing rapid urbanisation since the population boost in the 1970s. According to the Statistical Annex of the World Cities Report, in 2015 the country experienced 50% urbanisation and is foreseen to reach 60% in 2025 (UN-Habitat, 2016). Therefore, it is not surprising that the first shortcoming of this urbanisation phenomenon has been the increasing population in the urban centres, especially in informal settlements. Three main circumstances have worsened the conditions in the informal settlements: the increasing rural-urban migration, the mismatch between the ability of institutions to cope with increasing demand in a rapidly growing economy, and massive land speculation triggered by an ambiguous land use plan.

Since the economic advancement in the 1980s, considerable monetary reserves have been allocated towards social expenses, especially in terms of community-led upgrading. In 2000, the Community Organizations Development Institute (CODI), was created as a separate government agency. The main purpose of the agency was to strengthen poor communities through the promotion of saving groups, loans and housing microfinance (Nadkarny and Anderson, 2010). In 2003, CODI launched the Housing Programme called 'Baan Mankong', as a response to the informal settlements. Through relevant example, the essence of the programme in addressing informality is illustrated in the following sections.

## Baan Mankong: From Informal Settlements to Formal Communities

The Baan Mankong Programme (BMP) was the first official programme in Thailand that recognised the slum inhabitants as developers of formal housing (Dhabhalabutr, 2016). In a tacit sense, the programme provided extremely flexible loans and funds for communities to develop their houses and neighbourhoods on their own terms. Aptly, 'Baan Mankong' means 'secure housing' in Thai which has been recognised as a sustainable housing solution.

The novelty of the programme relied on how the funds were managed. For one, there was institutional support, from CODI, that provided capacity building and intermediation with other stakeholders in the city, such as NGOs, academics, construction professionals and other communities. On the other hand, the communities were given collective loans and were obliged to constitute a cooperative to pay their debt and solve any problem within the group (Dhabhalabutr, 2016). This effectively bridged the gap between the formal and the informal.

The rationale behind the programme was to provide financial freedom. Empowering the communities could become the principal driver and help them take decisions that were in their own interest. The unique characteristic of the stakeholders involved might be one of the reasons why the BMP has been extremely effective and successful for some communities and less for others. Let's look at two different cases.

## From Dynamo to Tawanmai: 'The New Rising Sun' Community

Located in Khon Kaen, the Tawanmai Community is regarded as one of the success stories of the Baan Mankong. For five consecutive years it has won the CODI 'Best Cooperative Award'. For outsiders, such as academics and planners, it has become a landmark of the possibilities that participative planning can accomplish. However, 14 years ago it was a different story for the residents of Tawanmai, with most of them living in Dynamo.

Dynamo was an informal settlement developed in the '70s and comprised rental shacks without direct access to public services, facilities and secure tenure (figure 1). They were looked down

*Left-* **Figure 1: Dynamo Community**
*Right-* **Figure 2: Tawanmai Community**

upon as 'the renters' and the poorest of the poor in the city. Dynamo residents thus, lived in vulnerable and hazardous surroundings, with exponentially increasing rent rates, lack of infrastructure and the overwhelming stigma of informality.

In 2004, the situation for the residents in Dynamo changed drastically when it was selected as one of the three pilot projects to implement the BMP in the North-East region of Thailand. Its nomination was based on CODI's strategy to find complex cases that could set an example for other informal settlers to get involved in the participative process of the BMP. Towards this, the national government negotiated with local actors who could provide support to the selected communities. With this support, the community gradually consolidated the cooperative, bought the land and started to develop Tawanmai Community, as shown in figure 2.

A number of factors contributed to the success of the project in Tawanmai. For one, the novelty of being a pilot project lured the stakeholders to engage in the project. For example, Khon Kaen University was proactive in organising on-field courses for their students to learn about participatory design. Likewise, the Municipality was quick to provide the site's services to show its commitment to the national agenda. On the other hand, one of the main advantages that they had within the community, and that continued having relevance in the subsequent years, was that the residents knew one another, which established a strong social relationship amongst them. Even more so as the families that were selected from outside the community had to be recommended by a Dynamo family.

The support system, built by the surrounding actors and the initial partial cohesiveness of the dwellers, gave Tawanmai a significant push at the beginning of the process. This by no means

implies that they did not face any challenge during its consolidation. The tensions caused by the uncertainties regarding the receipt of funds from the authorities and the rounds of negotiation between the members and the Khon Kaen University representatives were challenges that the community had to overcome and which brought them together.

Currently, the Tawanmai Community has completed the construction process and the community is expected to finish paying off the CODI loan by 2020.

### The Life Along the Railway

As seen in the previous experience, the BMP has been highly effective for some communities, such as Dynamo. However, its success cannot be generalised. In contrast to the Tawanmai Community, the 'railway slum', of Khon Kaen has faced significant setbacks that have prevented the community from acquiring a formal status. A major factor for this, among others, is its relation with the Railway State of Thailand (RST) defined by Boonyabancha (2009, 321) as "one of the most difficult public landlords".

While, in general, Thai culture is founded on the concept of being mutually accommodating, in the railway slums case, the urban poor are legally considered as squatters since they do not have any kind of approval from the RST. For this reason the informal settlements on the RST land are perceived to be the 'poorest and most insecure' slums (Boonyabancha, 2005).

In Thailand, these communities are the largest and most vulnerable. However, they are also the ones with the strongest network. In Khon Kaen alone there are two parallel community networks. The first one is linked at the national level, the 'Four Regions Slum Network' and the other is the network within Khon Kaen's grid. Thanks to both community

**The Baan Mankong Programme … provided flexible loans for communities to develop their houses and neighbourhoods on their own terms**

**Figure 3: View of the 20 metres where people were asked to move to build the double track railway**

networks, these dwellers have been able to reach an agreement with the RST; they have been granted the possibility to lease the land for a period of 3–30 years based on their distance from the railway track. Some of the families living within 20 metres from the railway line had to move, as illustrated in figure 3.

Besides this agreement, the majority of these communities did not upgrade, and accepted only some small interventions subsidised by CODI. Several reasons can be listed for taking this decision: financial instability, inability to run long-lasting saving groups, apparent disinterest towards the better living condition proposed by the BMP and the alleged lack of information from the Municipality.

However, another significant factor that derives from the usual challenges is that some communities simply did not want to move. The strategic location of the railways in Khon Kaen positions these communities at the centre of the city, which allows them proximity to their work places and to the main markets. As corroborated during further discussions, this was perceived more valuable by the settlers than housing upgradation.

In Khon Kaen there are 26 informal settlements, different in size, density, and housing conditions, along both sides of the railway path. The 8,000 odd residents of these informal settlements managed to build houses that ranged from shacks made of wood and rusted metal. The Theparak community presented in figure 4 is the biggest informal railway settlement and hosts more than 179 families.

## Tawanmai and the Railway Slums: Comparing Experiences

What is the difference then between these two communities?

In order to answer this question, some might refer to all the shortcomings of the BMP and the

collateral restrictions or difficulties of a community-driven process. Nonetheless, here, we are looking at two communities in the same city which, regardless of the similar initial conditions, ended up with two opposite results. There are two main points that make the railway community quite different from Dynamo – the tenure of the land and the characteristics of the community itself.

A strong actor such as the RST can create uncertainty in the lives of hundreds of people. As stated by a municipality officer (2018):

*The most headache for me is that we have never got any information from the RST. They told me they would have demolished the first 20 metre just 3 months before they did it. … The community nearby Central Plaza will be demolished after the high-speed train. The slum community over there is around 168 households. Where will they go to live then? Right?*

In the case of Tawanmai, a group from informal settlements built its organisation over time, resulting in a strong network and the strengthening of its approach towards collective ownership. These informal settlements host both the poorest of the poor in Khon Kaen who can certainly not move somewhere else, and also those who choose to live along the railway lines as a strategic choice.

It is clear that there is a tangible clash of power and intentions that determine this conflict between two strong, controversial and, to a certain extent, ambiguous actors that characterise the state of informality in the city of Khon Kaen. This conflict has been going on for several years and the agreement achieved between the Four Region Slum and the Railway State of Thailand is proof of their agreeing to meet halfway, typical of the Thai culture of negotiation. Nevertheless, despite the meeting point, there is still some leap to be made in order to let people in need find their own solution, without being trapped or crushed by power dynamics.

In contrast, the formal upgrading of Tawanmai with CODI support gave its residents the needed stability to consolidate and to access the advantages of a formal tenure, such as accessing the healthcare system and serviced land. Furthermore, the land they bought in 2004 was absorbed by the city growth and, as presented in figure 5, is now in a strategic position close to the city's medical centre and Khon Kaen University. Alongside, the fact that members of Tawanmai knew one another played a crucial role. Mutual trust helped unify them towards the same objective. In contrast, the heterogeneity of the people living along the rail lines made compromises difficult; there is no common set of priorities that can lead to a common path.

As both of these cases present a strong dichotomy, it is also important to highlight that both of them were presented with an option but each took a different path. While reviewing informality, there is hardly a definitive answer. The BMP has tried to cater to that challenge by providing flexibility for the communities to make their own decisions. However, by establishing the same principle to all communities it has also overlooked that some communities need more help than others and, more importantly, what happens to the poorest of the poor among them who get left behind.

## Moving Forward

The comparison between the successful story of the Tawanmai community and the resistance presented by the railway communities brings to light several aspects that drove us towards various persistent questions, that we will just leave here, as a memo: What are the chances of a betterment of life and adequate housing conditions for the people left out? What are the factors preventing the success of the BMP in Khon Kaen while addressing the housing needs of the most vulnerable group, the poorest of the poor? Are the BMP's loose limits and rules making it too dependent on the context and chances? Of course, these questions need proper room to be discussed and eventually answered. Ultimately, further research is needed.

However, the latter question leads us to another reflection about the replicability of the BMP, not only in other cities of Thailand but also in other countries. The flexibility of the programme is surely one of its main qualities, but probably also one of its main constraints.

Worldwide, the results of the Baan Mankong Programme have been praised. In 2008 the UN ESCAP recognised the BMP as being one of the best Asian practices for low-income housing development. Furthermore, the Asian Coalition for Housing Rights (ACHR) plans to replicate the Baan Mankong system in other countries within the South-East Asian Region. However, will this be possible? Each project is tailor-made according to the context, to the target group and to the stakeholders interacting with it. Moreover, the flexibility coming from the lack of a strict policy complements the Thai culture of compromise and negotiation. It surmises to say that, the extent to which this flexibility can be replicable perhaps relies on the culture and context. ●

**Figure 4: View of the housing condition of the Thepharak railway informal settlement**

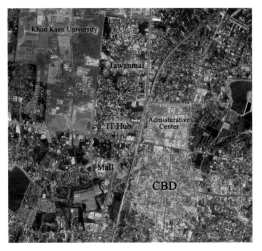

**Figure 5: Tawanmai location**

# Half of a Good House

**Amit Arya** and **Buvana Murali** explain Elemental's solution to the problem of incremental social housing

Provision of social housing for the poor on a government subsidy is the most challenging problem facing the global urban condition today. Effective solutions are scarce and much work needs to be done for a long-lasting impact in the urban environment. More importantly, 'out-of-the-box' ideas that challenge the status quo and demonstrate new attitudes to problem solving are the need of the hour. The problem is so widespread and the challenge so daunting that most architects and designers either shy away from this challenge or work with the problem in a disengaged manner. However, the work and ideas of Elemental, a group from Chile, has been seminal in addressing the complicated questions and challenges that face housing the poor in our cities. Their work and ideas on incremental social housing strategies over the last decade in several South American cities has, with repeated success, demonstrated new ways to resolve and engage with this issue.

Though the concept of structure and infill solution as a means to provide stable and incremental models of social housing is a well-established idea, Elemental's understanding of the challenges has been unique; that the biggest challenge in such projects is the initial capital cost of land and construction. So, rather than adapt the obvious solution of relocating the community to the periphery of the city where land is cheap in order to provide a bigger dwelling, Elemental propose to rehouse the families in their existing location. Thus maintaining the community's well established socio-economic networks, which form the backbone of the concept.

Furthermore, avoiding relocation makes the subsidy-based project by the government an investment into social housing by making it an 'appreciable asset' because of its central city location, an important quality for its sustenance in the future. Lastly, Elemental's concepts are based on the idea of infill solutions, which they aptly call 'half of a good house'. Since maintaining the land parcel within the city costs much more in terms of land value only smaller/inadequate sized houses can be built within the prescribed government budget, these are ineffective for future growth of the community and family. However, Elemental proposes design solutions that provide half the adequate area immediately along with the basic framework in order to add the other half in progressive increments by the homeowner based on their resources over time. It provides complete flexibility to adapt a house on the basis of the family's demands. To solve complex housing equations and yet design for flexibility within the preferred community context, within government prescribed budgets and making the community a stakeholder in its future development is a unique proposition at multiple levels. It is an exercise in learning how to conserve, adapt and prioritise the immediate needs while proposing social housing ideas in the heart of the city thus maintaining the city and its future as an opportunity for all economic classes.

> **Most architects and designers either shy away from this challenge or work with the problem in a disengaged manner**

**The Elemental Team from left: Alejandro Aravena, Gonzalo Arteaga, Juan Ignacio Cerda, Diego Torres, Víctor Oddó**

## Quinta Monroy, Iquique - Chile, 2001–2004

In the case of Quinta Monroy in Iquique, Chile, the equation was challenging. How do you provide social housing on a $7,500 government subsidy (cost of land + house) per family for 100 families who were squatting on half a hectare of land in the centre of the city for 30 years? To make houses in that budget meant providing a 40-sq.mt. dwelling unit after reducing the cost expended on buying the land. Such a size was inadequate for growth. However, looking at the problem from an incremental standpoint of providing the essentials and designing for the growth is what made Quinta Monroy the first successful prototype of the 'half of a good house' philosophy. It has provided 93 dwelling units in two typologies. Rather than provide separate houses on lots which would not achieve the desired density on the land, or a high rise typology which would provide land efficiency but no possible flexibility for the future, Elemental proposed a prototype that provides horizontally interconnected units at two levels (a duplex unit sitting over a ground floor unit) with equal amounts of built and open voids in the middle for future expansion without overcrowding and providing the same quality of light and air in the expanded unit. Units provided on the ground floor have potential for lateral expansion on the ground on two sides and duplex units on the upper two floors have potential for lateral expansion on one side at two levels.

SKETCHES: ELEMENTAL

*Left:* **Development stages of the Quinta Monroy prototype**
*Bottom:* **Quinta Monroy before and after**

PHOTOS: TADEUZ JALOCHA (BEFORE) / CRISTOBAL PALMA (AFTER)

**QUINTA MONROY**
**Before and after the residents moved in**

PHOTOS: TADEUZ JALOCHA (BEFORE) / ELEMENTAL (AFTER)

*Bottom Left:* **Components of the Las Anacuas housing prototype**
*Bottom Right:* **The Las Anacuas development: Before and after the residents moved in**

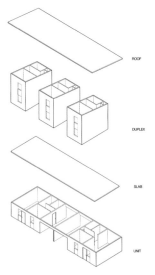

ROOF

DUPLEX

SLAB

UNIT

PHOTOS: RAMIRO RAMIREZ

## Las Anacuas Housing in Monterrey, Santa Caterina - Mexico, 2008–2010

A similar experiment in a different climate type at Santa Caterina in Mexico was designed keeping in mind the rainfall the city receives during the monsoon months. While replicating the Quinta Monroy typologies, a large continuous overhang roof was designed to facilitate the expansion during all seasons so as to keep feasibility of expansion through construction intact.

In the last decade Elemental has provided more than 2,000 dwelling units with these progressive urban social housing strategies. And though it should be noted that there are more challenging countries in the world like India and places in Africa that don't have effective policies for social housing subsidies and are dealing with far greater challenges of densities and budgets, the primary ideas of Elemental's work are

PHOTOS: RAMIRO RAMIREZ

**Las Anacuas development**

extremely relevant to all parts of the world. The skill to provide a decent, equitable and affordable future in our cities for all, by way of design, is a universal requirement and once again provides the opportunity for the architect to become relevant towards our most demanding urban challenges.

In conclusion, Alejandro Aravena, the founder member of Elemental, sums it up well in an excerpt from an interview in *The Guardian*: "One of the biggest mistakes in architecture is that we're expecting society to be interested in the specific problems of architecture. Instead, architects need to adjust to what society is discussing. We just provide the forms that can translate their problems into solutions." •

# Building the Dogon Way

Dutch office **LEVS architecten** on novel building technologies they use to create vernacular architecture in Mali

### Building Tradition

All over the world building with mud is a common way of construction. More than 50% of the world's population lives in mud or loam buildings. In West African countries, this tradition is well known because of structures like the Great Mosque, the biggest mud brick mosque in the world which stands along the River Niger in Djenne, the white Grand Mosque Bobo Dioulasso in Burkina Faso or the tombs in Timbuctoo. Building with mud was logical for these locations along rivers. However, there is, of course, an immense diversity of techniques and skills. The method of building in Mali is not the same as, for example, in Yemen or Afghanistan and the differences have led to variety in architecture. Climate change has also been an influencing factor in this development.

The Dogon Country, now predominantly in the desertification zone, has a very long tradition of mud brick building and handmade loam granaries. There are even buildings built before Christ that were constructed with special techniques for handmade bricks. The ancestors of the Dogon people, the Tellem, developed this method 2,500 years ago when there was much more water available. Today, this technique is still known, but only to a small part of the population. The buildings still exist because

they are protected by the rocks and preserved by traditional repair work. However, for contemporary building types, that traditional way of building is not a solution.

In the last century, there was a rising demand for new typologies to construct buildings such as schools. The government abolished the traditional techniques because buildings needed too much maintenance and did not appear as contemporary as the authorities wanted. The result: concrete block schools, plastered and painted in various colours. This led to the severance of any connection with tradition, architecture and vernacularism. Besides, the community couldn't identify with the buildings anymore because they were not built as a part of the village. Local inhabitants couldn't even contribute to the building process of communal buildings, which was once a Dogon tradition.

### Finding the Road

Building in partnership brought about the road to change. Though there was equal respect for all partners, part of our work included guiding the project in the right direction and highlighting possibilities. Over a period of 20 years, 30 schools were built. The first school was built with traditional mud bricks, which had to be repaired

> **For contemporary building types, the traditional way of building was not a solution**

*Left:* **Traditional granaries**
*Right:* **Yougo restoration**

*Top:* **Toguna**
*Left:* **Djenne White Mosque**

Through the use of the newly developed HCEBs, the building withstands both hot sunlight and heavy rainfall

every two years. Then we switched to natural stone blocks, but the mortar was expensive because of the enormous amounts of cement it contains. The concrete block schools that followed heated up and required a lot of energy for maintenance too. However, what was of paramount importance was the fact that people using these buildings did not feel connected to their community anymore. The turning point came with the reconstruction and restoration of the first school in the area, which is 100 years old today. It was built using the traditional method. That's why it has a comfortable interior climate and is architecturally connected to the place and the community. The restoration of this building in 2005 opened our eyes. At that point, building with HCEB (hydraulically compressed earth blocks) became the new and accepted approach. It became the mantra of a progressive and modern way of construction with endless architectural possibilities and, at the same time, connected to the Dogon tradition. And so Vernacular Building 2.0 was kick started.

## Primary School Tanouan Ibi

The Dogon plateau in Mali is underdeveloped, as the government hardly invests in this remote region of the country. Therefore, the development of new building techniques based on local construction methods, using local materials and training new masons, creates a spin-off for local development.

Dogon women with the HCEB

The new school building

Primary School Tanouan Ibi aims to safeguard the education and social development of the young generation of Malians in this area. It was developed and built together with the local community as an equal partner. This creates the highest commitment and a sustainable future because it isn't just any school building; it is their school building.

The school consists of three 7 x 9-metre classrooms for 180 pupils in total, a principal's office, a depot and a sanitation building. In the evening, it is used to educate women. The school is located at the edge of the village Tanouan Ibi in the vast plain of the Dogon region, next to the rock face of Bandiagara (World Cultural Heritage of Humanity, Unesco 1986).

The architecture is inspired by local building traditions and culture as well as by function. In the tradition of the Dogon area there is a doubtless

*Top:* **The pressing machine**
*Bottom:* **People celebrate their school building. In the background you see the old school building of Tanouan Ibi**

spiritual connection between people, culture and nature. Their minimalism in building with clay and the plasticity and immediacy of detail are remarkable. It is 'wealth in restrictions'. Nuances, personality and soul define the building; a majestic gesture is not necessary.

The building is erected using modern technology and built by local, newly trained masons. Because of the use of the newly developed HCEBs, the building withstands both hot sunlight and heavy rainfall much better than the traditional clay buildings. These bricks are non-fired and are produced using the soil on site, which reduces production costs and environmental degradation. They also provide an optimal cooling climate. The use of these blocks of compressed earth for floors, walls and roofs, leads to a supple integration into the environment, corresponding to the way the Dogon villages fit into the landscape. The language of form is a clear consequence of functional requirements.

The structure of the school building is unique with two verandas running parallel to the classrooms. These operate as buttresses to withstand the weight of the barrel vaults in the roofs over the classrooms. The roof and the eaves have been accentuated by an additional layer of stones and by dilatation stones, separating the barrel vaults. A thick layer of red earth, mixed with cement in order to achieve a waterproof and water resistant layer, covers the roof. The gargoyles, manufactured by the local people called Bozo, guarantee the swift drainage of rainwater. Custom made ceramic tubes have been inserted in the roof to provide ventilation for a pleasant inside climate, to allow daylight to filter in and to make a starry sky visible. During the rainy season (two months), these tubes can be closed.

The openings in the facades, with their window frames and blinds, are painted in a fresh yellow colour. The intricate floor pattern of the verandas with their benches establishes a meaningful place for the elders of the village community.

Tanouan Ibi is only one of the HCEB-buildings that have been built in Mali. All these projects were a very practical and pragmatic challenge: constructing buildings to ensure that education can be imparted and also provide housing for teachers and various other facilities. All this was done in collaboration with the local people. The contractor and the craftsmen work closely together with the students of a technical college. They are involved in every stage of the construction process in order to improve and to refine the construction methods, linked to already existing techniques, traditions

189

*Top:* **Building with HCEB**
*Bottom:* **Primary School**
**Tanouan Ibi**

and know-how. Educating people in building engineering is an integral part for the development of construction techniques and local architecture.

## Building Sustainably with HCEB

One of the most important issues to implement sustainable building methods is a careful study of available building materials. Using what can be found close to the building site to construct a building reduces transport costs to a minimum. The next important step is to design a building that will have a pleasant interior climate using the minimum energy possible. Each location asks for customised solutions. That is the true essence of sustainable thinking. There is no generic design solution that works all over Africa. In Mali, building with 'hydraulically' compressed earth blocks (HCEB) instead of traditionally compressed earth blocks (CEB) can make the difference.

Building with earth is not a new invention. Over the years, many different results have popped up. But then earth is seen as a cheap, inferior

**Inside the classroom**

ALL PHOTOS: LEVS ARCHITECTEN

material only good enough for low cost housing or for use as a wall filling. The production of such blocks was generally done with a hand press and occasionally even without adding cement. Sometimes blocks were pressed under low pressure with machines. This gave rise to two problems: the blocks were too weak to be used to support construction and the detailing of the joint was not waterproof.

The secret of HCEB blocks is that they are manufactured using 20 tonnes of hydraulic pressure. The production process, the composition of ingredients and the method of processing them are constantly in development. The objective is to minimise the amount of cement, which is very valuable because it needs to be imported. Even for the hydraulically compressed earth blocks, which contain less than 5% cement, it makes up 85% of the cost. The machine with which the earth or loam is pulverised is the key. If the grain is uniform, it is possible to make bricks that can bear up to 5KN (kilonewton). That means that an HCEB has completely different qualities than the earth bricks produced elsewhere around the world.

Without any cement, HCEB can be used for the indoor walls, for instance. They can also be used as floor stones and tiered roof stones, which require different characteristics. In the beginning the bricks were mostly produced in the factory in order to control the production process. Since 2011 the bricks have been produced on site, which has a significant effect on the transportation costs.

Building with compressed earth blocks demands a new approach to architecture and engineering. It also offers many benefits. One of them is using local materials. Another one is that the physical structure of the bricks creates an agreeably 'cool' building climate that adapts to the outside climate and cools down quickly at night. The bricks have a very high compressive strength, so they can be used to build bearing walls, even in multiple layers. Over the last few years we have made several designs for schools, housing, technical schools and a town hall.

As Dutch architects we have a broad tradition in designing brick facades and brick patterns. The dimension of buildings is based on the size, the natural quality and the possibilities of using the bricks. Within these limits we learned not only to use it as construction material, but also as decorating elements with a variation of patterns and reliefs. The buildings become more and more refined in their architectural expression. The reinterpretation of local traditions is a modern way of integrating the new buildings in traditional settings. ●

191

# The Artistic Rebirth of a Neglected Community

**Levi Wichgers** tells us about the colourful artworks of the Dutch artists **Haas&Hahn** and their vision

Artists Jeroen Koolhaas and Dre Urhahn are known as Haas&Hahn. Their worldwide reputation comes nowadays from their appearances on *CNN*, in the *New York Times*, the *Washington Post*, and their talks at *TEDGlobal*. But 10 years ago, it was a different story.

It all started when the duo were making a movie about the hip-hop culture in Rio de Janeiro. During their research, they discovered the social problems in the *favelas* and the painful lack of interest in those districts and their inhabitants. In retaliation they came up with the idea of initiating artistic projects together with the local community.

That's how the Favela Painting Project started. Not just for the artistic pleasure of painting, but because of a higher social purpose. As they describe it: To turn public urban spaces in deprived places into monumental artworks, to offer local youth education and job opportunities and, in the bargain, make their community a nicer place to live in.

In 2007 they started their first project, Boy with Kite, a 150 m² painting, followed by Rio Cruzeiro, a 2,000 m² painting in the Japanese style, depicting a river with colourful fish. However, their third project, Praça Cantão has probably become their most famous work.

Praça Cantão is 7,000 m². This artistic expression is comprehensive. The painting not only embellishes the *favela* and the city, but the colours used in the project are representative of the people and their identity. Therefore, Praça Cantão can be seen as a powerful social catalyst. To lead the project on track, the principle and concept of the painting were coordinated with the crew so that the workforce itself could complete it once Haas&Hahn left. They worked with a range of colours from which other colours could be derived. Initially, identical colour bands were painted, between which, house after house, new colours were applied. Haas&Hahn kept in touch with the crew to help

**Praça Cantão**

*Top:* **Dre Urhahn and Jeroen Koolhaas**
*Left:* **Praça Cantão earlier**

them realise the overall plan.

The Praça Cantão project made Haas&Hahn well-known all over the world and offered them opportunities to work on new locations in other countries, like North Philly in Philadelphia (USA). At this moment they are preparing large-scale community projects in Rio de Janeiro, Haiti and Curacao and are working on proposals for cities in Chili and Cuba.

In 2013 they started a campaign to raise funds to paint an entire *favela* hill and realise their ultimate dream.

Nowadays Haas&Hahn get invited worldwide to teach, to speak about their work and advise cities on community art projects. They search for ways to breathe new life into communities and give them a unique identity.

Today we might speak of a Haas&Hahn-system: a self-running production system in which art, architecture and social entrepreneurship are combined with optimal use of new media, PR and crowd funding. They are investigating the possibilities of setting up facilities for local paint production, creating even more opportunities and a higher sustainability.

Haas&Hahn have given us a great example of how artists can help to make the world a more loveable and liveable place. ●

# Streets as Drivers for the Transformation and Inclusion of Slums

**Banashree Banerjee** makes a case for putting slum settlements at the heart of the planning process

## Why Streets?

In 2014, the UN-Habitat brought out a flagship publication titled *Streets as Tools for Urban Transformation in Slums: A Street-Led Approach to Citywide Slum Upgrading.* The question is, why streets? The answer emerges from the policy and practices in use so far, that in turn explain the two simple premises on which the approach is based.

The first premise is that a focus on creating and improving streets and public spaces in existing slum settlements can catalyse significant improvements in livelihoods, living conditions and social interactions. A street is not only a physical entity for mobility and accessibility – under which water and sewerage pipes, power lines and drainage systems are laid – but also a public domain where social, cultural and economic activities are articulated, reinforced and facilitated.

The second, and related, premise that streets are the natural conduits which connect slums to the city, could prove to be the driving force for citywide slum upgrading and, ultimately, inclusive city planning. Slums are an integral part of the overall city system, but are spatially segregated as islands of poverty and informality. Creating streets or reinforcing and improving existing streets and accesses, with a view to integrating slums into overall city planning and management, can be the key to fostering urban regeneration.

Yet, what has been the experience so far? Can streets really play the key role assigned to them in the street-led approach advocated by UN-Habitat?

## What is the Experience?

Over the years, slum upgradation projects in many cities have helped people achieve an improved, healthy and secure living environment. They have clean water, paved streets, street lighting, drainage, waste disposal arrangements and some form of secure tenure. The scale of intervention differs from a few slums to citywide or multi-city coverage. As advocacy goes, slum upgrading is low cost, does not cause displacement and the results are immediate and highly visible (World Bank, 2000). Street-paving is perhaps the most visible result with dirt roads changing to all weather streets. Residents appreciate this as a hard surface,

### BOX 1: HOW MANY USES ARE THERE FOR A ROAD?

Site for hawkers

Play area for children

Space for girls to learn cycling

Dry place to sit in the cool breeze

Place to sleep in summer

Place for guests to sleep

Place for sorting garbage

Venue for social functions such as weddings and festivals

Parking of cycle rickshaws and carts

Site for washing and drying clothes

Allows daily money collection for savings and loans

Run-off for waste water

Relatives now able to visit

*From participatory field work for an impact assessment of slum improvement projects in Indore, India (Amis, 2001)*

*Clockwise from Top Left:* **Street activities: basket making, Howrah; informal meeting, Salvador; street vendor, Bangkok; children playing, Manila**

which apart from facilitating mobility, can be used for many public purposes, and for extending the living space of tiny homes in high density settlements lacking any other open space.

But the de facto multiple use of paved streets is not a cause for celebration. The contention of the street-led approach is that streets and public spaces need to be improved and opened up systematically to become the public domain for social, cultural and economic activities and for improved quality of life. Conventional slum upgradation projects are about retrofitting services and tenure into existing settlements. Most slums are characterised by high density and tiny plots along narrow winding lanes with many dead ends, where lack of street networks make it difficult to lay water and sewer pipes, power lines and drainage systems or for the entry of fire tenders and ambulances. There is also no space for community buildings and collective services. So, in spite of being upgraded, settlements continue to be vulnerable to disasters and devoid of facilities which are considered essential for human development.

On the positive side, there is ample evidence to show that tenure security and services lead to investment on the plot. In Senegal, for example, each dollar spent on public infrastructure on

World Bank supported projects was estimated to have stimulated about eight dollars in home construction and improvement (Kessides, 1997). Similar results emerged from research carried out in the Indian city of Bhopal on the long-term impacts of citywide implementation of tenure regularisation and basic service provision. Secure tenure has enabled private building activity to satisfy the growing demand – encouraged by improved services – for cheap rental housing, shops and workshops. But even as plots get built on and the settlement gets more people and activities, lanes remain narrow (sometimes just one metre wide) and get narrower still with overhanging upper floors and the spill-over of activities from buildings (Banerjee, 2006).

Significantly, building work is carried out without permission from the Municipal Corporation and even if permission was applied for, it would not be forthcoming because of non-compliance with the already lowered standards prescribed for low cost housing under the Madhya Pradesh Land Development Rules, 1984. Typically, plot sizes were below the minimum standard of 30 square metres and could be approached by lanes of less than 1.5 metres width, the minimum requirement. So, in spite of being regularised and

**Slums are an integral part of the overall city system, but are spatially segregated as islands of poverty and informality**

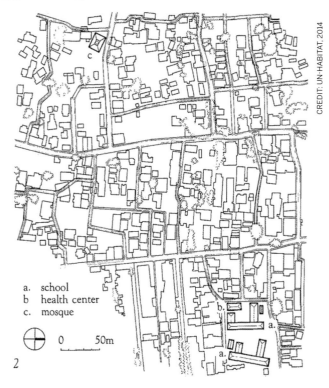

CREDIT: UN-HABITAT, 2014

a. school
b. health center
c. mosque

0    50m

2

PHOTO: BANASHREE BANERJEE

provided with municipal services, slums continue to remain outside the regulatory framework of city planning and building. Unregulated building on plots and increasing densities actually lead to worsening environmental conditions (Banerjee, 2006).

The point to be noted is that Bhopal is not an exception, but very much part of the pattern in the cities of developing countries. Ad-hoc infrastructure improvement that leaves intact the existing unplanned and haphazard land occupation of settlements is costly and counterproductive in the long-term. They remain low-quality enclaves and, even when all the slums in the city are included for upgrading, are rarely assimilated into mainstream urban planning and management. This calls for well-defined holistic strategies that put slum settlements at the heart of planning processes in order to upgrade and integrate them with the city.

## How is the Street-led Approach Operationalised?

The strategy being advocated by UN-Habitat involves a shift in approach to slum upgrading from thinking of slums as islands of poverty and informality to slums as deprived neighbourhoods. Slums are an integral part of the overall city system but they remain spatially segregated and physically disconnected due to a virtual absence of streets and public spaces. This is the main cause

for exclusion of slums from the city's urban fabric (UN-Habitat, 2014) and for limiting possibilities of their development as urban neighbourhoods. The street-led approach to instrumentalising citywide slum upgrading presents a practical and simple business case for maximising multi-dimensional outcomes for residents and gradually integrating slum settlements with the urban fabric.

The suggested planning and implementation strategy builds on the practical and symbolic role of streets as the key to linking up neighbours and neighbourhoods, businesses and economic activities situated adjacent to each other and sharing the common public space provided by streets. It recognises that informal settlements are vulnerable to multiple disasters such as floods, fires, landslides which are likely to be exacerbated with climate change. The layout and design of streets needs to build in the requirements of disaster management and rescue and relief operations.

The street-led strategy is well suited for phased and incremental development through strong participatory planning, rather than pursuing the complex implementation of a full-fledged upgrading and urban layout plan as a single-phased approach. The incremental approach based on the prioritisation of streets will ensure that strategic choices are made and that the streets selected

*Left:* **Kampung, Jakarta, Indonesia**
*Right:* **Bhopal, buildings on small plots on narrow streets**

## Unregulated building on plots and increasing densities actually lead to worsening environmental conditions

**Pathways and roads in Community Infrastructure Upgrading Programme, Dar es Salaam**

## BOX 2: 14 KEY URBAN PRINCIPLES: IMPLEMENTED THROUGH STREETS AS A PRACTICAL TOOL

1. Integrated citywide planning
2. Implementation in phases
3. Improved urban mobility and connectivity
4. Fostering economic growth
5. Creation of citizenship
6. Development through strategic participation and partnerships
7. Optimisation of density and promotion of mixed uses
8. Enable urban layouts through land readjustment
9. Laying the basis for the provision of security of tenure
10. Supporting safer cities
11. Providing alternatives to 'forced' relocation
12. Planning for disaster risk reduction
13. Ensure a steady flow of funds from a variety of resources
14. Making slum upgrading responsive to gender and youth as well as to children, the elderly and the disabled

for improvement or implementation initially are actually the ones that are likely to bring about the best outcome in terms of development opportunities, poverty reduction, optimisation of land use and generation of wealth as a result of increase in property values. The participatory approach will also ensure that the inevitable issue of relocation necessitated by opening and widening streets is acted upon when city level concerns for connectivity and mobility are considered. The participatory approach for layout and design of streets will also ensure that the inevitable issue of relocation necessitated by opening and widening streets are acted upon when city level concerns for connectivity and mobility are considered. Further, implementation targets can be set and gradually enhanced in keeping with the technical, managerial and financial capacity of the local government (UN-Habitat, 2014).

Citywide slum upgrading demands critical measures outside the domain of slum settlements as well as within. The street network becomes the binding element of these two domains, reinforcing their interconnections and interdependencies and creating value additions in both the city and the upgraded slum in a number of practical and symbolic ways. Thus streets facilitate the operationalisation and implementation of some of the key principles of urban planning and slum upgrading (UN-Habitat, 2014).

Although streets are ideal as the starting point for the physical integration of slums into the formal and official systems of planning and urban management that govern a city, the realisation of streets must be accompanied by a set of public policies and strategic interventions to complement and strengthen environmental and social inclusion strategies. These would include improving access to safe housing and employment opportunities and prevention of slums through developing new layouts that are affordable to the poor.

### Is it Practical and Feasible?

The street-led approach draws on practice and pragmatic lessons from international cases of slum upgrading where streets have been paramount for the transformation of slums into vibrant and included neighbourhoods of the city. Experience shows that this can be achieved incrementally through several strategic interventions incorporating some, if not all, of the principles of the street-led approach. A few of the examples which informed the conceptualisation and development of the approach are briefly presented alongside.

Among the well-known cases, the *Favela-Barrio* programme in Rio de Janeiro, Brazil, stands out for its innovative and practical use of streets and open spaces as key elements in the transformation of *favelas* (informal settlements) into city neighbourhoods. Simply the naming and numbering of streets has given a legitimate identity and location to dwellings and allowed the inclusion of *favelas* in city maps for the first time. Internal spaces of dense settlements have been re-organised as squares and children's play areas. New streets have allowed policing and extension of city services into the *favelas* while main streets have been widened and more streets opened up and provided with lighting and fire hydrants, improving accessibility, safety and security, especially for women and children. Opening up streets and open spaces has allowed interaction with the city in many ways. For example, in *favela* Parque Royal, new street alignments were created for the convenience of residents and to allow people from other parts of the city access to the newly created sports facilities and waterfront development. This required relocation of families, who were accommodated in apartments within the settlement.

Another well-known case is of Medellin, Colombia, where the focus was on reversing the process of social and spatial exclusion of the inhabitants of *barrios* (informal settlements) on steep hill-sides. An innovative public transport system based on cable cars (metrocable) was implemented to link these areas to the metro and municipal public transport systems. This physically connected these settlements with the rest of the city, improved accessibility and mobility significantly and created areas of regeneration with new streets, an increasing mix of commercial activities, housing improvement and good public services.

In the Citywide Slum Upgrading Project (CSUP) in Agra, India, geo-spatial and socio-economic data has helped participatory planning and integration of slum streets and services with the city. Linking up monuments in the slum through enhancing the street pattern is an innovative approach to upgrading in a heritage city. The presence of historic monuments in the Kachhpura slum was used to both open up streets for slum dwellers and to create a heritage walk for tourists, resulting in economic opportunities for residents.

A number of initiatives demonstrate the importance of participation of the local community. In Bissau (Guinea-Bissau) the perceived advantages of the urban layouts proposed for upgrading triggered voluntary demolition and rebuilding according to the layout plan. Strong citizen participation in Tirana, Albania, resulted in safeguarding open spaces and participatory opening up of streets by voluntary demolition of fences and walls and demarcating street boundaries to achieve better urban layouts. In a similar example of Ghousia Colony in Karachi, Pakistan, initial resistance to opening streets gave way to community participation in street demarcation

*Top:* **Street addressing in Bangalore slum**
*Bottom:* **Connection of *barrios* with the city through metro cables**

PHOTO: BANASHREE BANERJEE

CREDIT: CLAUDIO ACIOLY JR

CREDIT: CURE

**Street making in Kachhpura, Agra**

CREDIT: CURE

**Community square, Kachhpura, Agra.**

and voluntary cutting of plots and buildings for street widening. The Lusaka (Zambia) slum upgrading programme involved residents to plan roads and related decision making to implement layouts which led to the establishment of 'road committees' as a participatory tool to define the street pattern, demolition of houses and relocation of residents to nearby plots.

## In Conclusion

Therefore, it can be asserted that streets are a vital element in the transformation of slums and informal settlements into city neighbourhoods as well as their integration with city systems. The neglect of street and open space planning and design can largely be held responsible for the perpetuation of slum-like conditions in cities. It has been demonstrated in programmes from different parts of the world that upgrading strategies that build on the potential of streets are likely to produce better results. The street-led approach to citywide slum upgrading derives from both these perspectives and adds some innovative concepts. It has, so far, not been fully implemented anywhere since its articulation four years ago, but examples show that it is a practical and feasible strategy. ●

*This article is based on the UN-Habitat Working Paper published in 2012 and draws on the work carried out by the author to finalise the report and produce the strategy paper of UN-Habitat 'Streets as Tools for Urban Transformation in Slums: a street-led approach to citywide slum upgrading'.*

**Partial plan of Ghousia Colony, Karachi**

# Climate Adaptive Housing

**Paola Huijding** tells us what happens when climate change becomes a key opportunity to enhance people's livelihoods

Drawings of young children express the most precious aspects of their lives: a safe home, a happy family, a loyal pet and lovely trees, which all require cities that keep them safe and comfortable. It doesn't matter where in the world these children live or to which social class they belong. A safe home, provides families with a refuge from the climate. But what happens when the climate changes?

A safe home is also of concern for cities. When climate change is considered in the design or redesign of cities, the livelihoods of families are likely to remain stable for longer. Hence, climate change could be a key opportunity to improve the condition of people's daily life by creating alternative pathways for solving deeply rooted social and environmental problems that most affect vulnerable populations. The need for climate adaptive housing could help in rethinking the regular system offering a new understanding of exchanges between society and ecosystems. A socio-ecological approach to adapt to climate change can give cities the opportunity to reshuffle technologies and policies that are not helping vulnerable communities achieve resilience.

## Metropolis Baixada Santista and the city of Santos, Brazil

The metropolitan area Baixada Santista is situated along the coast, 70 kms from the city of São Paulo, about an hour's drive through a mountainous landscape of Atlantic rainforest and through mangrove forests close to the coastline. It's one of the most populated areas in the state of São Paulo and as a result of its port complex, has an important industrial role and is also a strong tourist attraction.

The city of Santos, founded in 1546 by the Portuguese nobleman Brás Cubas, is partially located on the island of São Vicente – which harbours both the city of Santos and the city of São Vicente – and partially on the mainland.

The city's first major boom came in the 1860s when the opening of rail links connecting the port to the rest of the state made it the key shipping point for coffee producers in the state of

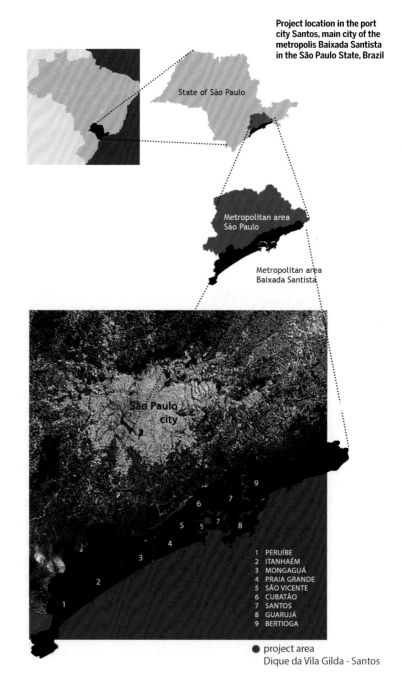

**Project location in the port city Santos, main city of the metropolis Baixada Santista in the São Paulo State, Brazil**

State of São Paulo

Metropolitan area São Paulo

Metropolitan area Baixada Santista

São Paulo city

| | |
|---|---|
| 1 | PERUÍBE |
| 2 | ITANHAÉM |
| 3 | MONGAGUÁ |
| 4 | PRAIA GRANDE |
| 5 | SÃO VICENTE |
| 6 | CUBATÃO |
| 7 | SANTOS |
| 8 | GUARUJÁ |
| 9 | BERTIOGA |

● project area
Dique da Vila Gilda - Santos

São Paulo. Today, the port exports far more than just coffee. It possesses a wide variety of cargo-handling terminals for solid and liquid bulk, containers and general cargo loads.

As a city in an estuarine area with South America's largest international port, Santos experiences a part of the battle against climate change and is trying to become a more resilient city. Santos has about 420,000 inhabitants and is facing significant impact from climate change, which has potentially serious consequences for human health, livelihoods and assets. Flooding in the city is a result of intense rain as well as the sea tides.

Situated in a sub-tropical mangrove system, the urban development of Santos has a long relationship with water; its economic importance – the port and tourism – as well as the master plan proposed by engineer Saturnino Brito in 1910, where water management, urban planning, infrastructure and climate control have all been integrated in one design for the East zone.

### Both prosperity and poverty face the same challenge: climate change

Due to the impact of climate change, the municipality of Santos is prioritising policies and plans to achieve a solution for the frequent floods. Ironically, the inhabitants of the prosperous neighbourhoods on the South and East zones are enmeshed in their properties depending mainly on adaptive measures and redesign of the infrastructure of their surroundings because their houses are not flexible enough for this adaptation. On the other hand, the structure of the poor neighbourhoods in the Northwest is so fragile that the value of the houses in this area is not an obstacle to finding new and innovative solutions. The ability of vulnerable communities to meet their most basic needs – water, energy, sanitation – has been threatened by the segregated governmental policies, and is also the source of its risks and weaknesses. Climate change may lead to new insights that may contribute to a sustainable and integrated future development of the Northwest towards climate adaptation and climate mitigation.

### Informal settlements

In the city of Santos, as in many others in Brazil, urbanisation has become synonymous with slum formation.

The slum's population – informally settled along the estuary's water edges – is one of the urgent issues. The very limited land available for construction purposes increases the price of the building land making it unaffordable for social housing, even if the area for this purpose is formerly indicated in the cities' spatial planning.

Officials are constantly looking for solutions for the resettling of the people living in the precarious stilt communities, which are nowadays illegally located in preserved mangrove forest areas.

Due to slum formation along the estuary, mangrove forests are disappearing. Santos is facing the consequences of having to invest in infrastructure projects to solve problems such as flooding, sedimentation and silting up of the water bodies, natural resource depletion, destruction of ecological services and sea level rise. These settlements have to be removed from the mangrove area to enable the local ecosystem services to recover.

**The need for climate adaptive housing could help in rethinking the regular system offering a new understanding of exchanges between society and ecosystems**

**Street in the Northern zone in Santos**

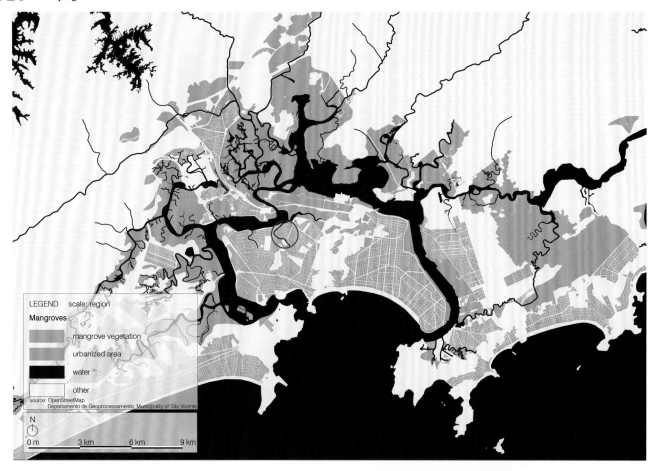

*Top:* **Location Vila Gilda and the conflict between urbanisation and mangrove forests**
*Left:* **Flood in East zone of Santos**

### Northwest zone

The Northwest is a very fragile zone in the city with about 90,000 inhabitants, mostly low-income families. The neighbourhoods in this area are built upon 40 metres of mud and some of them have an elevation that is lower than the high tide experienced every week. Flooding generally occurs when soils have reached their carrying capacity and from increases in ocean water levels. In addition, the port of Santos was filled to a higher elevation to protect against tidal flow. This action resulted in trapping the water in the Northwest, preventing water from naturally flowing into the estuary (ICF – GHK, 2012).

### Dique da Vila Gilda

The community of Dique da Vila Gilda, one of the informal settlements in the Northwest zone, is located on the island of São Vicente on the border between the municipalities of São Vicente and Santos. It expands over a river, with houses originally built in the 1950s on the slope of a dike that keeps the river from flooding the island on which most of the city stands. Over the last 65

years the community perched itself on stilts above the murky Rio Bugre and became the largest slum area on stilts in Brazil with about 30,000 inhabitants.

This slum is a medical danger zone. Solid waste covers the water surface; there is no sanitation and floods occur often compromising the quality of drinking water. This informal settlement is destroying the ecosystem of the mangroves, which provides a wide range of ecological services.

### Águas da Vila Gilda – Waters of Vila Gilda

The project Águas da Vila Gilda is tied to multiple environmental and socio-economic challenges such as ecosystems rehabilitation, water pollution and lack of sanitation, climate change, lack of housing and the fragile social-economical context of slums.

The required system innovation to achieve adaptive housing in this estuarine area is an interesting opportunity to democratise technology, something that can empower people. Combining the forces of democracy with the solutions for climate change, the slum of Vila Gilda can reshuffle

**Combining the forces of democracy with the solutions for climate change, the slum of Vila Gilda can reshuffle its system to ensure resilience and liveability**

Housing in the community of Vila Gilda

its system to ensure resilience and liveability.

Adaptive housing, as a matter of climate change, can safeguard people's well-being in the re-urbanisation processes of the Northwest. At the same time, climate mitigation can be increased when combining the design of adaptive housing with the rehabilitation of the mangrove ecosystem. This kind of forest has a huge capability of carbon sequestration. The recovered mangroves, as a matter of climate mitigation, give the people of Vila Gilda the basis for their new urban-ecological infrastructure: inspirational capital by passionate people, social capital by local employability and business, natural capital by biodiversity and also sanitation and energy supply. The circle is thus complete and the project's mission is accomplished when the economic value of this strategy makes the return of investments possible.

Águas da Vila Gilda is thus a neighbourhood-based concept for low-emission urban development incorporating solutions for adaptive housing. It proposes to house the slum inhabitants on a self-sufficient floating neighbourhood in the estuary of Santos in symbiosis with its direct surroundings, the city and environment. The overarching goal is the enhancement of capacity for resilience of the slum population through climate adaptation and climate mitigation actions. The development of an inclusive and social-ecological plan, which adds

economical value to the mangroves' ecosystem services, is the main instrument to achieving this goal. The strategy ensures equitable use of environmental resources encompassing all of the activities of a city in a single model. Focusing on adaptive housing models, infrastructure according to the principles of circular economy, implementing clean energy sources and ecological sanitation, the project addresses the most critical environmental issues of Santos like ecosystem depletion, flooding events and water pollution of the estuary.

*Top:* **Project proposition to re-urbanise the area of Vila Gilda integrating adaptive housing to the local ecosystem**
*Bottom:* **Project proposition focuses on the rehabilitation of the mangroves as a matter of climate mitigation. Adaptive housing is integrated in the urbanisation strategy providing the inhabitants of Vila Gilda with the development of a local economy as food production, fisheries and small business**

**Adaptive housing with self-supporting infrasturcture, biological sewage system and clean-tech energy production**

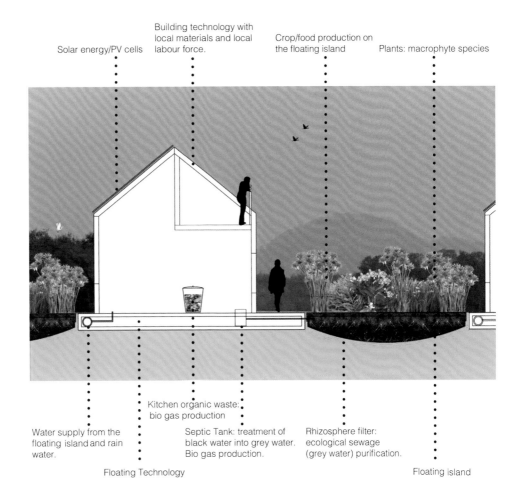

Solar energy/PV cells

Building technology with local materials and local labour force.

Crop/food production on the floating island

Plants: macrophyte species

Kitchen organic waste: bio gas production

Water supply from the floating island and rain water.

Septic Tank: treatment of black water into grey water. Bio gas production.

Rhizosphere filter: ecological sewage (grey water) purification.

Floating Technology

Floating island

The innovative strategy of the project strongly contributes to the parallel development of Santos's urban strategy regarding climate change and policies on sustainable urban development.

The resources produced by the mangrove's ecosystem and the ecological services will be integrated in the project; services such as protection against floods, reduction of the riverbank erosion, maintenance of biodiversity, water filtering, the incubator for fishes and the capacity of mangrove soil to increase in elevation in response to local rises in sea level.

## Behaviour change and commitment

Humans are affected by their surroundings, which can give us the conditions to make people feel more comfortable and safe. The collaborative and inclusive project approach aims to influence people's behaviour engaging the inhabitants towards a sustainable lifestyle and, by doing so, assuring their rights to the city.

Since successful innovations come from a process where the people who will ultimately benefit from the results are given a voice in its development, the project empowers the local community by involving them in the building activities of their own local affordable infrastructure, creating employability and providing safe and adaptive housing. In other worlds: the project democratises technology.

The project's approach builds capacity by helping the community to run and rule their lives by themselves. Initiatives to help stakeholders to obtain financing for their local and small-scale green economy business must have the municipalities' attention.

And finally, the project works on education, making it comprehensive and personal, thereby increasing the environmental awareness of the next generations in the transition to a sustainable community. The precious aspects contained in the drawings of the next generation of children will be safeguarded. ●

# References & Endnotes

## FOREWORD

1. This is drawn from the Global Sample of Cities comprised of 200 cities selected from a universe of 4,231 cities that had more than 100,000 inhabitants in 2010. On average, residential and housing use takes the land cover in cities in a range from 35% to 80%. The research was carried out by the University of New York, in cooperation with UN-Habitat and the Lincoln Institute of Land Policies. See *https://unhabitat.org/books/the-fundamentals-of-urbanization-evidence-base-for-policy-making/*

2. The Right to Adequate Housing includes: (1) Legal security of tenure; (2) Availability of services, materials, facilities and infrastructure; (3) Affordability; (4) Habitability; (5) Accessibility; (6) Location; (7) Cultural adequacy. In short, the right to Adequate Housing means "the right to live somewhere in security, peace, and dignity with adequate privacy, space, security, lightening and ventilation, with adequate infrastructure and location with regard to work and basic facilities – all at reasonable prices" Urban Jonsson (2015). Programmatic Guidance Note for UN-Habitat staff. Nairobi: UN-Habitat.

3. The Habitat Agenda was adopted by the 2nd United Nations Conference on Human Settlements, realised in Istanbul, 1996. It was endorsed by more than 170 countries.

4. The New Urban Agenda was adopted by the United Nations Conference on Housing and Sustainable Urban Development, realised in Quito, Ecuador, 2016.

5. Ibid., Acioly, C. (2017).

6. UN-Habitat (2016a). The Fundamentals of Urbanization. Evidence-base for policy making. Nairobi: UN-Habitat. https://unhabitat.org/books/the-fundamentals-of-urbanization-evidence-base-for-policy-making/. This publication draws on the Global Sample of 200 cities mentioned above.

7. Ibid., UN-Habitat (2016a)

8. UN-Habitat (2010). The State of the World Cities Report 2010–2011. London, Washington: Earthscan.

9. Ibid UN-Habitat (2016a).

10. Demographia (2017). 14th Annual Demographia International Housing Affordability Survey: 2018. Rating Middle-Income Housing Affordability <http://demographia.com/>; McKinsey Global Institute (2014). A Blueprint for Addressing the Global Housing Affordability Challenge. <*www.mckinsey.com/mgi*>; Property Prices Index for Country 2018 Mid-Year <*https://www.numbeo.com/property-investment/rankings_by_country.jsp*>; IMF's *Global Housing Watch Second* Quarterly of 2017 < *https://blogs.imf.org/2016/12/08/global-house-prices-time-to-worry-again/* >

11. Today, around one quarter of the world's urban population continues to live in slums. Since 1990, 213 million slum dwellers have been added to the global population. The expected global population increase of 1.18 billion combined with the existing housing deficit, implies that approximately two billion people will require housing in 2030. Today, 880 million urban residents are estimated to be living in slum conditions as opposed to 792 million in 2000. UN-Habitat (2013), Streets as Public Spaces and Drivers of Urban Prosperity; UN-HABITAT (2005). Financing Urban Shelter: Global Report on Human Settlements 2005. Nairobi: UN-Habitat ; United Nations (2015). The Millennium Development Goals Report 2015. New York: United Nations.

## INTRODUCTION

• **McKinsey Global Institute.** 'Tackling the world's affordable housing challenge' October 2014; https://www.mckinsey.com/featured-insights/urbanization/tackling-the-worlds-affordable-housing-challenge (last accessed January 2019).

• **World Bank, 'Inclusive Cities'** 2019. https://www.worldbank.org/en/topic/inclusive-cities; (last accessed January 2019).

• **World Economic Forum.** 'How many people will be living in cities in the future?' 26 May 2016; https://www.weforum.org/agenda/2016/05/how-many-people-will-be-living-in-cities-in-the-future (last accessed January 2019).

• **World Resources Institute,** 'Confronting the Urban Housing Crisis in the Global South: Adequate, Secure, and Affordable Housing.' July 2017. https://www.wri.org/publication/towards-more-equal-city-confronting-urban-housing-crisis-global-south (last accessed January 2019).

• **United Nations, 'World Urbanization Prospects',** New York, 2014 **Revision**; https://esa.un.org/unpd/wup/publications/files/wup2014-highlights.pdf (last accessed January 2019).

## SECTION 2- EDITORS' INTRODUCTION

**McKinsey Global Institute.** "Tackling the world's affordable housing challenge," October 2014;
https://www.mckinsey.com/featured-insights/urbanization/tackling-the-worlds-affordable-housing-challenge
(last accessed January 2019).

**World Resources Institute,** "1.2 Billion People Living in Cities Lack Access to Affordable and Secure Housing," July 12, 2017;
https://www.wri.org/news/2017/07/release-12-billion-people-living-cities-lack-access-affordable-and-secure-housing (last accessed January 2019).

## SECTION 3- EDITORS' INTRODUCTION

**State of the World's Cities**, 2006–2007, United Nations Human Settlement Program (UN Habitat);
**Earthscan**, London, 2006

## CHAPTER 5- Gendered Production of Spaces in Sri Lanka

Jacobs, J. (1992). The death and life of great American cities. New York: Vintage Books.

• **Perera, N. (1998).** Decolonizing Ceylon: Colonialism, nationalism, and the politics of space in • Sri Lanka. Oxford University Press.

• **Perera, N. (2002).** Feminizing the city: gender and space in colonial Colombo. Trans-Status • Subjects: Genders in the Globalization of South and Southeast Asia, 67–87. Perera, N. (2015). People's Spaces: Coping, Familiarizing, Creating. London and New York: Routledge.

• **Phadke, S., Khan, S., & Ranade, S. (2011).** Why loiter?: Women and risk on Mumbai streets. Penguin Books, India.

## CHAPTER 7- Children's Right to Play in Inclusive Cities

• **Chatterjee, S. (2018).** Children's coping, adaptation and resilience through play in situations of crisis. Children, Youth and Environments, 28(2), 119–45.

• **Chatterjee, S. (2017).** Access to Play for Children in Situations of Crisis: Synthesis of research in six countries, International Play Association working paper.

## CHAPTER 11- Dodoma: The Burden of Planning in Tanzania

'Tanzania: Dodoma Capital City Master Plan Ready', Tanzania Daily News, 4 December 2013, http://allafrica.com/stories/201312040468.html Unfortunately, the master plan is not a public document.

Garth Myers (2011), African Cities: Alternative Visions of Urban Theory and Practice, London: Zed Books, 43–69.

Wilbard J. Kombe and Volker Kreibich (2001), 'Informal Land Management in Tanzania and the Misconception about its Illegality', A paper presented at the ESF/N-Aerus Annual Workshop. "Coping with Informality and Illegality in Human Settlements in Developing Countries" in Leuven and Brussels, May 23–26, 2001.

The term 'urban fantasy' is kindly borrowed from Prof. Vanessa Watson, University of Cape Town. See: Vanessa Watson (2013), African Urban Fantasies; dreams or nightmares? Environment and Urbanization, 6 December 2013.

## CHAPTER 14- The Five Principles of Adequate Housing

• Angel, S., 2000. Housing policy matters. Oxford University Press Inc., New York.

• Ayala, A., Rabe, P. & Geurts, E., 2014. Best Practices for Roma Integration Regional Report on Housing Legalization, Settlement Upgrading and Social Housing for Roma in the Western Balkans. OSCE's Office for Democratic Institutions and Human Rights (ODIHR). Available at: http://www.osce.org/odihr/115737?download=true

• Fainstein, S.S., 2010. The just city. Cornell University, USA. Harris, R 2015. 'International Policy for Urban Housing Markets in the Global South since 1945'. In Cities of the Global South Reader. Miraftab F. and Kudva N. (eds.), 122–33.

• Harvey, D., 1988. Social justice and the city. 2nd edition. Oxford: Basil Blackwell.

• Huchzermeyer, M. and Karam, A., 2016. 'South African housing policy over two decades: 1994–2014'. In Domains of Freedom: Justice, Citizenship and Social Change in South Africa. Kepe, T., Levin, M. and von Liers, B. (eds.), 85–104.

• King, P., 2016. Principles of Housing. Routledge.

• McKinsey Global Institute, 2014. A blueprint for addressing the global affordable housing challenge. McKinsey Global Institute (MGI). In: http://www.mckinsey.com/global-themes/urbanization/tackling-the-worlds-affordable-housing-challenge (last accessed Aug 2017).

• Rawls, J., 1971. A theory of justice. The Belknap Press of Harvard University Press, Cambridge, Massachusetts, USA. United Nations Environmental Programme, 2009. Buildings and Climate Change Summary for Decision Makers, Yamamoto, J. & Graham, P. (eds.). Available at: http://www.greeningtheblue.org/sites/default/files/Buildings%20and%20climate%20change_0.pdf

• Piketty, T, 2014. Capital in the twenty-first century. Harvard College, USA.

## CHAPTER 26- Informal Housing in Venezuela

•Almandoz Marte, Arturo (1999): Transfer of urban ideas. The emergence of Venezuelan urbanism in the proposal's for 1930s Caracas. In: International Planning Studies, Vol. 4, No. 1, 79–94.

•Ayala, Alonso (2012): Urban upgrading intervention and barrio integration in Caracas, Venezuela. PhD dissertation. Geographische Grundlagen und Raumplanung in Entwicklungsländern, Fakultät für Raumplanung, TU-Dortmund.

•Baldó, Josefina; Villanueva, Federico (1995): Un plan para los barrios de Caracas. Concejo Nacional de la Vivienda, Caracas.

•Barroso, Manuel (1997): La Autoestima del Venezolano. Democracia y Marginalidad. Editorial Galac S.A., Caracas.

•Bolívar, Teolinda (1997): Densificación de los barrios autoproducidos en la capital de Venezuela. Riesgos y vulnerabilidad. Red de Estudios Sociales en Prevención de Desastres en América latina.

•Cartaya, Vanessa et al. (2007): Agenda para el Diálogo sobre la Pobreza en Venezuela. ILDIS. Friedrich-Ebert-Stiftung, Bonn, Germany.

•Harms, Hans (1997): To live in the city centre: housing and tenants in central neighbourhoods of Latin American cities. In: Environment and

Urbanization, Vol. 9, No. 2, 193–98.

•UN-Habitat (2006): State of the World's Cities 2006/7: The Millenium Development Goals and Urban Sustainability: 30 Years of Shaping the Habitat agenda. Earthscan, London.

## CHAPTER 29- Empowering Migrant Communities to Secure Housing

Boonyabancha, S., 2009, Land for housing the poor – by the poor themselves: experiences from the Baan Mankong Nationwide Slum Upgrading Programme in Thailand. Environment and Urbanization 21 (2), 309–29.

Mizzima Weekly April 28, 2016, Now the hard part: Yangon's new Chief Minister and the challenge of development, 14–18

Ra, A., 2016, Impact of self-help housing project on the livelihood of the beneficiaries: case study of self-help housing project in North Okkalapa Township, Yangon, Myanmar. IHS UMD 12 thesis, Sept 2016.

Save the Children, Myanmar, 2016, Lives on Loan

World Bank, 2016, Myanmar Economic Monitor. Anchoring economic expectations. World Bank Group, December 2016.

## CHAPTER 31- A Flexible Approach to Upgrade Informal Housing

•Dhabhalabutr, K., 2016. The Empowerment of the Slum Inhabitant as a Primary Agent of Low-Income Housing: Slum Upgrading in Thailand between 1980 and 2011. Procedia-Social and Behavioral Sciences, 216, pp.428–39. Available at: https://ac.els-cdn.com/S1877042815062370/1-s2.0-S1877042815062370-main.pdf?_tid=bd5b955f-8d80-46f1-bf22-4820cf9a7490&acdnat=1536335931_5888e2c9fbc68e680b214d561ae39e5d [Accessed: August 1, 2018].

•UN-Habitat, 2016. Urbanization and development: emerging futures (World Cities report 2016). Nairobi: United Nations Human Settlements Programmeme (UN-Habitat). Available at: http://wcr.unhabitat.org/?wcr_process_download=1&download_id=117118 [Accessed 04-01-2018].

• Nadkarny, S. and Anderson, M. 2010. SLUM UPGRADING IN THAILAND: CODI.

• Boonyabancha, S., 2005. Baan Mankong: Going to scale with "slum" and squatter upgrading in Thailand. Environment and Urbanization, 17 (1), 21–46. Available at: http://journals.sagepub.com/doi/pdf/10.1177/095624780501700104 [Accessed 23-02-2018].

• Boonyabancha, S., 2009. Land for housing the poor – by the poor: experiences from the Baan Mankong nationwide slum upgrading programmeme in Thailand. Environment and Urbanization, 21 (2), 309–29.

## CHAPTER 35- Streets as Drivers for the Transformation and Inclusion of Slums

• Amis, Philip (2001) "Rethinking UK aid in urban India: reflections on an impact assessment study of slum improvement projects", Environment and Urbanization, Vol.13 No.1 April 2001.

• Banerjee, B. (2006) Impact of tenure and infrastructure programmes on housing conditions in squatter settlements in Indian cities. In: Shaw, A. (Ed.) Indian Cities in Transition. New Delhi, Orient Longmans, India.

• Kessides, Christine (1997) World Bank Experience with the Provision of Infrastructure Services for the Urban Poor: preliminary Identification and Review of Best Practices, Washington, World Bank.

•UN-Habitat (2014) Streets as tools for urban transformation in slums: a street-led approach to citywide slum upgrading, Nairobi, UN-Habitat

• World Bank, Thematic Group on Urban Upgrading (2000), Cities Without Slums, Urban Notes, No. 2, May 2000.

# Author Biographies

**Amit Arya** is an architect with a Master's degree from Cornell University, New York. He has worked on projects in Asia, America and the Middle East and researches about architecture and its relationship with the public realm.

**Laura Amaya** is an architect and urban researcher, originally from Bogotá, Colombia, and currently based in Mumbai, India. Her main interest revolves around the role of design as a catalyst for development.

**Alonso Ayala** is an architect and spatial planner specialising in the fields of social housing and upgrading informal settlements. He is a lecturer at the Institute for Housing and Urban Development Studies of Erasmus University, Rotterdam (IHS).

**Sangeeta Bagga** is a Professor at the Chandigarh College of Architecture and has extensively researched the urban landscapes, environmental design and social issues in Chandigarh, India. She is currently Nodal Officer for the Trans-national Serial Nomination of the Architectural Works of Le Corbusier to UNESCO with special reference to Chandigarh's Capitol Complex.

**Banashree Banerjee** is an urban planner based in New Delhi, India. She works as an independent consultant and associate staff member of the Institute for Housing and Urban Development Studies, Rotterdam. The focus of her work is on inclusive approaches to urban planning and management.

**Vinayak Bharne** is a practicing urban designer, city planner and architect; an adjunct associate professor of urbanism at the University of Southern California (USC) in Los Angeles; and co-director of the India/Netherlands-based knowledge-platform, My Liveable City.

**Sudeshna Chatterji** is the CEO of the non-profit Action for Children's Environments (ACE). Trained as an architect and urban designer, she has a PhD in Community and Environmental Design. She is involved in research, advocacy, planning and design to improve the living environments of children in cities.

**Bruce Echberg** is the founding director of Urban Initiatives, a Melbourne based landscape and urban design studio that focuses on the design of public projects that enhance the quality of Australian towns and cities.

**Maartje van Eerd** is an assistant professor at the Institute for Housing and Urban Development Studies in Rotterdam. A human geographer by profession, she has extensive experience as a researcher, trainer and advisor on housing and social development issues. Her main expertise lies in housing rights, resettlement and gender, with a focus on Asia.

**Imran Hossain Foishal** is an assistant professor at the Department of Architecture of Khulna University, Bangladesh. He received his M.Sc. from the Institute for Housing and Urban Development Studies of Erasmus University in 2018. His research thesis on how resettled communities coped with the impact of spatial transformation in order to restore livelihoods received an honorary award by DAIDA.

**Ellen Geurts** is a housing expert at the Institute for Housing and Urban Development Studies (IHS) in Rotterdam, the Netherlands with nearly 15 years of experience. Her research has focused on public and social housing, housing finance, management of multi-family housing and housing needs, predominantly in sub-Saharan Africa and Central Europe.

**Sophie van Ginnekken** is an architectural historian and independent researcher, organiser and teacher in the field of urban planning, architecture and cultural heritage. She has an interdisciplinary focus on the 20th- and 21st-century city, with a focus on new towns.

**Prajakta Gawde** is an architect with a Master's degree in collective housing from UPM (Madrid)/ETH(Zurich), and an interest in sustainable social housing projects on an international scale.

**Shruti Hemani** is an architect and professor of urban design in Jaipur, India, and holds a doctoral degree from IIT Guwahati. She has worked with both government and design co-operatives in England. Her work focuses on design and research in the area of social dimensions of urban spaces.

**Kaushalya Herath** is a lecturer at the University of Moratuwa, Sri Lanka. Her research interests include gender studies, people's spaces, ethnographic research and participatory planning, specifically on how people negotiate space with regard to politics, culture, gender, age and other socioeconomic dynamics.

**Paola Huijding** holds two degrees in Architecture and Urban Planning, from Brazil and the Netherlands, and has over 20 years of experience in the field. She runs an architectural practice, Volpi Urbane in the Netherlands and has also provided a wide range of design services in Germany, Belgium and Brazil.

**Nathan Hutson** is an instructor of Public Policy and a PhD Candidate in Urban Planning and Development at the University of Southern California. He is an expert on transportation and infrastructure planning and is the author of the chapter 'Social Housing with a Human Face: Conserving Moscow's Soviet Era Housing Legacy', in the Routledge *Companion to Global Heritage Conservation*, (Routledge, 2019.)

**Shyam Khandekar** is an urban designer, city planner and architect with four decades of design experience in Europe and India. He is the founder-director of the Dutch design practice Khandekar Urban Design and Landscape that continues under the name BDP. Khandekar. From 2008–2012 he served as Company Director of BDP, headquartered in London. He is Co-Founder and Director of the Knowledge Platform, My Liveable City, and Editorial Director of its urbanism magazine.

**Siddharth Khandekar** is a consultant with Deloitte Real Estate in the Netherlands, working primarily for clients in the social housing sector. He is also a member of the non-executive board (RvC) of a Dutch social housing corporation. He studied at Oxford University and the Delft University of Technology.

**Jan Knikker** is a Partner at MVRDV and leads its Business Development and Public Relations efforts, which now also include a visualisation team. He began his career as a journalist and subsequently helped shape the public image of OMA for nearly a decade.

**Annemiek van Koldenhoven** is an associate in the multidisciplinary design studio of BDP in the Netherlands, and works as a landscape architect on large-scale projects internationally.

**Ashok Lall** is a practicing architect and educator based in New Delhi, India. He has helped develop curricula and teaching methods to address environmental issues, has published many articles and presented papers on environmentally sustainable design and is an active member of institutions and groups promoting awareness and building competence in sustainable design of buildings.

**Hélène Leriche** is a French architect and urban designer based in the Netherlands, and has been working for several years on major international urban design projects in India and beyond.

**Rajeev Malagi** is an architect, urban designer and a documentary filmmaker. He currently works at World Resources Institute, India, as a senior associate on urban development projects. He explores places through the lens of people, culture and spaces. He is also the founder of Janaa Creations.

**Nikos Margaritis** graduated as an architect from the University of Thessaly and received his Master's degree in landscape architecture from Delft University of Technology. Currently located in the Netherlands, he is part of the BDP Rotterdam Studio.

**Mirjana Milanovic** is an urban designer and adviser at the City Planning Department in Amsterdam, with experience in leading new large housing projects. Her previous work activities include research at the TU Delft, State Planning agency and Social Housing Department in Amsterdam.

**Buvana Murali** is an architect and urban designer with a Master's degree from the University of Michigan. She has worked for over a decade in architecture and on urban projects at all scales on three continents. Her interests also include photography and the use of the image as a story-telling device.

**Dorcas Nyamai** is an academic researcher on Urban Development and Management. She is currently involved in research on Complex Urban Land Markets in Uganda and Somaliland, and on Urban Mobility and Spatial Justice in Nairobi, Kenya.

**David Rudlin** is a director of URBED, Honorary Professor at Manchester University, Chair of the Academy of Urbanism and winner of the quarter of a million pound Wolfson Economics Prize in 2014.

**Liesl Vivier** is the director of Studio BDP in the Netherlands. She works as an urbanist on large-scale projects of urban regeneration in the Netherlands and abroad.

**Levi Wichgers** is a Netherlands-based urban designer and planner with over a decade of professional experience. He is particularly interested in the strategy of growth and mobility in urban centres.

**Rene van Zuuk** studied building production technology at the Technical University of Eindhoven and worked for SOM in London and Chicago. In 1989 he won the Ongewoon Wonen ll competition on the Fantasie in Almere where he started his own firm. His projects include the architectural institute in Amsterdam ARCAM, the housing project Block 16 and the pavilion De Verbeelding in Zeewolde.

**LEVS architecten** is an Amsterdam-based architecture office that works with a team of 35 people on projects in Europe and Africa. Their interests include architecture and the development of new building techniques and how architecture can be part of the social debate concerning building for humanity and developing sustainable techniques. LEVS supports the non-profit organisation Partners Pays-Dogon by designing different kinds of sustainable projects.

**Alessia Guardo, Lucia Valenzuela, Dhruv Bahl, Revathi Konduru and Samidha Patil**, met while studying at IHS, Rotterdam and lead the formation of "The Thailand Project" (https://www.facebook.com/TheThailandProject/).